327.41
F41t   110901

DATE DUE			
Nov 16 79			

The *Trent* Affair

A Diplomatic Crisis

The *Trent* Affair

A Diplomatic Crisis

BY NORMAN B. FERRIS

THE UNIVERSITY OF TENNESSEE PRESS
KNOXVILLE

~~~~~~~~~~

Library of Congress Cataloging in Publication Data
Ferris, Norman B   1931–
   The Trent affair.
   Includes bibliographical references and index.
   1. Trent Affair, Nov. 8, 1861.   I.   Title.
E469.F387   327.41′073   76–28304
ISBN 0–87049–169–5

To Kathleen

Preface

In almost every historical account dealing with nineteenth-century Anglo-American relations, one of the key episodes is the *Trent* affair. The basic elements of the story are well known. Two emissaries of the Southern Confederacy en route to Europe were seized from the deck of a British mail steamer by the captain of a Yankee warship. This led the English people to cry out for war and Queen Victoria's cabinet to demand an apology and the return of the captives to British protection. The American people, however, vowed to fight rather than to yield the "traitors." Then, at the crucial moment, President Lincoln decided to relinquish the prisoners and war was narrowly averted.

What historians have heretofore failed to explain is *why* a relatively trivial maritime incident threatened to touch off a trans-Atlantic war at the end of the year 1861. For the *Trent* seizure could not have precipitated such a violent explosion of wrath in England without the existence already of a strong barrier of misunderstanding between the political leaders of the two English-speaking nations. I have tried to delineate the main elements of that barrier in the pages that follow.

Another important factor in precipitating the *Trent* affair was an excessively legalistic attitude on the part of the elderly gentlemen who held the highest civil offices in England. Fortunately, however, the younger members of the British cabinet were far from united about how to treat the incident, and while they awaited the American reply to their ultimatum they grew progressively more pacific, reflecting, indeed, a national trend. I have tried to set forth in detail the progress of this "cooling down" process in England.

In the United States, national political leaders seemed bewildered by the *Trent* affair. Mesmerized by the jargon of jurisprudence, and apparently oblivious to the destructive forces set in motion by the crisis, they offered the American people little more than windy rhetoric at a time when calmness and prudence were requisite if war was to be avoided. A notable exception to this kind of behavior was the secretary of state, William H. Seward. To him should go much of the credit for the preservation of peace.

Journalistic opinion in both countries altered significantly as it passed through several distinct stages. My somewhat limited study of the subject leads me to suggest that the press did not play the inflammatory role throughout the *Trent* affair which some historians have attributed to it.

Finally, I have discussed in the pages following not only the activities of the leading players in the drama but also their motives and their relationships with each other—decisive factors that other historians have virtually ignored. My work on this book will be justified if readers learn from it how easily a serious international crisis may accidently arise, and how afterward—through the exercise of diplomatic statesmanship— such a crisis may be terminated without war.

All those who aided in this undertaking have been thanked in person, and I hope to have the opportunity to thank at least some of them again in various ways. Formal acknowledgments have been inserted at appropriate places in my bibliography.

Murfreesboro, Tennessee   Norman B. Ferris
November 25, 1976

Contents

Abbreviations

ALP	Papers of Abraham Lincoln
AP	Papers of Adams family
AT	Archives of the *Times*
BM	British Museum
BPCUS, G&B	Belgian Political Correspondence, United States, General and Bound
CP	Papers of George William Frederick Villiers, 4th earl of Clarendon
ESD	Dispatches of Edouard Stoeckl
FMAE, AD	Archives of the French Ministry of Foreign Affairs, including "Archives diplomatiques, Angleterre"
FMAE, MD	Archives of the French Ministry of Foreign Affairs, including "Memoires et Documents, Papiers de Thouvenel"
FO	British Foreign Office
CGLP	Papers of Sir George Cornewall Lewis
HL (or HM)	Manuscripts of Charles Sumner, Francis Lieber, and Thomas Dudley, Huntington Library
HSSP	*See* SaP
HWLP	Papers of Henry W. Longfellow
JBP	Papers of John Bigelow
JMMP	James Murray Mason Papers
JSPP	James Shepherd Pike Papers
LC	Library of Congress
LP	Papers of Richard Bickerton Pemell Lyons, 1st earl Lyons
MHSP	Massachusetts Historical Society *Papers*
MLN	Papers of Sir Alexander Milne
NA	National Archives

NeC	Papers of Henry Pelham Fiennes Pelham Clinton, 5th duke of Newcastle
ORA	*War of the Rebellion: Official Records of the Union and Confederate Armies*
ORN	*Official Records of the Union and Confederate Navies in the War of the Rebellion*
OsC	Papers of John Evelyn Denison, viscount Ossington
PP	Papers of Henry John Temple, 3d viscount Palmerston
PRO	Public Record Office, London
RCP	Papers of Richard Cobden
RCSA	Records of the Confederate States of America
RHDP	Papers of Richard Henry Dana, Jr.
RSD	Dispatches of Rudolf Schleiden
SaP	Papers of Henry Shelton Sanford
SeP	Papers of William H. Seward
WP	Papers of Thurlow Weed

Wal, wal, two wrongs don't never make a right;
Ef we're mistaken, own up, an' don't fight:
For gracious sake, ha'n't we enough to do
'Thout gettin' up a fight with England, too?

JAMES RUSSELL LOWELL,
"Mason and Slidell: A Yankee Idyll,"
The Bigelow Papers.

The *Trent* Affair

A Diplomatic Crisis

I.

The Departure of Mason and Slidell

*Mr. Mason is a high and mighty Virginian. He brooks
no opposition to his will. . . . Whatever a Mason does
is right in his own eyes. He is above law.*

MARY BOYKIN CHESNUT,
Charleston, S. C., 1861.[1]

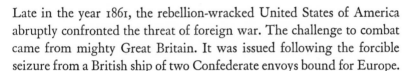

Late in the year 1861, the rebellion-wracked United States of America
abruptly confronted the threat of foreign war. The challenge to combat
came from mighty Great Britain. It was issued following the forcible
seizure from a British ship of two Confederate envoys bound for Europe.

One of these emissaries, James Murray Mason, was old and arrogant.
Under a receding hairline and bushy brows a constant glower in his eyes
warned strangers that this proud grandson of the legendary George
Mason was insistent, domineering, and conscious always of his prerogatives. After fourteen years as a United States senator from Virginia,
Mason had resigned from the national legislature early in 1861 to join
his state in seceding from the Union. But he had hardly reached his plan-
tation home near Winchester when he was asked to undertake the mission that was to ensure for his name a place in American history.

Appointed as special Confederate commissioner to the United Kingdom of Great Britain and Ireland, Mason hurried to Richmond to receive
instructions about his mission.[2] Praised by Confederate President Jefferson Davis in a letter to Queen Victoria as one of the "most intelligent,
esteemed, and worthy citizens" of the South, he was granted the authority to negotiate with the British "concerning all matters and subjects
interesting to both nations."[3]

His instructions commanded Mason to proceed "with as little delay
as possible" to London, where on arrival he was at once to present the

Confederate government's case for recognition of its independence. In behalf of the Confederate States he was to appeal "not for material aid or alliances offensive and defensive, but for . . . a recognized place as a free and independent people." The eleven states of the Confederacy, covering over seven hundred thousand square miles of territory and containing a population of over nine million people, were unconquerable; therefore, "the sooner the strife be ended the better for the cause of peace and the interest of mankind." The Southerners were committed both to a policy of free trade and to an agrarian economy based on cotton production, which guaranteed that many years would have to pass "before they would become the rivals of those who are largely concerned in navigation, manufactures, and commerce." They would rather content themselves with being "valuable customers" and exporters of cotton to Great Britain, as reliable "as if these States were themselves her colonies."[4]

The political interests of British leaders, Mason was instructed additionally to remind them, lay in the establishment of a "balance of power" between two great confederacies on the North American continent. For the old American "manifest destiny," which had led to invasions of both Canada and Mexico and filibuster expeditions elsewhere in the Hemisphere, would die with the old Union.[5]

Finally, the Confederate commissioner was instructed to argue against the legality of the Northern maritime blockade. He was to "be furnished with abundant evidence" that the blockade of the coasts of the Confederate States had not been effectual or of such a character as to be binding under international law. And he was to suggest that by attempting to cut off the great Southern supply of cotton "from the general uses of mankind," those who imposed the blockade were levying war "as much against those who transport and manufacture cotton as against those who produce the raw material." It was therefore "the duty of the nations of the earth to throw the weight of their moral influence against the unnecessary prolongation" of the civil war in America.[6]

Thus furnished with his commission and with moral, economic, political, and legal arguments for immediate British recognition of Confederate independence, Mason hurried to Charleston, South Carolina, to take passage to London on a ship capable of running the Northern blockade. He was accompanied on the week-long journey from Richmond by his former colleague in the United States Senate, sixty-eight-year-old John Slidell. Unlike Mason, whose only "diplomatic" experience had been ten years of service on the Senate Foreign Relations Committee, Slidell had been sent by the Polk administration to Mexico in 1845 as a special commissioner to seek a settlement of the Mexican-Texas boundary dispute and to purchase New Mexico and possibly California as well. This mission had ended in failure. Slidell had also visited Europe in 1853 to sell bonds of the New Orleans and Nashville Railroad Company. These foreign travels, as well as his marriage to a Louisiana Creole, and his own fluency in the French language, helped to qualify him for the post of Confederate commissioner to France. Furnished with letters of credence and introduction similar to those given Mason, and with instructions containing arguments for recognition and noncompliance with the Northern blockade that differed only in slight detail from those given his colleague, this wily Louisiana political boss—the leading wire-puller in the Federal government during the presidency of James Buchanan—planned to take part of his family with him to Europe. His wife, three daughters, and a fifteen-year-old son, as well as several servants, accompanied him to Charleston.[7]

Also present in the city whose inhabitants had only a few months before witnessed the siege and capitulation of Fort Sumter were the two prospective Southern secretaries of legation. Ordered to accompany Mason to London was James E. Macfarland of Virginia, while Slidell's aide at Paris was to be a Louisiana lawyer and former United States congressman named George Eustis, who was married to the daughter of W. W. Corcoran, a wealthy banker and philanthropist. Because the white-haired Slidell lacked the vitality of his younger days, Eustis contemplated taking a large share of the work in Paris on his own shoulders, but his wife was with him to ease the burdens that might be waiting in the French capital.[8]

The Southern envoys planned to slip through the blockade on the paddle-wheel steamer *Nashville*. This vessel, originally built for the coasting trade between New York and Charleston, had been purchased by the Confederate navy department at the outset of hostilities and had been made into a cruiser, but she was too weakly armed to risk close combat with the formidable Federal ships blockading Charleston. She had to trust to surprise and to superior speed to get away.[9]

Two Yankee blockaders, a steam frigate and a sloop of war, awaited the *Nashville* beyond the reach of Southern shore batteries, but her captain calculated that he could run safely past them through the main channel on a moonless night. Mason and Slidell waited for several days, during which the tide would not permit departure after dark; then came strong winds which made passage over the sand bar at the channel entrance unsafe. When the wind finally calmed, another obstacle appeared: a very fast-looking, propeller-driven clipper ship had joined the blockading force. Mason and Slidell and the other members of their party held consultations with the captain of the *Nashville* and several local pilots, in which they were joined by William Henry Trescot,[10] a former assistant secretary of state in the administration of James Buchanan, who was then living as a private citizen in Charleston. "It was then projected," Mason later reported, "to make the attempt through the Maffitt Channel, though without the full sanction of the pilots, and this I believe we should have attempted but for the appearance at that time of another steam frigate, thus making the squadron to consist of three steamers besides the sloop of war. Such sudden and unusual accessions to the blockade of the port made us infer (as a high probability at least) that our presence here and purpose had reached the enemy, and we were the cause of the unusual preparation we witnessed."[11]

The dangers of the projected voyage now appeared so great that Mason and Slidell determined to take an overland route from Charleston to Texas. Once they had crossed into Mexico at Matamoras, they hoped to find a British ship to take them the rest of the way to England. But after sending a telegram to Richmond detailing their plans, the two envoys realized that by taking the Mexican route they would be delayed excessively in reaching Europe. Both men had been specifically ordered to get to their diplomatic posts as soon as possible. Finally, taking the advice of Trescot and George A. Trenholm, a merchant who was deeply involved in blockade-running projects in behalf of the firm of Fraser and Company, the two diplomats determined to charter a vessel with a shallower draft than the *Nashville*, one capable, if necessary, of taking them close along the shoreline and out past the blockaders by a circuitous route.[12]

A privateer named the *Gordon,* which had for several months been chartered by the local authorities for harbor service, was selected for the venture. At a charge of $210 per day she had proved to be a very effective scout vessel, used nightly to reconnoiter the Federal blockade ships, approaching to near gunshot range, and then either outrunning any attempt to catch her or slipping into shoal water where the larger vessels dared not follow. According to the Southern naval officers stationed at Charleston, the blockading squadron had become so familiar with the *Gordon,* through her nightly and sometimes daytime visits, that they appeared to ignore her presence in their midst; and it would be a simple matter to run her directly through them out to sea, after which it would be impossible for them to overtake her. The owners wanted $10,000 to take the Confederate envoys to either Nassau or Havana in the West Indies, with "the privilege of bringing back some $7,000 worth of cigars and other light articles." Alternatively, they were willing to sell the vessel outright for $62,000.[13]

On October 4 the *Gordon's* captain took Slidell, two of his daughters, and several of the *Nashville's* officers on a demonstration cruise out the main channel to within three miles of the blockading squadron, whose captains did not even bother to raise anchor when they saw the vessel approach. The passengers on the *Gordon* noticed that a fifth warship had joined the Federal squadron. But Mason and Slidell wrote the Confederate secretary of state that "come what may, . . . we will embark at once in the *Gordon,* and doubt not can make the voyage successfully."[14]

By the evening of October 11, the time for the venture had come. "If nothing goes amiss," Mason wrote Jefferson Davis, ". . . we shall be off about midnight tonight, as soon as the moon disappears." The *Gordon,* her bunkers bulging with extra coal, her cabins crowded with the charter passengers, and with several Confederate naval officers supplementing her regular deck force, put to sea through a heavy rain. Crossing the bar about two in the morning in pitch blackness, she slipped through the midst of the Federal cruisers, guided partly by their lights a mile or two away; and by morning she was well beyond their horizons, running before a strong northwest wind toward Nassau. "Here we are, my dear wife," Mason wrote ebulliently, "on the deep blue sea; clear of all the Yankees. We ran the blockade in splendid style." And though a heavy swell had made all the passengers but himself seasick—"I have never felt the slightest qualm," he boasted, "but had a good appetite and a clear head all the time"—the Bahamas and safety from Union cruisers lay only a few miles ahead.[15]

About four in the afternoon on October 14, the *Gordon,* which had been renamed the *Theodora* "to confuse the enemy," arrived at Nassau in the Bahamas. She did not anchor, however, because the pilots who came on board to assist in docking informed the passengers that the only regular steamer service from that port was to New York. But a British mail steamer was scheduled soon to leave Havana, Cuba, for St. Thomas, in the Virgin Islands, where connections were habitually made for Southampton. At once the *Theodora* dropped the pilots and got underway for Cuba. Two days later, nearly out of coal and approaching the Cuban port of Cardenas, about one hundred miles down the coast from Havana, the Confederates encountered a Spanish warship, and Slidell and Eustis boarded her, only to be informed that they had barely missed catching the English mail steamer and would have to wait three weeks for the next one. This was disappointing, but, as Mason wrote his wife, "at any rate, we are safe from the Yankees . . . henceforth under a foreign flag."[16]

Escorted into port by the Spaniards, the Southerners were greeted at Cardenas "with great kindness and hospitality." Mason reported to his chief at Richmond that the Spanish governor, "with some of the principal men of the town have called on and proffered us every attention, and, so far as we can gather opinion from conversation and on the streets, the sympathies of the people are entirely with us." A planter named Casanova, who had married a Virginian during a long stay in the United States, and who was acquainted with Slidell, rode thirty miles on horseback into the town to invite the entire party of Southerners to visit his estate, and he arranged for a special train to pick up the party of about fifteen people and transport them to a terminus near his house. As Casanova's guests from Saturday, October 19, until the following Tuesday, the Southerners were, according to Mason, "sumptuously entertained" amidst hospitality that seemed "profuse" even to a member of one of Virginia's first families. Mason catalogued Casanova's assets with relish: "The estate," he wrote, ". . . yields two thousand hogsheads of sugar, and he has two coffee plantations adjoining, besides other estates in the island; carriages, horses, and negroes without stint. There are . . . on the estate twenty or thirty negroes just from Africa and plenty of Coolies (Chinese) as much slaves as the Africans."[17]

While Mason and Slidell and their party made preparations for the overland journey westward to Havana, news of their departure from Charleston had finally reached Washington. Gideon Welles, secretary of the navy, learned of the escape from distorted stories in the New York newspapers. On October 15 he telegraphed Admiral Samuel F. DuPont "that the steamer *Nashville* has run the blockade at Charleston, with Messrs. Mason and Slidell on board." If a fast steamer could be spared, DuPont was requested to send it out to intercept the *Nashville*.[18]

DuPont was quick to respond. By midnight the same day he had written out a set of orders to Commander John B. Marchand, whose ship the *James Adger* was fueled and ready to sail, commanding him to leave at once and attempt to intercept the *Nashville* on her way to England. Marchand was also ordered to watch for three or four blockade runners reportedly on their way from England to the coast of Georgia or South Carolina with munitions and other military stores. The *James Adger* was ordered to carry the chase after the *Nashville* all the way to the English Channel, if necessary, before returning for a fresh assignment. Off she sailed on her futile hunt, even as Mason and Slidell, languorous in the humid heat of Cuba, waited for their British mail steamer, and the *Nashville* lay comfortably at her pier in Charleston harbor.[19]

Mason and Slidell were preceded to Havana by another Southern representative, Charles J. Helm, who had already been appointed special agent of the Confederate States in the West Indies. Orderd to proceed to those islands "with all convenient dispatch" and to promote with every resource at his command "the establishment and cultivation of friendly commercial relations with them," as well as to provide "a sure and safe channel of communication" between Confederate authorities in Richmond and their representatives in Europe, Helm left his Kentucky home on August 17 and traveled north to Canada and thence to England, arriving in London one month later. There he held discussions with other

Southern agents to arrange "the mode of my cooperation with them," and then, on October 2, he sailed for Havana, where he arrived three weeks later, to "find a large majority of the population . . . zealously advocating our cause." While Mason, Slidell, and their party journeyed toward Havana from the east, Helm addressed a letter to the captain general of Cuba, His Excellency Don Francisco Serrano. He recalled their earlier friendly association when Helm had been United States consul general in Havana, from 1858 until early in 1861, and he submitted his commission and a letter of accreditation, along with a request for an official interview. On the following day, although he was received by the general as "a private individual" only (inasmuch as Her Catholic Majesty's government had not yet granted *de jure* recognition to the Confederate States), Helm reported to Richmond that Serrano was "perfectly cordial" and gave "assurances of sympathy in our cause." The governor promised that Confederate ships would be admitted to all Cuban ports under their own flag, "for all the purposes of legitimate commerce."[20]

Mason and Slidell arrived in Havana on the same day that Helm had his initial interview with General Serrano. After checking into Helm's hotel, the Cubano, the two envoys were soon in close consultation with him about the problems, generally, of blockade-running with "necessities of life" for the Southern economy. The three men envisioned a system whereby large cargoes would be purchased and shipped from Europe by Mason and Slidell and their associates there, consigned to Helm and his agents in the West Indies, and then carried to the Confederacy by small, fast, shallow-draft vessels which could evade the blockaders by approaching their destinations close along the shoreline through the shallow and narrow inlets and across the bars where larger Northern cruisers could not follow.[21]

Mason wrote his wife on October 29 that the Havana heat, ranging in the daytime between 98° and 100° F., forbade any enjoyment of the sights and sounds of the city; "to walk a few hundred yards," he complained, "disables you for the day." Moreover, the streets were "so narrow; and the sidewalks don't allow two persons to pass; narrow balconies over the streets are so near that persons in opposite houses can converse without raising the voice." But he and Slidell had both "been received here with marked attention by the inhabitants, all of whose sympathies are with the Confederate States, from the Captain-General down. As an evidence, the ladies of Havana got up a large silk flag and presented it to the ship that brought us here, and under which, floating from the mast-head, she sailed out of the harbor on her way home."[22]

The Virginian declined invitations "to balls innumerable," but wherever there was good food to be consumed, he made an effort to be on hand. "The fruit here is certainly exquisite," he wrote home. Beginning in the morning about seven he was habitually served "a cup of coffee, and after that orange; breakfast a la fourchette at 10 o'clock, stews, haricots, fish, etc., and claret; at 1 o'clock lunch of fruit all pulled fresh from the trees, pineapples in perfection, oranges of every shape and flavor, and delicious bananas, guavas, yuccas, and a long catalogue of others, the beverage cocoanut water, from the cocoanut fruit; dinner at five, and very recherche; and a dozen servants." Almost regretfully he added that the commissioners expected to sail from Havana on November 6 for St. Thomas, about eight hundred miles down the British West Indian chain of islands, there to transfer to a second steamer, which was scheduled to reach London about November 28. In the British capital, he hoped to have "accounts from home, for which, Heaven knows how much I long."[23]

II.

The British Anticipate a Crisis

*Mutual distrust had produced mischief. England &
America seemed each to suspect the other of hostile
intentions, while it was possible that both were quite
mistaken.*

Lord Russell to an American Diplomat.
September 9, 1861.[1]

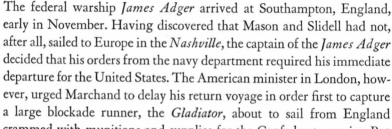

The federal warship *James Adger* arrived at Southampton, England,
early in November. Having discovered that Mason and Slidell had not,
after all, sailed to Europe in the *Nashville*, the captain of the *James Adger*
decided that his orders from the navy department required his immediate
departure for the United States. The American minister in London, however, urged Marchand to delay his return voyage in order first to capture
a large blockade runner, the *Gladiator*, about to sail from England
crammed with munitions and supplies for the Confederate armies. But
Marchand seemed little interested in this adventure, and Charles Francis
Adams might not have suggested it to him, had he known that the prime
minister of England was intensely interested in the *James Adger* and its
mission.[2]

Believing that Marchand's ship had come to British waters in search
of the West Indian mail packet which was supposed to be carrying Mason and Slidell, the venerable Henry John Temple, Lord Palmerston,
wrote the Foreign Office that the crown law officers "should be asked,
among other Questions, what would be the Rights of the American
Cruiser with Regard to the Passengers & Crew and lawful Papers and
Correspondence on Board our Packet, on the assumption that the said
Packet was liable to Capture & Confiscation on the ground of carrying

enemies [*sic*] Despatches." The premier also wanted to know whether the *James Adger* would be legally justified in carrying the packet with passengers and cargo all the way back to America, or whether she "would be obliged to land in this Country or at some near Port all the People and all the unseizable goods." In his opinion, to carry the passengers back to America, after their having traveled as far as the English Channel, would be "an intolerable Hardship."[3]

A preliminary report supplied by the undersecretary for foreign affairs, Edmund Hammond, was hardly encouraging. Travers Twiss, a leading authority on international law, had informed Hammond that it seemed "very doubtful whether the American vessel might not be justified in taking the Confederate Envoys out of the English Ship." Therefore, Hammond recommended that the mail steamer be contacted off the coast of Ireland and its captain be asked to "make some excuse for running into Cork and landing her mails and passengers there." Alternatively, he suggested that a warship might convoy the packet at least up the Channel to Southampton and prevent "her from being searched on the ground that she was coming as a mail from the British West Indian Islands."[4]

Hammond's recommendations went to the prime minister on Saturday, November 9. On the following Monday, Palmerston convened a special meeting at Downing Street, to which he summoned the lord chancellor, the home secretary, and the first lord of the admiralty, for the purpose of hearing an opinion on the case delivered by Sir Stephen Lushington, a distinguished admiralty jurist. Lushington asserted that "it was out of the question to attempt to protect the packet in any way beyond British waters from the interference of the American cruiser." His opinion was endorsed by Her Majesty's three law officers,[5] who joined the meeting after it was underway; hence Palmerston was finally convinced, "much to my regret," he later wrote,

> that, according to the principles of international law . . . practised and enforced by us . . . this American cruiser might . . . stop the West Indian packet, search her, and if the Southern men and their despatches and credentials were found on board, either take them out, or seize the packet and carry her back to New York for trial.[6]

At the same meeting, consideration was given to Hammond's suggestion, which had since been endorsed by the foreign minister, that the packet be convoyed into port by an English man-of-war. But, having granted the right of search outside the three-mile limit of territorial waters, Palmerston and his fellow conferees saw little justification for sending out a convoy vessel. The group did decide, however, to send a frigate, the *Phaeton*, to Yarmouth Roads, on the north coast of the Isle of Wight, where its captain could intervene if the *James Adger* attempted to stop and search the mail steamer *within* territorial waters as it headed into port at Southampton. In a memorandum of the meeting, Palmerston wrote that "we thought it would not be well that the Phaeton should keep Company with the American, & stand by and see the Packet searched & possibly Captured at Sea," and not be legally able to interfere. To this opinion, the foreign minister, who had been too ill with a bad head cold to attend the meeting on the question, reluctantly yielded.[7]

Both the *Gladiator* and the *James Adger* had put to sea by the morning of November 12. A thick fog heavy with coal smoke screened off the sun. At the United States legation, the Adamses were breakfasting by lamplight when a messenger delivered a note from Palmerston. "My Dear Sir," it read, "I would be very glad to have a few minutes conversation with you; could you without inconvenience call upon me today at any time between one and two." Surprised that the head of Her Majesty's government should want to see him in such haste, Adams spent the morning worrying whether some diplomatic crisis might be impending. Then, soon after the hour of one o'clock, he was ushered into the library of the premier's London residence, Cambridge House in Piccadilly. Lord Palmerston was cordial and businesslike. Without wasting time with amenities, he told the American minister that he had information that the object of the *James Adger* in frequenting British waters was to intercept the British packet carrying Mason and Slidell to England and to take them out of it by force, if necessary. Having got drunk on "some excellent brandy" the previous Sunday, Captain Marchand had then put to sea leaving the impression that he intended to wait for the mail packet's appearance off the Channel coast in a day or so.[8]

Whether a United States warship had a legal right to commit such an act against a foreign vessel, Palmerston said, was a question he would set aside, for the moment, "for those whose province it was to discuss it." But even admitting the right to take such a step, the exercise of such a right would be "highly inexpedient." For "it would be regarded here very unpleasantly," Adams reported the premier as saying,

> If the Captain, after enjoying the hospitality of this country, filling his ship with coals, and with other supplies, and filling his own stomach with brandy (and here he laughed in his characteristic way) should within sight of the shore commit an act which would be felt as offensive to the national flag. . . . [Regarding the Southern commissioners] it surely could not be supposed that the addition of one or two more to the number of persons who had already been some time in London on the same errand, could be likely to produce any change in the policy already adopted. He did not believe that the Government would vary its action on their account be they few or many. He could not therefore conceive of the necessity for resorting to such a measure as this which in the present state of opinion in England could scarcely fail to occasion more prejudice than it would do good.[9]

Having taken it for granted that the United States government had ordered the *James Adger* across the Atlantic Ocean to seize Mason and Slidell from a British ship, the prime minister had tried to convince Adams that he should prevent the execution of the alleged scheme not so much because of its impropriety as because of its inexpediency. This, thought Adams, furnished "a curious example" of the tendency of English minds to examine questions in terms of whether they were "politic," rather than on the basis of principle. The American minister quickly informed Palmerston of the true purpose of the *James Adger*'s mission. He had seen Captain Marchand's instructions, he asserted, and they directed him merely to seek out and capture a Confederate steamer called the *Nashville*, which the American officials believed to have evaded the blockade with Mason and Slidell on board. Adams "took it for granted that his Lordship had no objection to make to that proceeding." Having discovered on his arrival in England, however, both that the two Southern envoys had stopped in the West Indies, and that the *Nashville* was nowhere to be found, Captain Marchand had announced his intention to depart for home. Adams had urged that he linger long enough in English waters to keep his eye upon a steamer leaving the Thames River

15

about the same time carrying contraband of war for the insurgents in the United States, under the protection of the British flag. Americans "had been very much annoyed" by continuous shipments of arms and supplies to the Southern rebels from England. Such contraband carriers as the *Bermuda* and the *Fingal* had already become notorious. Now the *Gladiator* had loaded and left London "with scarcely any pretence of concealment." Adams had advised Marchand "to keep on the track of her and the very first moment he could form a reasonable conviction of her intent to land anywhere in the United States to snap her up at once if possible." With this single exception, Adams declared, he "thought the destination of the *James Adger* might be depended upon."[10]

Palmerston appeared "tolerably well satisfied" with this explanation.[11] He intimated, however, that before such an attack took place, proof that the vessel contained contraband destined for a Southern port should be well established. Adams replied that the United States government would do everything in its power to avoid "opening questions" with Great Britain. But it was undeniable "that these proceedings in England were excessively annoying, and that there would spring up a strong desire to arrest them as decisively as possible."[12]

As soon as the interview terminated, the prime minister wrote a brief note to the editor of the London *Times*, saying that he had seen Adams,

and he assures me that the American paddle-wheel was sent to intercept the *Nashville* if found in these seas, but not to meddle with any ship under a foreign flag. He said he had seen the commander, and had advised him to go straight home; and he believed the steamer to be now on her way back to the United States. This is a very satisfactory explanation.

Having duly informed the press, Palmerston then proceeded to acquaint the Foreign Office, the Home Office, the Admiralty, and the lord chancellor with what had transpired in his conversation with Adams, but characteristically he did not write the queen about it until the next day.[13]

On the same afternoon that Palmerston had his tension-easing talk with Adams, the Foreign Office received the written opinion which the prime minister had requested from the crown law officers three days before. The opinion was based on the assumption "that the United States' man-of-war steamer now lying at Southampton, or any other similar steamer of the United States, should attempt to intercept the West Indian mail steamer, with a view of getting possession of the persons of Messrs. Mason and Slidell, or of their credentials or instructions," beyond British territorial waters. The law officers declared that the officers of a belligerent warship might board the mail steamer, might examine her ship's papers and public mailbags, might "put a prize-crew on board the West India steamer, and carry her off to a port of the United States for adjudication by a Prize Court there; *but she would have no right to remove Messrs. Mason and Slidell and carry them off as prisoners, leaving the ship to pursue her voyage*."[14] The presence of "enemies [*sic*] despatches" on board the packet would alone entitle a captor "to carry her and everything in her, to America." No British warship would be justified in preventing the seizure on the high seas because all decisions about the legality of the act, belonged, under international law, "to the Prize Court of the captors."[15]

Now that the lawyers had finally decided the state of the law, the stage was set for a serious Anglo-American controversy. All that was required to create it was that a naval captain of the United States should seize the Southern envoys from a British mail steamer without also carrying the ship back to America for adjudication in a prize court. The fact that Palmerston had taken the unusual step of bypassing his foreign minister in order to speak directly to Adams on the subject indicated how apprehensive the prime minister was of trouble and how anxious he was to avoid it. Several days previously he had written to the colonial secretary that every report received from America, public and private, showed "that our relations with the Washington government are on the most precarious footing."[16] He feared that the excitement sure to follow any Yankee attempt to seize the Southern envoys from the deck of an English ship would furnish the Washington government what it had apparently long sought, a pretext for a serious quarrel with the government of Great Britain.

III.

Twisting the Lion's Tail

*I would throw up my cap if Lincoln will announce not
only his determination to hang every one we catch as a
pirate, but to catch him wherever he can find him, even
in English ports.*

HENRY SANFORD TO THURLOW WEED,
May 18, 1861.[1]

Captain Charles D. Wilkes, U.S.N. was sixty-two years old[2] when the
Civil War began. Unlike many naval officers who had been his close
acquaintances for several decades, he was staunchly loyal to the Union
and considered Southern secession a "great catastrophe." Two of his
sons, however, were ardent sympathizers with the Confederate cause,
and he had relatives and many close friends living in the South. Despite
having won fame early in his naval career as a scientist and Antarctic
explorer, Wilkes had been barred from assignment to important com-
mands and hindered in the struggle for promotion by a well-deserved
reputation for insubordination and ill temper. When the guns began
booming at Fort Sumter, he had been stationed at Washington in the
innocuous billet of chairman of the lighthouse board. Anxious to obtain
a command that would enable him to see combat before his imminent re-
tirement, he was bitterly disappointed to be sent, early in 1861, to the
coast of Africa to take command of the U.S.S. *San Jacinto*, a relatively
modern fighting ship, for the sole purpose of returning her to the Philadelphia Navy Yard for repairs and refitting.[3]

Wilkes took charge of the *San Jacinto*[4] at Fernando Po on August 28.
Violating his orders, which stipulated that "as soon as you can be ready,
you will proceed to the port of your ultimate destination," stopping only
for "coal or other supplies," he cruised along the African coast for nearly

one month, vainly seeking action against Confederate privateers. He then altered course westward, heading his ship not, however, for Philadelphia, but for the West Indies, where he hoped to find and sink the Southern commerce raider *Sumter*.

Touching at Jamaica, Grand Cayman, Boca Grande, and at Cienfuegos on the south coast of Cuba, Wilkes learned from the United States consul at the latter port that Mason, Slidell, their secretaries, and members of their families, were at Havana en route to Europe. Abandoning his search for the *Sumter*, Wilkes hurriedly loaded his ship's bunkers with coal and put to sea with the intention of intercepting the *Theodora*, which he assumed would continue to carry the insurgent envoys further on their journey.

Arriving at the Cuban capital on October 30, Wilkes found that the Confederate blockade-runner had already departed for Charleston, leaving the rebel envoys behind to await the sailing on November 7 of a British mail packet, which would take them to the island of St. Thomas, east of Puerto Rico, and thence to England. Wilkes heard that the consul general of Great Britain had presented Mason and Slidell to the captain general of Cuba as ministers of the Confederate States of America on the way to their respective posts at London and Paris. He also heard that the Englishman, with full knowledge of the missions of the rebel emissaries, had personally booked them for passage in the mail packet *Trent*.[5]

Two of the *San Jacinto*'s officers called on Mason at his hotel and had a long conversation with him but learned, according to him, "nothing touching our plans or purposes, beyond what was already generally known in the town." That the Southerners intended to sail on the *Trent* was part of this general public knowledge. Captain Wilkes had a choice to make. He might pursue the *Theodora*, which had almost a two-week headstart on him, on the unlikely supposition that he could overtake her before she ran the blockade. He might resume his search for the *Sumter*. He might, indeed, follow his orders from the Navy Department, from which he had already departed, calling upon him to deliver the *San Jacinto* to the Philadelphia Navy Yard. Finally, the daring notion struck him that he might intercept the *Trent*, once it had left Spanish territorial waters, in order forcibly to seize Mason and Slidell from under the protection of the British flag. After poring over charts and law books, and after consulting Lieutenant D.M. Fairfax, his executive officer, Wilkes reached a decision. Overriding Fairfax's earnest argument that the seizure of Mason and Slidell from the deck of the *Trent* might well touch off a war with England, the *San Jacinto*'s captain calculated the exact spot in the Bahama Channel where he might ambush the *Trent* on November 8. In the meantime he determined both to seek assistance from other United States warships in preparing his trap and to resume his search for the *Sumter*.

Starting his intentions to U.S. Consul General Robert Shufeldt,[6] and asking him to telegraph the exact time of the *Trent*'s departure to the Cuban port of Sagua la Grande where he would call for the message, Wilkes put to sea on November 2 and cruised his vessel along the north coast of Cuba, his lookouts alert for any sign of the *Sumter*.

In broad daylight on the following morning the *San Jacinto* collided with a French brig, *Jules et Maria*, sailing from Liverpool to Havana. Damage to this latter vessel was extensive, and Wilkes had to take her in tow to keep her from sinking. Altering his course, he reluctantly accompanied his victim most of the way to the nearest port with a repair yard.[7] At Key West, his next port of call, he was disappointed to learn that no recent news of the whereabouts of the *Sumter* had been received there. In vain did Fairfax beg Wilkes to consult Federal District Judge William Marvin, whom the lieutenant considered "one of the ablest maritime lawyers" in the country, before going through with his plans to stop the *Trent*. Wilkes had already "determined to take the steamer as a prize; the grounds of capture," he declared, "I have duly considered." He believed that no action he might take against the Southern rebels "would so effectively non-plus their diabolical schemes" as the capture of Mason and Slidell. He obviously wished to hear no opposition to his plan. Fairfax "therefore ceased to discuss the affair."

Back to the north coast of Cuba sailed the *San Jacinto*. She sailed alone; no other United States warship had been found at Key West to aid in Wilkes's daring venture. At the port of Sagua la Grande he went ashore to inquire for the expected telegram from Shufeldt, giving the *Trent*'s time of departure from Havana. Although Shufeldt had in fact sent a telegram, its message was garbled and of little help. Wilkes would have to depend entirely on what he already knew about the *Trent*'s sailing schedule. "If she left at the usual time," he calculated, and if the *San Jacinto* was positioned in the center of the fifteen-mile wide Bahama Channel near the Paredon del Grande lighthouse, "she must pass us about noon on the 8th and we could not possibly miss her."

At 11:40 A.M. on November 8 the cry rang out from the *San Jacinto's* crow's nest: "Steamer ahoy!" Emerging from his cabin, Wilkes anxiously raised his telescope. The approaching vessel was less than ten miles away. As drums beat "to quarters," Fairfax mustered sailors on deck and selected boarding parties for two of the ship's boats. Gradually the *Trent* drew near. When after an hour and twenty minutes had passed, she had approached to within a few hundred yards of the American warship, the British ensign fluttered to her masthead. Wilkes shouted an order, and as the American flag was hoisted in reply, a cloud of smoke spewed from one of the *San Jacinto's* portholes and a round shot flew through the air across the packet's bow and splashed several hundred yards away. Wilkes waited for the British captain to issue the order to heave to, but the small steamer maintained a steady pace. Another order rang out, and a shell was fired from the pivot gun at the bow, which burst uncomfortably close to the *Trent*, its fragments kicking up small spumes over a wide area of blue water. At once the *Trent's* engines were reversed, and slowly she came to a halt about two hundred yards away.

Wilkes summoned Fairfax and handed him a written set of instructions which called upon him to board the *Trent* and seize her papers, especially her passenger and crew lists. "Should Mr. Mason, Mr. Slidell, Mr. Eustis and Mr. Macfarland be on board," Wilkes had written, Fairfax should

> make them prisoners and send them on board this ship immediately and take possession of her as a prize.
>
> I do not deem it will be necessary to use force [but the prisoners] . . . must be brought on board. All trunks, cases, packages and bags belonging to them you will take possession of and send on board this ship. Any dispatches . . . will be taken possession of also, examined and retained if necessary. . . .
>
> I trust that all those under your command in executing this important and delicate duty will conduct themselves with all the delicacy and kindness which becomes the character of our naval service.

21

Wilkes had also ordered Fairfax to offer members of the families of the four Southern envoys passage on the *San Jacinto* to the United States, and to promise "all the attention and comforts we can command." If "necessaries or stores" unavailable on the American cruiser were needed by these additional passengers, Fairfax was to "procure them" from the *Trent*. Wilkes's paymaster would reimburse the British captain.

As a boat was lowered down the *San Jacinto*'s side, Wilkes shouted through a megaphone that preparations should be made to receive a boarding party. Soon more than "twenty men armed with cutlasses and pistols in their belts"[8] were on their way, paddles splashing, to the *Trent*. Concluding that they "meant mischief," James Mason sent his secretary, Macfarland to "take the dispatch bag which contained my public papers, credentials, instructions, etc., and which was in my state-room, and deliver it to the mail agent of the steamer, to tell him what it was and ask him to lock it up in his mail-room, and I told him at the same time to make the same suggestion to Mr. Slidell." Before Fairfax's boat reached the *Trent*'s side, the British mail agent, a retired commander of the Royal Navy, bustled up to Mason and whispered conspiratorially that he had locked both dispatch bags in his mail room, to which, he added, "I have the key in my pocket and whatever their objects may be they must pass over my body before they enter that room." Asked by Mason, in the event that the Southern commissioners were unable to complete the trip to England, to deliver the bags to Confederate agents already in London, Commander Richard Williams promised that he would see them safely to their destination.[9]

Instructing his boat crew to remain seated and quietly to await further orders, Fairfax climbed to the *Trent*'s main deck, where an indignant Captain James Moir awaited him. A hostile crowd of seventy or eighty passengers and crewmen, edged forward to listen. Upon being introduced to Moir, the American lieutenant said that he had been informed that enemies of the United States named Mason and Slidell were on board the *Trent*. He asked to see her passenger list. Hearing his name mentioned, a paunchy, white-haired gentleman stepped toward Fairfax and certified himself as Slidell. Soon the thin-lipped, red-nosed Mason joined the group, and at a gesture from the portly Virginian, Eustis and

Macfarland joined the others crowded around the captain. Fairfax then announced that he had orders "to arrest Mr. Mason and Mr. Slidell and their secretaries, and send them prisoners on board the United States war vessel near by."[10]

Hearing these words, some of the passengers, many of whom were Southerners, bristled with anger and indignation. One drawled: "Throw the damned fellow overboard!" Others began threateningly to advance toward Fairfax. Shouting over the threats and catcalls, the American lieutenant observed, with a significant gesture toward the menacing bulk of the *San Jacinto*, that his every move was being closely scrutinized through spyglasses, that a heavy battery of loaded guns was trained upon the *Trent*, and that any injury or indignity to an American officer or sailor might lead to "dreadful consequences." At once the British captain called for peaceful behavior on board his ship. Gradually the commotion subsided, and Fairfax began to breathe more easily.

A few moments later, however, the uproar resumed. The officer whom Fairfax had left in command of his boat, hearing all the noise, and fearing ill-treatment of his executive officer, had rushed up the ladder to the rescue, bringing with him six or eight sailors armed with bayonetted muskets. As the Americans, flourishing their ugly-looking weapons, hurried to Fairfax's side, Captain Moir swung around, saw them, and immediately demanded that they leave his ship. The Southern men muttered and growled once more, and their women looked frightened. Amid the renewed commotion, Williams kept chiming in that he was in charge, that he solemnly protested "this act of piracy," and that Fairfax must refer all questions to him for decision.[11]

Shaking off the insistent grip on his arm of the querulous mail agent, Fairfax ordered the American sailors to return to their boat and hurried the process of gathering the baggage of the rebel envoys and their secretaries. He also sent a paymaster's clerk below to purchase supplies "to add to the comfort of the new guests."

Having asked Moir to allow a peaceful search of his vessel, and having received a blunt refusal, Fairfax did not attempt to use force to ransack the *Trent* for Confederate dispatches or letters. To search the vessel against her captain's determined opposition would have entailed taking command of her as a prize, which Fairfax, anticipating that such an act might cause the British government later to declare war against the United States, wished to avoid if at all possible.

While her husband was locating his baggage, Mrs. Slidell came forward and asked who commanded the *San Jacinto*. Fairfax answered: "Your old acquaintance, Captain Wilkes." Mrs. Slidell looked surprised. She expressed amazement that Fairfax's chief should commit an act certain to rouse the hostility of England. "Really," she asserted, "Captain Wilkes is playing into our hands!" At this juncture, however, Mason broke in to suggest that it was an inopportune moment to discuss such matters, and Mrs. Slidell soon walked away. Both she and Mrs. Eustis firmly rejected Fairfax's offer to let them accompany their husbands aboard the *San Jacinto*.

At first Mason and Slidell appeared docile. They accompanied Fairfax down a ladder to the lower deck, but there, at the entrance to the ship's lounge, off which their staterooms opened, both balked at going further, unless compelled to do so by the use of force. While Fairfax sent a boatswain to the gangway to bring help, the Southerners retreated inside the lounge, followed by Slidell's wife, son, and three daughters, and many other passengers. Summoning Lieutenant James Greer from his boat, along with eight Marines, Fairfax followed the Confederate commissioners into the lounge, accompanied by a young petty officer, and eventually the two Americans reappeared, firmly propelling Mason between them.

While Mason remained in custody on deck, Fairfax went back inside to seek Slidell. There he was berated by one of Slidell's daughters, who insisted that her father would not leave the ship, and who barred the way to the stateroom where Slidell was still conversing with his wife. Passengers and even ship's officers crowded around Fairfax, "making all kinds of disagreeable and contemptuous noises and remarks."

Soon the petty officer who had accompanied Fairfax into the lounge re-emerged and suggested that Greer send the Marines inside to help the executive officer, who was getting nowhere in his attempt to enter Slidell's stateroom. As Greer hesitated, a Southern voice from within shouted: "Shoot him." At once Greer ordered the Marines forward, and they rushed into the lounge flourishing their weapons. The passengers fell back. At almost the same moment the ship rolled over a large wave, and Commander Williams, standing at one side of the large cabin, saw the still arguing Slidell girl lose her balance and fall against Fairfax, who steadied her for a moment.[12] Apparently, Slidell decided that it was now time for him to reappear. There was a crash, the window burst outward, and the Louisiana lawyer half stepped, half fell, into the midst of the excited spectators. Meekly, he allowed Fairfax to take his arm and escort him, along with Mason and the two secretaries, outside the lounge and across the deck towards the gangway.[13]

Seeing her father thus convoyed, the Slidell girl gave vent to a hysterical scream,[14] which was followed by cries of "pirates" from some of the passengers, and a general surge forward, apparently with the idea of blocking the exit of the party from the ship. At an order from Fairfax, however, the Marines advanced, grimly raising their muskets, bayonets pointed toward the "vehemently excited" crowd. A pathway quickly opened to the ship's side. As Commander Williams loudly threatened that the British navy would retaliate within a few weeks by destroying the entire Northern blockade, the captives gingerly descended into Captain Wilkes's personal cutter.[15] As Greer ferried them to the *San Jacinto*, Fairfax supervised the loading of their baggage onto another boat, and hurried the evacuation from the *Trent* of the handful of American sailors and Marines still aboard her.[16]

When they arrived at the *San Jacinto*, the four Southerners found Wilkes waiting on deck. Introducing himself,[17] he led them to the captain's cabin, where he turned over the two staterooms there to Mason and Slidell, and he invited Eustis and Macfarland to occupy the best officer's quarters in the wardroom.[18] Calling in his steward, Wilkes said, according to Mason: "Steward, you will understand that the cabin, and all the stores belonging to it, are at the command of these gentlemen, and you will obey their orders accordingly."[19]

While Mason and Slidell stared out the captain's portholes at the boats scurrying back and forth between the two ships, Fairfax, having brought the boatload of baggage for the Southerners, reappeared on board the *San Jacinto*. He told Wilkes that he had not yet carried out that portion of his orders requiring him to make the *Trent* a prize of war. While the captain frowned impatiently, Fairfax argued that in view of Wilkes's previously announced intention of sailing next to Port Royal, South Carolina, there to participate in a Northern naval attack on that Confederate stronghold, it would be dangerous to weaken the fighting capacity of the *San Jacinto* by leaving a large prize crew on board the *Trent*. Furthermore, if the mail packet was taken to Key West for condemnation as a prize of war, many "innocent persons," both passengers, among whom were a large number of women and children, and also the addressees and consignees of the large amount of mail and specie (allegedly worth one million dollars), would be seriously inconvenienced. Hence Fairfax begged Wilkes to reconsider his original order.

After a few moments of thought, Wilkes finally agreed to do so. He told Fairfax to return to the *Trent* and to inform Moir that he was free to resume his voyage. He then went below and invited his Southern "guests" to come on deck to ascertain whether their possessions were all accounted for. When the Confederate emissaries found "some little parcels of our stores" missing, Wilkes sent another boat to the *Trent* to pick up the absent items. He also ordered additionally that "some dozens of sherry, with pitchers and basins, and other conveniences for the toilet" be purchased for the enjoyment of his passengers. No sooner had this mission been performed than the *Trent* steamed off to the southeastward, while the *San Jacinto* prepared to sail north to the American coast.

The entire incident had lasted less than three hours. The principal participants had shown each other great courtesy and forebearance throughout the ordeal.[20] Even the officious Williams had come forward as Fairfax was stepping off the deck of the *Trent* for the last time, to bid the American officer a pleasant good-by, and the retired British commander had complimented Fairfax on his "moderate and gentlemanly manner throughout this very embarrassing and perplexing duty."[21]

As the prisoners on board the *San Jacinto* prepared for sleep that night, Wilkes scribbled elatedly in his diary that the day of November 8 "has been one of the most important in my naval life." He had seized the Southerners with a minimum of unpleasantness, had "made them as comfortable as we could, and [he wrote] I shall continue to treat them well."

The almost exaggerated courtesies and compliments exchanged among the *San Jacinto*'s officers and their captives continued for the duration of her long voyage north. Wilkes's immediate purpose was to join Admiral

DuPont's fleet off Charleston in time to participate in the Port Royal expedition. As he headed his ship northwest through the Santaren Channel toward the east coast of Florida, St. Petersburg came into view off the port side and then slowly slipped into the distance off the stern. Veering several miles seaward, the cruiser picked up speed in the Gulf Stream.

While the prisoners sat on deck gazing wistfully at the tantalizing green shores of the Georgia coast, Wilkes collected a thick sack of depositions from his officers giving their respective accounts of the seizure of the Southerners from the *Trent*. On their first day at sea following their capture, the rebel envoys had handed Wilkes an elaborate memorandum containing their agreed-upon version of the incident, along with a request that it be transmitted to the United States government as a statement offered by on-the-spot witnesses to the events described therein. Realizing that he had not seen with his own eyes many of the details of the actual seizure, and that serious questions of international law, and possibly also questions of war and peace, were involved in that incident, Wilkes had decided to arm himself with written statements from his own subordinates.

Perhaps he had been able to overhear the garrulous Mason, pacing the deck with his secretary, Macfarland, declaring that the "piracy" of his host would "produce a profound sensation" in England, followed by a "categorical" demand for the Southerners' release. For the public indignation would be such, Mason had proclaimed, that "no ministry could live an hour, which did not fully respond to it." If the demand met with a refusal from the authorities at Washington, Mason had gleefully calculated, the British would join the Confederates in common cause. (This theme was also repeated several times during the voyage by Eustis, in conversations with Fairfax.)

Wilkes, who claimed to have consulted "all the authorities on international law to which I had access, viz, Kent, Wheaton and Vattel, besides various decisions of Sir William Scott and other judges of the Admiralty Court of Great Britain which bore upon the rights of neutrals and their responsibilities," had satisfied himself before stopping the *Trent* that he was legally justified in ridding her of the rebel envoys. But in the fervor of preparation for the seizure, his study of international law had been cursory at best, and the fact that he refused Fairfax's request to consult the Admiralty court judge at Key West before waylaying the *Trent* indicated that he was not completely sure of his legal ground and that the real basis for the capture was expediency, not legal authority.

Wilkes's worries momentarily appeared justified when late on the afternoon of November 10 a warship flying the British flag bore down upon the *San Jacinto* from the north. As Mason and Slidell stood hopefully on deck, the American crew dashed to their battle stations, while the cry of "general quarters" reverberated throughout the ship. But the British vessel proved only to be the gunboat *Steady*, regularly used as a courier between Halifax, New York, Washington, and Bermuda, where the admiral of the West Indian Fleet had his headquarters. Exchanging hails of identification, the two warships passed without incident. The seizure of Mason and Slidell was as yet unknown to the British navy.

Two days later the *San Jacinto* sailed in among the Federal blockading fleet off Charleston. Mason and Slidell could dimly see the Confederate flag waving over Fort Sumter, which bulked menacingly in the blue harbor from which they had so recently departed. After boarding several of the Northern warships and learning that the Port Royal expedition had already sailed, Wilkes decided at once to resume his northward voyage, stopping only at Hampton Roads, Virginia, to replenish his dwindling supply of coal. Arriving there during the afternoon hours of November 15, he sent off a special messenger to the Navy Department with his voluminous official reports on the seizure of Mason and Slidell. When the Confederate envoys asked for the bills for some barrels of oysters which they had requested be brought aboard for them, the steward informed them that Wilkes had ordered his purser to pay for them out of the ship's funds. Perhaps overwhelmed by this last act of generosity, the four Southerners signed a brief acknowledgment that they had "uniformly been treated with great courtesy and attention" during their entire stay on board the *San Jacinto*.

On the morning of November 16 the voyage northward was resumed. Already military telegraphs in Washington had tapped out the news of the capture of the rebel commissioners; and early in the afternoon, Wilkes's dispatches and letters were delivered at the Navy Department by Captain Alfred Taylor, who had traveled by boat to Baltimore and thence to Washington by special train. Before the government working day was over, several telegrams went off to the United States marshal at New York to board the *San Jacinto* on her arrival there and escort "Mason and Slidell and Suite" to Fort Warren at Boston. Enterprising journalists dug up enough of the story to file reports for publication the next day, while the Associated Press service telegraphed its own account of the *Trent* incident to catch a steamer already approaching Cape Race, Newfoundland, on its way to England. A telegraph company official reported from New York: "The excitement here is great. All hands seem rejoiced. The stock brokers are working for a fall on the strength of difficulty with England. The people are glad to see John Bull taken by the horns. It is suggested . . . to stop Mason's oysters and Slidell's whiskey."

As the news of her heroics became the leading topic of conversation all over the United States, the *San Jacinto* steamed onward, those aboard her oblivious to the growing furor, as each day's newspaper headlines fed on the growing intensity of argumentative commentary about the case. At New York, Wilkes's vessel was intercepted in the narrows by a tugboat, and while Mason and Slidell and Macfarland played backgammon in the cabin, two Federal marshals came aboard in a late evening rainstorm with orders from the secretaries of the navy and state to deliver the prisoners "immediately" to Fort Warren. So the *San Jacinto* did not dock at New York but continued her voyage. The seasick marshals were kept away from the Confederate prisoners during the time it took to reach Boston Harbor; indeed, Wilkes confided to Mason, he had ordered that "they could have nothing to do with you gentlemen, whilst you were on board my ship."

As the vessel made its way along the coast of Long Island, the weather grew "most uncomfortably cold" for the thin-blooded Southerners. Upon hearing their complaints, Wilkes stilled their shivering by supplying the cabin with glowing red shot, fresh from the ship's furnaces, hauled up several ladders in large buckets of sand.

After pausing briefly at Newport for more coal and for a stove to be installed in the cabin for the comfort of his passengers, and after putting into Martha's Vineyard for about twenty-four hours until a thick fog lifted, Wilkes finally brought the *San Jacinto* around the tip of Cape

Cod; and at 7:30 on the morning of November 24, he gave the order to drop anchor at Fort Warren, about eight miles from the city of Boston. It took almost four hours to get the Southerners and their vast amount of baggage moved off the ship; then, with a snowstorm blowing up, the *San Jacinto* steamed quickly across the bay to the Charlestown Navy Yard, where the officers and crew were at last free to go ashore, there to luxuriate in the pleasing warmth of mass adulation.

Colonel Justin Dimick, commanding officer at Fort Warren, apologized profusely to his distinguished "guests" for being ill prepared for their arrival. He invited them to take their ease in his personal quarters until comfortable rooms could be made ready for them. When the Federal marshal from New York searched the prisoners' baggage,[22] according to Mason, Colonel Dimick allowed him to do so with the greatest reluctance, saying to his captives: "Gentlemen, I hope you will understand that I have nothing to do with it." After a superficial search, the marshal left to send a telegram to Secretary of State Seward announcing that after he had personally "delivered" the prisoners to Dimick, he had "thoroughly searched and examined their baggage but found no papers of any description whatever." The written evidence requisite for a successful Admiralty court prosecution of the four Confederates as carriers of enemy dispatches had all been left behind on the *Trent*.

Early in the afternoon of their first day at Fort Warren, the Southern envoys were conducted to their rooms, which were small but clean and warmed by large fires. The furniture of each room consisted of "a plain pine table, a few camp stools," the baggage of the occupant, a wooden bedstead, with a straw mattress and pillows, and heavy woolen army blankets. When they wandered outside, the Confederate emissaries discovered that the fortress was approximately circular in shape[23] and filled all but the beaches of an island in Boston Bay. The stone barracks for the officers and men of the garrison, where Mason and Slidell were billeted, had been constructed against the outer fortifications, and between them and the interior buildings, where most of the prisoners were crowded into large drafty halls, were courtyards used for exercise and visiting. The two distinguished latecomers were from the outset singled out by the "respectful and deferential" commanding officer of the fort for special treatment, such as being allowed to have lights and visitors until late at night. Moreover, Mason and Slidell were able to avoid the daily prison ration (twenty-two ounces of flour, twelve ounces of bacon, one-half pound of potatoes, and a little coffee, sugar, salt, and vinegar) by joining a select mess which Dimick had allowed to be established in a large room in one of the barracks. There, professional cooks brought from Boston prepared hot dinners with food purchased there each morning. The "mess fee" was a dollar a day. In later years, Mason could still smack his lips at the recollection of innumerable meals of canvasback ducks, terrapins, oysters, and turkeys, topped off by some of the thousands of fresh Havana cigars that had accompanied the slaveholder diplomat into captivity. Afternoon toddies, evening teas, and perpetual games of whist enabled them agreeably to pass the time. An occasional letter reached them from home, and each day they could receive fresh newspapers and magazines from England, as well as from Boston, New York, Philadelphia, and other Northern cities. It was not an uncomfortable situation.

IV.

Union Opinon-makers Confront the *Trent* Crisis

Welcome to Wilkes! who didn't wait
To study up Vattel and Wheaton,
But bagged his game, and left the act
For dull diplomacy to treat on. . . .

Who talks for exploit such as this
Of government's assured displeasure?
A country's gratitude instead
Outspeaks in large, unstinted measure![1]

From newspapers a few days old the Confederate commissioners were able to learn how the Yankee journalists had "vied with each other in laudation of the act of capturing the 'rebel emissaries.'" Most Northerners had learned of the capture of Mason and Slidell on November 16, when afternoon newspapers announced the event in front-page headlines. Few journals were published on the following day, Sunday, but those which appeared that morning gave the capture of the Southern commissioners extensive coverage. By Monday, November 18, the Northern press seemed universally engulfed in a massive wave of chauvinistic elation.[2] As a writer for the Boston *Transcript* put it, the capture of Mason and Slidell "was one of those bold strokes by which the destinies of nations are determined." Captain Wilkes had "dealt a heavy blow—at the very vitals of the conspiracy threatening our national existence."[3]

Journalists everywhere in Yankeeland jumped at the opportunity to gloat over the humiliation of the captive slaveholders. Mason was labeled a "knave," a "coward," a "bully," and a "snob," as well as a "pompous, conceited, shallow," depraved "traitor." Slidell was described

32

as "cold, cruel, selfish," rapacious, and utterly corrupt—"the most accomplished scoundrel, and the ablest engineer of [the secession] conspiracy in all the South." The "caged ambassadors" embodied the evil arrogance of slave society. If the Northern military forces had been able to "search the whole of Rebeldom, no persons so justly obnoxious to the North could have been found."[4]

So ecstatic were Northern journalists about the capture of the hated former senators that they discounted the possible dangers of the deed. How would the British government react to the kidnapping of civilian passengers from a British ship? "We do not know," Horace Greeley editorialized, "and we do not greatly care." As another writer declared, the "heavy blow" dealt by Wilkes at the Southern conspiracy justified "hazarding the displeasure of a powerful nation." Northern newspapermen, in various ways, reflected a widespread conviction that the British government would probably not even remonstrate. For "the gallant act of Lieut. [*sic*] Wilkes so full of spirit and good sense" had been "an exact imitation" of longstanding British belligerent maritime practice.[5]

Such remarks, however, had a perceptible quaver about them. Within twenty-four hours of the time people in Boston learned of Wilkes's feat, a visiting Englishman noticed that a strident "clamour of justification" broke out "among the lawyers," and was soon taken up by the populace, until "every man and every woman in Boston were armed with precedents." The British consul in that city reported that every second citizen was "walking about with a Law Book under his arm and proving the *right* of the Ss. Jacintho [*sic*] to stop H.M's. mail boat." In New York, also, uneasiness intensified as prominent citizens attempted, through prolonged discussion of the legal aspects of the incident, to convince themselves that international law justified Wilkes's daring venture. And in Washington, although "everybody . . . rejoiced that the arch rebels are in custody. . . . The circumstances connected with their arrest have created some apprehensions of consequences. . . . There is a casting about for precedents, and in the streets even Grotius, Puffendorf, Vattel and Wheaton are learnedly appealed to for justification."[6]

Chanting quotations from anachronistic decisions and interpretations of Western legal luminaries, Northern editors marched confidently into the foggy morass of international maritime law, hurling "precedents" right and left in justification of the *Trent* seizure. For about one week the legality of that act seemed unquestionable. Then, one by one, the "precedents" so confidently cited earlier were revealed by publicists to be erroneous or inapplicable. On November 24, an editorial writer for the *New York Times* admitted that there appeared to be "not on record a single case precisely similar" to that of the *Trent* seizure. Although, "so far as general principles and the scope and spirit of international law go, we are clearly justified," the same writer added, there was unfortunately enough "vagueness in the matter" to allow the British to "construe" the case otherwise. Americans could only hope that Englishmen would be reluctant "to take advantage of a quibble . . . to rush into war." In the *Daily Tribune*, editor Horace Greeley suggested that the Lincoln administration "could very well afford" to surrender Mason and Slidell to the British, in order to establish a "precedent and principle" requiring that "belligerents on board neutral ships" should be considered immune from capture. In the *Albany Evening Journal*, whose long-time editor, Thurlow Weed, was a close friend and political associate of Secretary of State Seward, an editorial suggested that if Captain Wilkes had "exercised an unwarranted discretion, our Government will properly disavow the proceedings and grant England 'every satisfaction' consistent with honor and justice."[7]

"Observer," the Washington correspondent of the *New York Times*, soon revealed that "the surrender of the culprits" was being seriously discussed in the nation's capital. In the same newspaper readers also discovered that since Wilkes and Fairfax had neglected to search the *Trent* for the papers of the Confederate captives, evidence which was necessary to justify the condemnation of the vessel, the abduction of Mason and Slidell probably had no legal basis. Early in December a spokesman for the *Times* warned that journal's readers that Wilkes's "bold deed" might not, after all, be "justified by the principles and precedents of international law." Should that, indeed, be the case, there could "be no hesitation as to the course to be pursued—however gratifying the seizure of the rebel Ambassadors may have been, it is not worth the sacrifice of a single principle of the public morality of nations." Secretary Seward should be left entirely free to pursue "such a course as, on a full examination of the question in all its bearings, may seem to be dictated by right and the law of nations."[8]

Although many of those who wrote about the *Trent* difficulty persisted in treating it entirely as a legal question, perceptive readers could see that the possibility that it might precipitate a serious conflict with England, an outcome vigorously deprecated in many newspaper editorials, would be a factor affecting the final disposition of the insurrectionary emissaries, quite as much as the narrow and slippery pathways of international law. Americans were soon allowed a preview of the probable reaction of the British government. From nearby British Canada, from British subjects in Central America and in the West Indies, and from Englishmen currently residing in the United States, came expressions of violent indignation and an almost universal demand either for restitution of the captives or for war against the United States. Reacting to this outburst of feeling, a writer for the *New York Times* cautioned his fellow countrymen that the naval armaments of the United States were "insignificant" compared to those of either England or France, and he expressed a hope that American leaders would not "permit the country to drift carelessly into a war with any foreign power at the present time." Such acts as that committed by Wilkes did not justify talk of war. Whether Mason and Slidell remained in a Northern prison could not, in itself, affect the outcome of the Civil War. Hence the United States government would "lose nothing by restoring matters to their original status," and releasing the rebel commissioners to British custody.[9]

As leading American journalists awaited the British reaction to the *Trent* abduction, therefore, their oft-repeated theme was conciliation rather than defiance. Well before the English position on the seizure could be explicitly ascertained in America, a placatory press had begun to condition the American people to the unpleasant possibility that the Southern prisoners might be set free.[10]

In recorded expressions of opinion by private citizens of the North, a trend similar to that encountered in newspaper editorials may be discerned. At first well known Boston lawyers like Edward Everett (a former secretary of state), Richard Henry Dana, Jr., George Sumner, and Theophilus Parsons, justified Wilkes's act by citing precedents from international law. But many Northern politicians less dogmatic and more realistic, asserted openly, as did former President James Buchanan, that "the prisoners would of course be given up as soon as the facts came officially before the government," for passengers sailing under the British flag were entitled to its protection. Such venerable politicians as Thomas Ewing, a former senator and previously a member of two presidential cabinets; Lewis Cass, formerly a senator, a secretary of war, and a secretary of state; and Robert J. Walker, a former senator and secretary of the treasury in the Polk administration; all pointed out that it was vital for the future of the nation to settle the *Trent* affair peaceably, even if that meant relinquishing Mason and Slidell to Great Britain. By the third week of December even members of the Boston bar had begun to reflect the prudence of the amiable statesmen who had held power during the 1840s and 1850s, before New England righteousness had joined the anti-Southern economics of the Middle West to overthrow them. George T. Curtis mirrored the new cool-headed approach, which had also become the theme of most Northern newspapers, when he wrote the editor of the Boston *Journal* that the British had the right, under international law, to demand the return to the protection of their flag, of the Southern commissioners, and "all Europe" would probably support them. Americans should not expect their national government "to do the impossible"— to uphold "the lawfulness of this capture."[11]

Unfortunately, loyal Americans in Europe had no means of learning that many influential segments of public opinion in their homeland espoused relinquishing Mason and Slidell, if that became necessary to avoid war with Great Britain. Not until the last few days of the year did reports reach London indicating that Northerners generally comprehended both the enormity of their danger and the precariousness of their legal position. Before this news could cross the Atlantic Ocean, however, Americans in England suffered through a plethora of desperate days.

V.

On the Verge of War

*There is hardly any amount of violence to which a
captain of an American man of war, if he were clearly
in superior force, might not be expected to resort. . . .
And however outrageous in itself and opposed to International Law the conduct of the American officers
might be, it would meet with enthusiastic applause from
the multitude, and consequently the Government would
not dare to disavow it.*

Lord Lyons to Lord Malmesbury,
May 30, 1859.[1]

On the morning of November 21 the American minister at London
learned that the Southern warship *Nashville* had just arrived at Southampton after having captured and destroyed a Northern merchant ship,
the *Harvey Birch*. Here, Adams thought, was "a sudden turn in the
wheel of fortune." When the news reached America, the excitement
would be "prodigious," and if the *Nashville* received hospitality in England, as seemed probable, the demand in the United States for Adams's
recall would be "universal." So, he thought, "I may as well be making
preparation for that contingency."[2]

Soon William H. Nelson, the portly master of the *Harvey Birch*, arrived to tell his story. He related glumly how he had been sailing in
ballast from Le Havre bound for New York, when he had been stopped
by the *Nashville*, his papers seized, his crew and himself made prisoners,
and all his fresh stores transferred on board the Southern cruiser, after
which the *Harvey Birch* had been set on fire. The chronometer and
barometer belonging to the *Harvey Birch* had been taken by Captain
Robert B. Pegram of the *Nashville* as "spoils of war." Repeatedly, while
on board the Confederate steamer, the Northern captain had been told

by some of her officers that she had not yet been fitted out completely as a vessel of war, but was on her way to England for that purpose, and that she carried Confederate naval officers instructed to take command of two other vessels then also being prepared in British ports as Southern men-of-war. Nelson had also been informed that the crew, composed almost entirely of English and Irish seamen, had originally signed articles at Charleston, S.C., to sail to Liverpool, "but that before sailing the officers were all changed, and new articles were brought on board, which the crew were compelled to sign by threat of force."[3]

Adams directed Nelson to repeat his story in the form of a sworn statement, so that it might serve as the basis for a representation to Lord John Russell, the foreign minister, that the *Nashville* ought to be seized as a pirate. For Adams decided that perhaps the best way to prevent his countrymen "from getting embroiled" with Great Britain over this latest question would be to submit it at once to the methodical machinery of the British judicial system, rather than to allow it to become the subject of a spirited diplomacy.[4]

On Saturday afternoon, November 23, Adams completed an elaborate note to Russell, attached the supporting papers, and sent the documents by messenger to the Foreign Office. "The act of wilfully burning a private merchant ship," he wrote, would have been barbarous even if committed by a vessel duly commissioned as a ship of war by a recognized belligerent, or sailing under letters of marque, "but when voluntarily undertaken by individuals, not vested with the powers generally acknowledged to be necessary to justify aggressive warfare, it approximates too closely within the definition of piracy to receive the smallest countenance from any Christian people." Adams requested the British government to institute an inquiry to determine both whether the Southern vessel was not "subject to due process of law as a common disturber of the peace of the world," and whether she had not come to England to arm herself further "for carrying on a war against the people of a friendly nation." Should the latter accusation be true, Adams asked, was this "recognized belligerent" to be allowed "with impunity to violate the terms of her Majesty's proclamation forbidding the fitting out within the ports of Great Britain of any armament intended to be used against a nation with which she is at peace?"[5]

The minions of the Foreign Office and of the Admiralty had already warmed the telegraph wires to Southampton with inquiries about the *Nashville*. From the customs office at that port came information about the destruction of the *Harvey Birch* and a declaration by the captain of the *Nashville* that his vessel had been commissioned as a regular man-of-war in the Confederate navy. To prove his contention, Captain Pegram produced copies of officers' commissions. Maintaining that his ship had passed through heavy weather, he said that he desired "to place her in dry dock for calking and other repairs." At once Foreign Minister John Russell issued instructions that the *Nashville* "shall not be allowed to equip herself more completely as a vessel of war or to take in guns or munitions of war." He also decided to ask the crown law officers to determine whether the ship had violated international law and whether, if so, any legal action should be taken by the British government against her.[6]

Before receiving Adams's remonstrance, Russell ordered additionally that the *Nashville* should be prevented by the Royal Navy from "going out of Dock before we have settled the right & wrong of the case," for "important & difficult questions of international law are involved in her proceedings." If the Confederate captain suspected that his vessel was being held, Russell wrote, "she may get away in a hurry." To Adams the foreign minister wrote hurriedly that the American protest would "receive the immediate attention of her Majesty's government." Instructions had already been issued "that no infringement of the foreign enlistment act shall be permitted in regard to the *Nashville*." Inquiries were still being made about the sinking of the *Harvey Birch*. This message, brief though it was, pleased Adams, "first by its promptness, and secondly by its manifestation of willingness to do something. Upon this much of the preservation of good feeling in America must depend."[7]

Adams had advised Captain Nelson of the *Harvey Birch* to consult legal counsel about reacquiring his property taken by the commander of the *Nashville*. He hoped thus "to throw the question of the vessel's character into the Courts." A search would be sought to locate and attach Captain Nelson's goods. When the *Nashville*'s status under international law was thus made a matter of judicial inquiry, her officers would be forced to produce the authority under which she sailed, and if they had no regular navy commission or letters of marque for privateering, then there was only one possible ruling for a court to make—that she was a pirate ship. A judgment of this kind would not only end the career of the *Nashville*. It would also give Adams a powerful lever to use in subsequent cases involving armed vessels sailing under the Confederate flag.[8]

While Adams waited to see how the affair of the *Nashville* might be resolved, he had to discourage efforts to sponsor armed expeditions against her. George Schuyler, a Union arms agent from New York, wrote from Paris that the *Arago*, a large, powerful Northern mail steamer, "partly armed already," was in the English Channel, and he believed that Adams might have the authority to purchase her on behalf of the United States government in order to take "active measures" against the *Nashville*. Should Adams agree, Schuyler added, "please consider me at your dispatch to assist in any capacity you think proper." Adams replied, however, that inasmuch as he was even then remonstrating with the British government against similar proceedings by the Southerners, the New Yorker might "see at a glance that I must carefully abstain from any equivocal act."[9]

Next came the energetic Captain Edwin Eastman, who had been so anxious in October to assist the *James Adger* in intercepting the *Gladiator*. The New Englander arrived at the legation "full of fight" and with plans to purchase a ship called the *Adriatic* and use her to pursue the *Nashville*. But Adams could not furnish him with the requisite funds, and apparently neither the banker George Peabody, nor any other wealthy American citizen in London, was disposed to finance such an expedition.[10]

At the instigation of the British prime minister, meanwhile, the queen's advocate was induced to provide a quick unofficial comment on Adams's double-barreled demand—that the *Nashville* be condemned as a pirate, or that, if not thus detained, at least she should be prevented from adding armaments. Sir John Harding responded that no evidence had been offered to justify the ship's detention. The Southerners had produced papers to show that the *Nashville* was a regular ship of war commissioned by a recognized belligerent nation. The destruction of the *Harvey Birch* had been accomplished outside English jurisdiction, and no proof had been produced to show that the Southerners fell within the terms of the Anglo-American extradition treaty. Hence all that could be done was to give "orders that the enlistment act shall be enforced." Later, still at Palmerston's insistence, the two remaining crown law officers were consulted regarding Adams's note, and they gave substantially the same opinion as their colleague. Russell, therefore, wrote the American minister on November 28 that the *Nashville* appeared upon investigation to be "a Confederate vessel-of-war," whose action in capturing and burning, on the high seas, an American merchant ship, was deemed by Her Majesty's government a legitimate act of war. The fact that several of the Southern steamer's officers had exhibited regular naval commissions was, Russell wrote, sufficient evidence that she was a warship and not a pirate. Adams's remonstrance, however, had "been the subject of careful and anxious consideration," and Russell assured the American envoy that great care would be taken "to prevent the *Nashville* from augmenting her warlike force within Her Majesty's jurisdiction."[11]

Captain Nelson was unsuccessful in his lawsuit. The authorities at Southampton would not issue a search warrant without the sanction of the foreign minister, which was denied them in a letter saying that Russell had "no power to give authority . . . to issue any summons or warrants or do or abstain from doing anything in relation to the matter." Hence, Captain Nelson returned, baffled and dejected, to America; the *Nashville* went into drydock at Southampton, while her officers were lavishly entertained by many citizens of that town; and the attention of the American minister at London was soon diverted to other even more serious questions.[12]

While awaiting Russell's response to his inquiries on the subject of the *Nashville*, Adams decided to take his wife, who was anxious momentarily to escape from London, on a visit to the Yorkshire country home of Richard Monckton Milnes, English poet, biographer, member of parliament, patron of the arts, and self-professed friend of the Northern cause.[13] The minister's son, meanwhile, struggled "to resist complete nervous depression in the solitude of Mansfield Street." Like the other two secretaries, young Henry Adams was bored with his tiresome office chores. But his tedium was soon relieved, when he received a startling telegram from the American consul at Southampton, announcing the abduction of Mason and Slidell. At first the three secretaries shouted with delight. But, on reflection, Second Secretary Benjamin Moran saw clearly "that the act will do more for the Southerners than ten victories, for it touches John Bull's honor, and the honor of his flag." Now, he believed, the malicious Palmerston had been presented with a pretext for indulging "his satanic object" of hostilities with the United States. The prime minister could be expected quickly to grasp the opportunity. "Age will soon lead him to the grave, and he must glut his ire before he goes." Henry Adams, meanwhile, declared with boyish bravado that since England was waiting only for the right moment before attacking the war-weakened United States, it had been wise for the Americans to strike first with an act which was virtually a declaration of war. The news was hurriedly telegraphed to the minister and the secretaries settled down nervously to await his return.[14]

In ancient Fryston Hall, eight prominent Englishmen, among them William Forster, Lord and Lady Wesleydale, and the historian James A. Froude, had joined the Adamses as overnight guests. Rain beat against the windows of the spacious manor-house library, as host and guests were served a late breakfast on the morning of November 27. Milnes, famed throughout England as a raconteur, showed some of his gift for sprightly conversation; others strove to match his wit; and the quiet little American minister listened alertly to intimate anecdotes about public figures of the day.[15]

After breakfast, Adams went to his room upstairs to answer a letter from Edward Everett which he had brought from London to show his English friends. Much of the distrust and enmity that had arisen during the past year between the peoples of Britain and America, Adams wrote, could be attributed to the issuance of the Queen's Proclamation of Neutrality before he had been given an opportunity to announce the policy of the new administration to Lord Russell. Nevertheless, during the past few weeks he thought that he had begun to gain the good will of the ministry for his country. The future of Anglo-American relations looked promising. The only real remaining danger lay in the intense desire of some of the most powerful members of the English aristocracy for the disintegration of the American Union. As one of the Milnes servants knocked on his door to announce that luncheon was served, Adams had just written: "If the ghost of democracy can be laid the gentry think. . . ." He left his writing at this point, and the passage was never finished.[16]

The weather began to clear during luncheon and the Adamses decided to join Milnes and half a dozen others in a visit to the ruin of nearby Pontefract Castle. As their carriage drew near the hill upon which towered the great torn shell of the ancient keep, flanked by the skeletons of what had once been thick sandstone walls, the sky again darkened and a steady drizzle began. The sightseers left their carriages at the castle gate, and Adams was passing under the portcullis when a telegram from his London office was placed in his hands. It brought him his first news of the seizure of the Confederate commissioners from the *Trent*.[17]

Under the weathered walls of Pontefract Castle, Adams fretted over the probable consequences of the act of Captain Wilkes. As he strolled about the site, staring up into the drizzle at the surviving portion of the towering keep, peering curiously into a remnant of the room where Richard II was said to have been murdered, or looking through an open trap door into the dungeon, Adams could not keep his mind on the many historical associations of this venerable ruin. Thoughts about the important role the castle had played in the War of the Roses were thrust aside by visions of an Anglo-American war growing out of the *Trent* incident. Adams had little relish left for further diversion in the country. At such a grim moment, his proper place was in London. He was glad when the onset of darkness and a sudden heavy downpour drove the little group back to the carriages.[18]

As these conveyances, when covered against the rain, could conveniently accommodate only the ladies, the men walked back to Fryston Hall. Plodding through the mud, Adams conversed most of the way with William E. Forster, the quiet, hardy Yorkshireman who in Parliament more than any other member thus far had made the Northern cause his own. The American minister found relief in ruminating aloud to this sympathetic listener about the events of the past six months—"how I had seen this breach slowly but certainly widening from the first moment when Lord Russell made his wrong departure, without the power to check it more than for a moment." The two men talked earnestly about the *Trent* case—Forster mainly interested in knowing whether Wilkes had violated international law; while Adams viewed the legal aspects of the abduction of Mason and Slidell as no more than historical curiosities. What concerned him was how diplomacy might be used to keep the incident from creating a war.[19]

The Adamses returned home the next evening. The minister found on his writing table a note from the foreign secretary requesting that he call at the Foreign Office. It seemed that Russell, too, viewed the *Trent* affair with concern.[20]

The first intelligence that the Southern commissioners had been forcibly taken from a British ship reached the British Foreign Office early on November 27. Recalling the opinion of the crown law officers, sought in regard to the *James Adger*, "that she could have no right to remove Messrs. Mason & Slidell and carry them off as Prisoners, leaving the ship to pursue her voyage," Foreign Undersecretary A. H. Layard quickly brought the news to the attention of Lords Russell and Palmerston. The foreign minister's first thought was to summon all of the members of Her Majesty's ministry within reach of London to a cabinet meeting on the following day. Prompt action was in order, for Americans, he declared, "are very dangerous people to run away from." But Palmerston cautioned: "We shall not be ready for a Cabinet till we get the opinion of the Law Officers" once more. Judicial precedents should be carefully searched "to see whether any similar cases have happened." And Captain Moir, as well as the government mail agent on board the *Trent*, should both be brought to London to give depositions under oath for the consideration of the law officers. This would all take time. But if Russell could not wait longer—and the foreign secretary was insistent, writing his colleague that "whatever may be the opinion of the Law Officers there must be a cabinet on so grave a matter,"—the members of the ministry might meet in two days, on Friday, November 29.[21]

In the meantime, Palmerston sent a note to the War Office to suggest that previously planned reductions in British military spending for 1862 be reconsidered. "Relations with Seward & Lincoln are so precarious," wrote the premier, "that it seems to me that it would be inadvisable to make any reduction in the amount of our military force." Reinforcements earlier planned for Canada which had been held back on the ground that housing was not available, should be sent anyway. For there was "no Doubt that Seward is actuated in his Conduct towards us by the Belief that Canada is insufficiently defended: while he treats the French with great Respect because they have no vulnerable Point, but have a Fleet which could do the Northerns Mischief."[22]

The prime minister's messenger brought back a hurriedly scribbled reply from War Secretary George Cornewall Lewis, indicating the latter's belief that even if Wilkes's act was not expressly ordered by his government, it "will probably not be disavowed. Moreover, we would not," the Secretary for War apprehended, "be satisfied with anything short of the surrender of the persons removed by force from a ship bearing the English flag. The present aspect of affairs seems to me to be inevitable war."[23]

On the morning of November 29, Palmerston prepared for an afternoon cabinet meeting to be held in his Downing Street office. Although he had held an informal caucus with several cabinet members on the previous day, he had not yet decided on a course of action to propose to the full council. He asked the law officers personally to attend the afternoon's session, "in case we should want any further explanations from them." As an afterthought he notified Gladstone that he wanted the famous Admiralty jurist, Sir Robert Phillimore, to attend; and he also asked one of the undersecretaries at the Foreign Office to prepare a digest of certain cases, "of the same nature as the Mason Slidell Case," which had been that morning cited in the London *Morning Post*. Having reflected overnight "on American matters," he wrote Russell, he tended now to agree with "what I think your Conclusions yesterday were, namely that we ought to demand from Seward and Lincoln apology and Liberation of the Captives, and that if this is refused Lyons ought to come away, and not to remain as the Representative of a Country deliberately insulted."[24]

Some of the queen's ministers doubted whether the *Trent* case would require positive action. Lord Stanley of Alderley, for example, wrote his wife, when he first learned about the incident, that it might "possibly require a Cabinet," but that he was uncertain whether he would have to stay in London to deal with what appeared an "ill advised proceeding of the U. States government," which *might* involve "important consequences." On the other hand, the duke of Argyll, usually friendly to the North, wrote from a vacation resort in France, after reading in the newspapers about "this wretched piece of American folly," that he was "all against submitting to any clear breach of International Law, such as I can hardly doubt this has been. Even the doctrine of contraband of war, as applicable to civilian passengers, does surely not apply in the case of a vessel *going away* from both of the Belligerent Powers."[25]

Argyll was apparently the only member of the cabinet who did not meet at Downing Street on November 29. But he kept himself informed of developments, both by soliciting letters from ministerial colleagues and by assiduously keeping up with the English newspapers. London journalists seemed quite certain of the course of action to be taken. The *Times*, on November 28, had related the story of the seizure of Mason and Slidell from the *Trent*, including the fact that all of the dispatches of the Southern commissioners had "escaped the vigilance of the boarding officers," and had safely been delivered to Confederate representatives in Europe.[26] Also published was an inflammatory letter from the purser of the *Trent*, testifying, among other things, that "a most heartrending scene" had taken place between Fairfax and Slidell's eldest daughter, "a noble girl," who "with flashing eyes and quivering lips, . . . threw herself in the doorway of the cabin," resolved to defend her father "with her life, till, on the order being given to the Marines to advance, which they did with bayonets pointed at this poor defenceless girl, her father ended the painful scene by escaping from the cabin by a window." Thus had been made manifest "the meanness and cowardly bullying" of the Americans, during an abduction which Lieutenant Fairfax was reported to have said was carried out "under orders"—but under *whose* orders, whether those merely of Wilkes or some sent from Washington, was not entirely clear.[27]

A spokesman for the *Times* commented that although the right of search was well established under international law, the numerous Admiralty court decisions upholding that right

> were given under circumstances very different from those which now occur. Steamers in those days did not exist, and mail vessels carrying letters wherein all the nations of the world have immediate interest were unknown. . . . Moreover, if we gave full scope to all this antiquated law it remains still to be asked whether the men who have been taken from beneath the protection of our flag were liable to seizure.

... even if it were necessary to admit [that Mason and Slidell had a] contraband character on board the English vessel, it is, we believe, the opinion of very eminent jurists that this was not a question to be adjudicated on by a naval officer and four boat's crews. The legal course would have been to take the ship itself into port and to ask for her condemnation, or for the condemnation of the passengers, in a Court of Admiralty ... if the proceeding was irregular we surely have a right to demand that these prisoners shall be restored.[28]

Recognizing that it was the duty of a responsible journalist "to calm—certainly not to inflame—the general indignation" over the *Trent* incident, the *Times*'s editor continued:

We cannot yet believe, although the evidence is strong, that it is the fixed determination of the Government of the Northern States to force a quarrel upon the Powers of Europe. We hope, therefore, that our people will not meet this provocation with an outburst of passion, or rush to resentment without full consideration of all the bearings of the case. On the other hand, we appeal to the reasonable men of the Federal States ... not to provoke war by such acts as these."[29]

Other British newspapers, however, contained commentary much less conciliatory than that published in the *Times*. A writer for the Manchester *Guardian*, for example, declared: "It is clear that the American government are determined to test to the utmost the truth of the adage that it takes two to make a quarrel." Readers of the London *Chronicle* were told that England had been "piratically outraged." The assault on the British flag was "unendurable" and "must not go unavenged." In the Birmingham *Daily Post* an editorial spokesman proclaimed: "Englishmen can put up with bluster, but not with blows. ... A challenge has therefore deliberately been thrown down to this country." And an editorial in the London *News* referred to the *Trent* seizure as "wanton folly" by an "imbecile" government at Washington, which rendered it necessary for Her Majesty's ministers "to insist on ample, complete and immediate satisfaction." Unless the Washington government was possessed by "madness," it would at once "disavow the act, restore Messrs. Mason and Slidell, and tender the fullest apology. Nothing short of this reparation can be accepted."[30]

Those who wished to learn the opinions of the prime minister habitually turned to the editorial columns of the London *Morning Post*. On the morning of November 28 a writer in that journal predicted that the crown law officers would decide that the seizure of Mason and Slidell was a violation of international law. "If we are right," the editorial continued, "the British Government will be entitled to reparation and apology, and no reparation could be complete without the restitution of the passengers taken from under our flag." Even if found to be sanctioned by law, Wilkes's act was an "insult . . . most gratuitous; and if, as we think, it was unwarranted by the code of nations, it will not only be deeply felt, but duly resented."[31]

Thus as the cabinet ministers assembled on November 29, they probably knew that British journalistic opinion strongly advocated that a demand be made on the Americans, both for an apology and for the surrender of the captured Southern commissioners. The London *Times* that same morning had reported that the crown law officers had ruled that it was "contrary to International Law for the officer of an armed cruiser to make himself a judge at sea." The *Trent* should have been taken to a port with facilities for adjudication. If not, the *Times*'s editor inquired, "for what reason have we Prize Courts, and Admiralty Judges, and codes of law and libraries of admiralty decisions . . . if any valorous lieutenant, with his drawn cutlass, is to stand upon a ship's deck and decide all questions of contraband and nationality offhand?" Even in Britannia's "most haughty days," her leaders had "never ventured . . . to insist that our naval officers should perform in a summary way the functions of Admiralty Judges." That an American officer had presumed to do so was "an unjustifiable outrage." As the members of the cabinet prepared "to consider what action should be taken upon the opinion of the Law Officers," the *Times*'s spokesman offered guidance. Only "one reparation" was "adequate to the affront." The four Confederate emissaries "must be restored with a sufficient apology."[32]

The American minister rose early on November 29. Grimly he perused the morning newspapers, full of hints and guesses, all seeming to signify great danger of Anglo-American war. Particularly did the *Times*'s pronouncement worry him. Before tackling his official correspondence, Adams dashed off a doleful postscript to his unfinished letter to Edward Everett: "The clouds have strangely gathered in the sky since this was written. I fully expect now that my recall or my passports will be in my hands by the middle of January." He then turned to the business of the day. Allowing Legation Secretary Charles Wilson to deal with the steady stream of anxious visitors, mostly Americans, who had been alarmed by press accounts of the *Trent* incident and wanted to know whether war was imminent, Adams composed a long note to Russell, in which he tried to terminate the long-standing Bunch controversy before the new one came to a head in England. With this note, and with several dispatches to the secretary of state, Adams kept his son Henry and Moran hard at their copying until dusk. "The excitement caused by the late news of the seizure of Messrs. Mason and Slidell," Adams wrote Seward, "is so great as to swallow up every other topic for the moment." Prudence dictated that older subjects, such as the case of the *Harvey Birch* and the harboring of the *Nashville* at Southampton, all be allowed to "lie in abeyance until the heats stirred by the new one shall subside." [33]

That afternoon when Adams arrived at the Foreign Office for his appointment with Russell, he observed that the foreign minister greeted him with no apparent ill will, but with slightly more gravity than usual. Russell said that it was of course too early to enter into any discussion about the seizure of the Confederate envoys. His present object was to learn, in advance of a cabinet meeting to be held in a few minutes, whether Adams possessed any information that might shed light on the matter. Adams replied that the whole affair was new to him and that he was not prepared to discuss it in any way. He did not, he declared, even know to what extent Captain Wilkes had acted under authority. [34]

Russell then alluded to Adams's conversation with Palmerston on November 12. The prime minister, he said, had understood Adams to assert that the captain of the *James Adger* had been instructed not to stop any British ship. Adams replied that this was not strictly true; what he had said was that the primary mission of the Northern warship was to intercept the *Nashville* and, failing in this, to return to the United States, keeping alert, however, for British ships bound for American shores with contraband of war for the insurgents. But Captain Marchand was not instructed to take the Confederate commissioners from a British ship. The conference lasted only ten minutes, after which Adams returned to his office to continue work on his dispatches. [35]

As soon as Adams left him, Russell went directly to the cabinet meeting, where he reported what the American representative had said. The opinion of the crown law officers, that Captain Wilkes's act had been "illegal and unjustified by international law" because the *Trent* "was not ... carried into a port of the United States for adjudication as a prize," was then read. It was endorsed in person by the eminent Dr. Phillimore. Much of the legal research of the lawyers had been accomplished at the time the *James Adger*'s arrival had precipitated the "hypothetical" opinion on November 12. It had been clear then that a naval captain could not legally usurp the proper function of a prize court, in order personally to decide the fates of passengers aboard a neutral vessel stopped at sea, and it was clear now that Her Majesty's government would "be justified in requiring reparation for the international wrong which had been on this occasion committed." The members of the cabinet soon agreed that the British minister in Washington, Lord Lyons, should be sent instructions to demand an apology by the United States government and the return of Mason and Slidell to British protection. If these stipulations were not met, the British minister in Washington should demand his passports.[36]

That evening, Palmerston wrote the queen that "it appeared to the Cabinet that a gross outrage" had been committed against a British ship, and that the ministers would "demand" reparation and redress. This was strong language, but the prime minister was momentarily influenced by several pieces of misinformation about the *Trent* incident. First of all, despite an affirmation by Mrs. Slidell that Wilkes had acted on his own, without instructions from Washington, Palmerston preferred, instead, to believe a newspaper rumor that General Winfield Scott, recently arrived in Paris, had asserted that he had been present at a cabinet meeting in Washington, at which the seizure of the Confederate emissaries had been "deliberately determined upon and ordered," even though Lincoln and his advisers were entirely aware that this step might lead to war with England. Moreover, declared Palmerston, "it was known that the *San Jacinto*, though come from the African station, ... had been at St. Thomas, and had there received communications from New York"—probably including orders to abduct the Confederate commissioners from the *Trent*.[37]

The British cabinet reconvened on Saturday, November 30. Although some members apparently agreed that the intent of the Americans "to bring about a collision" by means of the "monstrous" outrage against the *Trent* was self-evident, the secretary for war could not believe that the act was deliberate. Lincoln's cabinet might indeed have "been desirous of catching the Southern envoys, and may have caused their wish to be known; but it does not follow that they gave the instructions to board the 'Trent.' It seems incredible that Seward can seriously desire to provoke a war with England."[38]

In this atmosphere of uncertainty whether Wilkes's act had been authorized at Washington, the cabinet considered two draft dispatches to Lyons, submitted by Russell. These were "softened and abridged" in the course of active debate among fourteen participants, each proposing at least one alteration. The principal dispatch, as finally modified, recited what appeared to be the facts of the case, and stated "H.M.'s. Govt. are unwilling to imagine that the U.S. Govt. will not of their own accord be anxious to afford ample reparation for this act of violence," and said that the queen's ministers expected (1) "The liberation of the four gentlemen captured, and their delivery to [Lyons]," and (2) "an apology for the insult offered to the British flag." A second dispatch instructed Lyons to remove himself to London within seven days if the British demands were not met.[39]

Off to the queen at Windsor went the draft dispatches, arriving at the castle that evening. The foreign minister wished Her Majesty's opinion on the papers "without loss of time," as a large mail steamer was already being held up in order that it might carry the dispatches to America. But the queen had a dinner party, which came first. While she entertained a company that included Mr. and Mrs. Gladstone, the prince consort, who had pleaded illness in order to excuse himself from attending, sat down at his desk by lamplight and took up the drafts from Whitehall. Influenced by conciliatory editorials in the London *Times*, he completed a draft memorandum for his wife's signature. Containing in places the very language of the *Times*'s commentary, the prince's memorandum suggested that the principal dispatch—the one for communication to the United States government—was "somewhat meagre," and that, while the restoration of the Southern commissioners should be required, and a suitable apology requested, there should also be expressed "a hope, that the American captain had not acted under instructions, or, if he did, that he misapprehended them." Thus would the United States be furnished a loophole through which to retreat with honor. [40]

Palmerston concurred in the royal suggestions that the British demands be softened. The queen's "proposed alterations," he wrote Russell, "seem to me to be in their general character very good," and he advised the foreign minister to incorporate them into his dispatch. Thus the paper which was finally sent to Lyons closely followed the form of the queen's modifications, referring to the "friendly relations which have long subsisted between Great Britain and the United States," declaring that Her Majesty's government were "willing to believe" that Wilkes had either acted without authority or that he misunderstood his instructions, and only then calling for a restoration of the four captives and a "suitable apology." [41]

Several companion dispatches gave Lyons his private instructions about the manner in which he should broach the British demands. He was directed to allow Seward a delay of no more than seven days before answering the ultimatum, with noncompliance to result in Lyons's closing of the British Legation in Washington and the removal of its personnel outside the United States. British consuls in that country would, however, "continue to discharge their consular functions until further orders, unless prevented from doing so by the government of the United States." And Lyons was given minute instructions about arguments buttressing the British position which he could present to Seward. Although "strictly consonant to Maritime Law," they were also based on the idea that it was "essential for British interests" that foreigners must be protected "when under the safeguard of the British flag." Russell hoped faintly that Seward might understand a declaration of self-interest, even if he failed to appreciate the British legal arguments. [42]

At the last moment before handing the package of dispatches to a messenger, who was to rush them to the still-waiting mail steamer, Russell added a private note. "At your first interview with Mr. Seward," he instructed his Washington representative, "you should not take my despatch with you, but should prepare him for it." Lyons was to "abstain from anything like menace." The main objective of the demand was the liberation of the Southern commissioners. This done, the British government would probably "be rather easy about the apology," for which an "explanation" sent through Adams might suffice. The French in Washington would probably be ordered to add "moral support to the British case; "so that," Russell added, "you may as well keep the despatch itself a day or two before you produce it." The British people were "quiet, but very decided." They would fight the Americans if necessary. But "the best thing would be if Seward could be turned out and a rational man put in his place."[43]

VI.

England Mobilizes for War

*We are a very illogical people, with brute combativeness
which is always ready for a quarrel and which can be
excited at the will of a governing class that has subsisted
for centuries upon this failing in John Bull's character.*

RICHARD COBDEN TO REV. HENRY RICHARD,
August 17, 1861.[1]

The steamer carrying the British ultimatum in the case of Mason and
Slidell had hardly passed beyond sight of Ireland on its way westward
to North America, when a bundle of dispatches from the British minister at Washington reached London. Lord Lyons's appraisal of the significance of the *Trent* seizure seemed to corroborate all the dark suspicions
which had developed in England during 1861 of the aggressive designs
of William H. Seward.[2]

Reminding the foreign secretary that he had long "been in constant
apprehension of some violent proceeding on the part of this government
towards Great Britain, which would render the maintenance of friendly
relations between the two countries no longer possible," Lyons declared
that he had devoted the most "minute attention" for many months to

> the perplexing and disagreeable questions which have arisen almost
> daily [*so*] as to ward off this danger. It has been my constant care to
> prevent these questions coming to a point, at which it would be neces-
> sary for Her Majesty's government either to give way to unreasonable
> pretentions and violent conduct on the part of the United States or to
> take strong measures to resist them.

Now, however, all of Lyon's "laboriousness"—all the inconveniences
and irritations which he had chosen to endure rather than to risk an

Anglo-American conflict—seemed to have been wasted because of an event which was bound to "have a baleful effect" on Anglo-American relations.[3]

Although he was still unacquainted "with the essential facts" of the *Trent* incident, beyond what had appeared in Northern newspapers, and therefore could not offer an opinion about its legality, Lyons thought it ominous that "the American people at large" viewed the capture of Mason and Slidell "as a direct insult to the British flag." Although "the exultation which is undoubtedly felt" because of this had been "in some degree subdued" by a widespread "apprehension of the consequences," it was apparent to the British minister that most Americans were "very much pleased at having . . . insulted the British Flag."[4]

Reminding the foreign minister of dispatches written during May and June, in which he had warned of Seward's propensity to insult the British and of a mad scheme allegedly authored by the secretary of state to unite North and South by a war against England, Lyons remarked "that the apprehensions expressed in my former despatches are considerably increased—while my opinion of the best means calculated to meet the danger remains unchanged." Advocating a show of strength in the form of immediate preparations for an Anglo-American war, Lyons had strongly recommended military reinforcements for Canada and the assignment of additional warships to the British West Indian fleet.[5]

"In the present imperfect state of my information," Lyons wrote, he had

> hazarded no conjecture as to the course which will be taken by Her Majesty's government. On the one hand I dare not run the risk of compromising the honour and inviolability of the British flag by asking for a measure of reparation which may prove to be inadequate. On the other hand I am scarcely less unwilling to incur the danger of rendering a satisfactory settlement of the question more difficult by making a demand which may turn out to be unnecessarily great.[6]

Hence Lyons did "not propose to take any decided step without orders from Your Lordship."

The British minister assumed that in due course he would receive some kind of ultimatum to deliver to Seward regarding the *Trent* affair.

There was, of course, a slight chance that Wilkes's act might be "so far sanctioned by international law, as to render it unnecessary or undesirable for Her Majesty's government to require the release of Mr. Mason and Mr. Slidell." This would induce a feeling of relief in the North—but, in Lyons's opinion, it would greatly weaken "the hope of maintaining friendship in future." For "however clear the case might prove to be in point of international law, the people would never be convinced that no insult had really been offered. . . . They would be confirmed in their idea that England will bear anything from them." Even greater "insults and unpardonable acts of violence would only too probably follow; and the danger escaped for the moment would at no distant time recur." No official of the United States government was currently "willing to sacrifice his own popularity" by advocating, "from a sense of justice," spontaneous reparation to Great Britain,

> without at least waiting to see how the thing is taken in England. If Mr. Seward, in particular, may be supposed to hope that no serious measures may after all be deemed necessary by Her Majesty's government he will then be able to present himself to Congress and the public as a high spirited and successful Secretary of State. But success in doing this now will fatally lead him to seek popularity again by the same means. The subordinate officers and especially those in the Navy, will be encouraged in this unfortunate tendency to court popular favour by acts of oppression against foreigners. The people will more than ever applaud such acts. The government will less than ever be able or willing to repress them.

All of which added up to a set of "discouraging circumstances" portending, later if not sooner, the likelihood of Anglo-American war.[7]

On December 3 each member of the British cabinet was provided by the foreign office with "a full abstract of Lord Lyons's despatches about the 'Trent' affair." The same information was sent to the queen. The permanent undersecretary of state for foreign affairs thought that it seemed "pretty clear from the account given by Lord Lyons that the only chance of avoiding a rupture, is to act upon the apprehensions entertained in the United States of the consequences of the capture of the [Southern] delegates." The British government should "ostentatiously" prepare for war. Palmerston agreed. He was "afraid," he wrote, "that we shall not get what we ask for, without fighting for it."[8]

Lyons's dispatches had a profound influence on most members of the British cabinet. Lewis, for example, had "little hope of a peaceful solution" after reading them. They indicated to the secretary for war that Seward would not be likely to comply with the British demand, especially in view of the great joy expressed in the New York newspapers at the capture of Mason and Slidell. However, Lewis wrote, "we shall soon *iron the smile* out of their faces." Meanwhile, Edward Cardwell, chancellor of the duchy of Lancaster, wrote the undersecretary for war: "I quite share your feeling that we must prepare for war," and Stanley of Alderley found the newspaper reports of exultation in the Northern States "grave and serious" enough to portend an almost certain trial of arms.[9]

The chancellor of the exchequer, who had argued in the cabinet meetings a few days before "that we should hear what the Americans had to say before withdrawing Lyons," had nevertheless acquiesced in the general feeling that Wilkes, in seizing the Southern emissaries from the *Trent*, had "gone far beyond" the most odious British precedents of international maritime law; thus making the British ultimatum inevitable. The affair was "very sad and heartsickening," and William E. Gladstone was "not confident" that war with the United States could be averted. Upon hearing from him that the cabinet had agreed to send Lyons instructions to demand the restoration of the Southern commissioners and an apology for Wilkes's act, Argyll agreed that his ministerial colleagues could not have adopted "any milder or more procrastinating expression." The British, Argyll wrote, had conceded that "sheer necessity" might have justified the United States government in overriding its own "municipal" laws by the use of "military force; but as regards international law, Seward ought to have been more than usually scrupulous." The lord privy seal hoped that the secretary of state and his associates in the American cabinet would not "be so foolish as to drive us into a quarrel about this absurd seizure of men whom it will have done them no good whatever to have caught."[10]

The two most liberal members of the British cabinet, after reading

Lyons's dispatches, had both endorsed the ultimatum to the American government. Thomas Milner-Gibson (whom a close friend of Seward's testified "is unreservedly our friend") wrote Richard Cobden that the Americans had been "wrongheaded" to seize the Southerners; while Charles P. Villiers wrote John Bright about the same time that the British demand had been "inevitable"—for Lyons had written that if the Americans "found that we bore it meekly, every fellow in the command of a government vessel would have vied with the other in heaping fresh & further insults upon us—with a view to the glory and perhaps promotion it would get him." As the earl of Clarendon, who had close ties with several cabinet members, expressed the prevailing idea: "mealy-mouthed . . . flinching" by the ministry "would only delay the evil hour" of chastising the Yankee "bullies." The temptation was great to end the suspense at a time when it was "a hundred to one" that another incident might occur in which the English "were so clearly right" and the Americans so wrong.[11]

Much of the indignation expressed by prominent Englishmen over the *Trent* "outrage" may be traced to a conviction that unnecessary "violence" had been used to arrest the Southern envoys. As the foreign minister put it, in a remonstrance based almost entirely upon information provided by the captain and the purser of the *Trent*, "(1) the stoppage of the 'Trent' was attended with unnecessary and dangerous acts of violence, and accompanied by an offensive display of armed force;" (2) the four passengers had been carried off forcibly without a search of the vessel first being conducted "*in the ordinary way*;" and

> (3) It is an invariable principle that under no circumstances can any violence or force be justifiably used by a belligerent against an *unresisting* neutral ship, except just so much as is necessary to bring her intact before the nearest tribunal of the belligerent, administering international law. . . . the outrage therefore is of the most wanton nature.[12]

As the lord chief justice of England proclaimed: "I must unlearn Lord Stowell and burn Wheaton if there is one word of defence for the American Lieutenant. . . . How a great and gallant nation can *en masse* confound safe swaggering over unarmed and weak foes with true valor, I cannot understand." And the famous historian George Grote fulminated: "What a precious 'hash' these Yankees are preparing for themselves! Their stupid, childish rage against us, seems to extinguish all sense, in their braggart minds, even where the instinct of self-interest ought to supply it."[13]

Not only did an editorial writer in the London *Morning Post* characterize the *Trent* incident as a calculated affront, which, even if legal, had been "most gratuitous," but another journalist, in the Liberal Manchester *Guardian*, lamented that "nothing which could add to the insulting character of the outrage appears to have been omitted." Even if the seizure of the Southern envoys should turn out, unexpectedly, to have been justifiable under international law, "such experiments" touched the English "on two points on which we are particularly sensitive, our freedom of action on the seas, and our reputation for political hospitality. These feelings are so perilous to meddle with that the United States cannot be too strongly warned against abusing the occasional licence for impertinence conferred on them by their present weakness and distress."[14]

While quotations on the British stock and commodity exchanges wavered wildly in response to every flitting rumor regarding the case of Mason and Slidell, "An Occasional Correspondent" named Karl Marx wrote the *New York Daily Tribune* that since the Crimean War he had "never witnessed an excitement . . . equal to that produced by the news of the *Trent* affair." On the evening of November 27, as the story of the *Trent* seizure began to take shape in London, wild tales circulated "to the effect that the American Minister had forthwith been sent his passports, that orders had been issued for the immediate seizure of all American ships in the ports of the United Kingdom, and so forth. . . ." Although the editorial tone of "the ministerial press" was calm and conciliatory for the next three days, while "Tory scribblers . . . gave full vent to their savage satisfaction at . . . finding a *casus belli*," and the cabinet members began their consultations with the crown law officers, it had become known on November 30 through "all the London papers," save the Liberal *Morning Star*, that the Lincoln administration was to be confronted with a choice of "reparation . . . or *war*." Marx, fervently pro-Northern, warned his American readers that a war between the United States and Great Britain would inevitably result in a victory for the rebel slaveholders, and he urged that the captured Southern emissaries be relinquished on demand.[15]

"Of one thing you must be sure," the author of the *Communist Manifesto* cautioned,

> Palmerston wants a legal pretext for a war with the United States, but meets in the Cabinet councils with a most determined opposition on the part of Messrs. Gladstone and Milner Gibson, and, to a less degree, of Sir Cornewall Lewis. 'The noble viscount' is backed by Russell, an abject tool in his hands, and the whole Whig Coterie. If the Washington Cabinet should furnish the desired pretext, the present Cabinet will be sprung, to be supplanted by a Tory Administration. The preliminary steps for such a change of scenery have already been settled between Palmerston and Disraeli.

Continuing his imaginative discourse, Marx traced what he described as the pattern of Palmerston's "designs," beginning with the premature issuance of the queen's neutrality proclamation, followed by the shipment of some three thousand British soldiers to Canada, after which had come an effort to obtain agreement in the cabinet to an armed intervention, jointly with France, for the purpose of ending the American Civil War on the basis of Confederate independence. When this last measure encountered strong objections during cabinet discussions, Palmerston had substituted a Mexican intervention instead, which "was from the first set on foot, not for its ostensible purpose, but for a war against the United States."[16]

There is little concrete evidence that Palmerston had any desire overtly to intervene in the American Civil War by aiding the Southern Confederates; nor can Russell or Lyons be shown consciously to have favored the slaveholders. But it is difficult to suppress a suspicion that Lyons's unsympathetic attitude toward "Yankees," and toward their institutions and folkways, so distorted his reports to Russell regarding the American side of the *Trent* affair, that the British foreign minister, and the premier as well, lacked the means accurately to evaluate a dangerous situation. Reports from Lyons continued to be pessimistic. All his "peaceful plans and hopes," he wrote, had been dashed by the seizure of Mason and Slidell. And he was "so worn out with the never ending labour of keeping things smooth, under the discouragement of the doubt whether by so doing I am not after all only leading these people to believe that they may go all lengths with us with impunity, that I am sometimes half tempted to wish that the worst may have come already."[17]

Should "the capture be unjustifiable," Lyons continued, "we should ask for the immediate release of the prisoners, promptly, imperatively, with a determination to act at once, if the demand were refused. . . . For they have made up their minds that they have insulted us. . . ." It was "a case for an extreme measure." The "fiery legislators" in Congress, disappointed at the failure of Northern generals to win military victories after so many "preposterous boastings beforehand," might be assumed collectively to be in a malignant mood, ready to instigate war against England at the slightest indication of hesitation or sign of squeamishness on the part of Her Majesty's government. Meanwhile the Morrill tariff, the Americans' "last brilliant discovery in political economy," was not working satisfactorily; indeed, the Federal finances generally had been allowed to fall into a precarious state, thus adding to the national desperation. A "curious sign of the confusion into which things are falling," the British minister wrote, was a project contemplated by the Federal commanding general, George McClellan, who was said to plan first "a great victory, and then, with or without the sanction of Congress and the President, to propose the most favorable terms to the South, if it will only come back."[18]

About the time Russell received this caustic commentary on affairs in the Northern states, he also heard it rumored that General McClellan had told Lincoln that the seizure of the Southern commissioners "was quite unjustifiable." The British foreign minister was out of patience with the American president and his secretary of state. "I wish," Russell said, "McClellan could be made DICTATOR." Sarcastically, in much the same vein as his representative at Washington, he described for an old political friend what he expected from "the Yankee Government." "I cannot imagine," he wrote, "their giving a plain yes or no to our demands. I think they will try to hook in France, or if that is, as I hope, impossible, to get Russia to support them. . . . Their Government has all the genius of a country attorney." But Mason, Slidell, and their secretaries had to be returned to the protection of the British flag. Although "all the Yankees in the world" protested that they would never yield the

traitorous prisoners, British determination, Russell thought, would in
the end force compliance "I guess, I calculate, I reckon they will do so,"
he scoffed, "indirectly it may be, but substantially." If the men were
released, he would "not care much" whether the British also received
the formal apology which the cabinet had demanded.[19]

Visualizing "the possible evasive answers of Mr. Seward falling short
of substantial compliance with our demands," Russell sent Lyons some
private "contingent instructions," to prevent his becoming entangled
"in endless arguments on Vattel, Wheaton, & Scott." This letter was
timed to reach Washington before the expected deadline for American
compliance with the British ultimatum. "What we want," the foreign
minister declared, "is a plain Yes or a plain No to our very simple demands, and we want that plain Yes or No within seven days of the
communication of the despatch." Should Lyons "receive the Confederate
prisoners under the protection of the British flag," Russell stated, "we
shall be satisfied. But if that is not to be obtained, you will only have to
obey your instructions & withdraw."[20]

With no time remaining to reach Lyons with additional instructions
regarding the *Trent* affair, Russell and his cabinet colleagues concentrated on military preparations for the war they feared might follow
the expected American rejection or evasion of their demands. One of the
first measures taken was to order an embargo on American shipments
from England of large quantities of saltpeter, the principal ingredient of
gunpowder. Within a few hours of receiving the news of the *Trent*
"outrage," Russell set in motion machinery for "the saltpeter to be
stopt." He also wanted to forbid the exportation of all munitions, arms,
and other warlike stores to America. This suggestion was, however, rejected as premature at the cabinet's first meeting on the *Trent* crisis.
Palmerston had not supported it. But that evening, November 29, the
prime minister wrote Russell that he had decided to join, after all, in
espousing an embargo.

> For how do we stand? We have reason to suppose that Seward & Lincoln
> mean a Rupture with England, and would it not be folly . . . to allow
> [Americans] . . . to supply themselves obviously from our warehouses
> and workshops with materials and implements to make war against us?
> By stopping their supplies we should not only cripple their means of

making war . . . , but by restricting their Resources we lessen the Probability of their risking a Rupture. I shall tomorrow at the Cabinet renew your proposal and press it on our Colleagues.[21]

To win support for the measure, the premier wrote individually to several other cabinet members. As he had told Russell, such a proclamation "would be a good political warning to Seward & Co. of which they could not justly complain, but which would probably be understood." Moreover, with war quite "possible," he wrote the lord president of the council, it would "be an act of folly amounting to absolute imbecility to let those who may soon be our enemies, and whom we believe intending to be so," to continue acquiring in England "the means of war against us." Some influential merchants and manufacturers might complain; nevertheless "the interests of the few must yield to the welfare of the many."[22]

From the moment that the British ultimatum left London on its way to Lyons, members of the ministry began to worry whether the American response might be a sudden invasion of Canada. The first lord of the Admiralty believed that Great Britain "could not defend Canada against a serious attack from the Federal States," and that "if Canada be overrun and occupied by a Federal army . . . reconquering Canada [would be] a task which we could not accomplish except at a cost far beyond its value." Therefore, the duke of Somerset suggested, before great expenditures were made to fortify lower Canada and send more English troops there, the cabinet should consider whether "a very different system of hostilities should be adopted." A naval war, rather than a struggle on land, was indicated. To propose parliamentary expenditures for additional land forces in Canada "would be a course inviting defeat in the House of Commons," which might in the end leave the colony's defenses "in a much worse position."[23]

The prime minister's reply to Somerset's objections was a shrewd amalgam of visionary imperialism and practical party politics. "I must say," Palmerston declared, "that I cannot think the loss of our North American Provinces a light matter, or one which would not seriously affect the position of England among the nations of the world. It would lower us greatly, and if reputation is strength, would weaken us much." Quebec, at least, could be defended until blows struck elsewhere against the Americans and a rush of reinforcements across the Atlantic Ocean relieved the pressure against it. "As to the expediency of proposing a vote to Parliament," the premier wrote, he was not prepared to endanger "national & imperial interests" by shirking criticism in the House of Commons. Far better to take "the straitforward course" and ask the House for the funds necessary to fortify Quebec at once. True, the money might be denied. But a failure to request it might be even more politically damaging.

> Suppose a war to break out, and Quebec to be taken, and the present gov't. to be reproached for having left it in the present defenceless state, ... what would be our excuse? All we could say would be that we *thought* that Parliament would not vote the money. The answer would be, why did you not try? What right had you to assume to take for granted that Parliament would refuse necessary means? I can imagine Dizzy & Derby[24] tumbling us over much on such a topic.[25]

While bridling at the hesitation shown by Somerset, and earlier by the colonial secretary, the prime minister had nothing but praise for the energetic military preparations initiated by the secretary for war. Within the week, Lewis proposed to send thirty thousand rifles, an artillery battery, and some officers to Canada, after which, he wrote Palmerston, "I propose to engage a Cunard steamer & to send out one regiment & one battery of artillery next week," followed as quickly as possible by three additional regiments of troops and more artillery.[26]

Perhaps worried that Lewis, backed by the prime minister, would initiate military arrangements so precipitately that any slight remaining chance of peace would be endangered, Russell requested that "a small committee . . . assist Lewis, & the Duke of Somerset" in formulating plans for waging war against the United States. "I shall," Russell wrote, "be quite willing to attend it."[27]

Palmerston replied: "I agree with you that . . . Lewis should be assisted, and his personal responsibility shielded by the assistance of a Committee of the Cabinet and the Commander in Chief." Such a group could convene at the War Office on December 9. Much had to be done, for "the rabid Hatred of England which animates the . . . northern newspapers, will so excite the masses, as to make it impossible for Lincoln & Seward to grant our Demands; and we must therefore look forward to war as the probable Result."[28]

Amid a spate of wild rumors, such as one pertaining to a "dodge" for transferring American-owned ships to English registry, while control remained in the hands of the Yankees, the special cabinet war council met on December 9.[29] Among those present were Palmerston (presiding), Lewis, Somerset, Newcastle—as the ministers whose departments, besides the Foreign Office, were most affected by the war preparations —and the queen's cousin, the duke of Cambridge, whose title of "commander-in-chief" at the Horse Guards required that he be consulted on all military movements. Russell's absence from this meeting may have been owing to illness, although it is also possible that he was purposely excluded. The members of the war council were told that current British military strength in Canada and on the North American station included approximately five thousand regular troops in the North American Provinces, as well as about the same number of "ill-trained" volunteer militia. This was a pitiful force to match against a potential enemy army of several hundred thousand men. There was, moreover, a severe shortage of modern arms and ammunition in Canada, including a dearth of weapons for the forthcoming reinforcements. A special advisory committee, composed of three high-ranking army officers who had Canadian experience, had already been chosen by Lewis, and its members had already agreed that five thousand additional regular troops and huge amounts of munitions should be sent as soon as possible to Canada. Lewis presented these recommendations to his colleagues on the war council, and they quickly endorsed them, approving, as well, the advisory committee's recommendation that the most vital strategic points in Lower Canada, especially at Quebec and Montreal, ought to be heavily fortified, and that a fleet of gunboats adequate to seize control of the Great Lakes should be assembled there. To the British fleet on the North American station, already containing about thirty vessels, the members of the war council agreed to send enough warships to raid Union shipping, to break the blockade of the Southern coast, and to impose a counterblockade, ultimately, of the Northern coast. Already, during the previous week, the Admiralty had ordered that three battleships, two frigates, and a corvette be detached from various squadrons in the

Mediterranean Sea and in the English Channel, in order to join Admiral Alexander Milne's fleet. During the rest of December these early reinforcements were to be joined by two more frigates and a sloop. As Milne later wrote Somerset: ". . . to make war felt it must be carried against the enemy with energy and every place must be made to feel what war really is."[30]

On the day following the meeting of the war council, Lewis wrote a friend:

> We are making all our preparations on the assumption that there is to be war. They will cost a great deal of money; but, if we have war, everybody will approve of them; and if, by some marvellous inspiration of good sense and moderation, Lincoln's govt. yields to our demands, and preserves peace, the public will probably think that the preparations had something to do with the decision of the American govt.

The queen heartily approved of the war preparations. A war with the United States, she predicted, would bring about the "utter destruction" of the Yankees.[31]

If the members of the cabinet seemed dangerously ardent about the possibility of war, ordinary Englishmen appeared positively enraged. The excitement in the country, reported Henry Wilding, the American vice consul at Liverpool, was much greater than he had ever encountered during many years of residence in England. Popular feeling, he wrote, was "almost universally adverse, & very bitter." Consul Freeman Morse reported likewise from London that the *Trent* incident had "caused immense excitement among, so far as I can judge, nearly the whole British people. Hardly any other subject is talked of . . . and many call openly for war, at once." As soon as the crown law officers pronounced the capture of the Southern envoys illegal, London merchants had been heard openly to "speculate on the fortunes that will be made, with the Northern ports blockaded, Northern ships driven from the sea & Southern trade open." In London dockyards, Morse noted "the greatest possible activity" accompanied the fitting out of "a strong fleet, . . . with double gangs working the whole 24 hours, including Sundays." After more than one week had passed, the consul was able to discover "no abatement to the war spirit among the people. Nearly the whole nation appears to be aroused in opposition to the North, & to be in sympathy with the South."[32]

At the Tower of London, "the greatest activity" was evident from the first day of December. Workmen labored from dawn "until a late hour at night in packing up firearms and every kind of article necessary for active service abroad." Out of the huge arsenal, gangs of panting long-shoremen hauled enough boxes on one Sunday evening alone to fill eight barges on the Thames River with cargoes of weapons destined for Canada. An elderly American felt "the old feeling" of enmity to England, forgotten since the War of 1812, surge through his venerable body as he watched a regiment of redcoats march up the gangway onto a Canada-bound steamer. Everything in England, he warned the American secretary of state, "is upon a war footing. Such prompt and gigantic preparations were never known." If the seizure of Mason and Slidell from the *Trent* should be "avowed and maintained, it means war. . . . The indignation is wild and permeates all classes."[33]

A few sober Englishmen objected to the outburst of bellicosity. A retired general wrote the *Bradford Advertiser* that it made him sad to see "all the little boys are mad with joy for war, & there is nobody in the country above 12 years old." Despite such cautionary admonitions, however, the popular excitement continued unabated; the belligerency of the British press seemed actually to intensify; and each seemed to feed on the other. As the American minister's son, who was writing secretly as a "Special Correspondent" for the *New York Times*, declared in his London letter of December 7, it had been "a weary, anxious, troubled week." Although assurances had been received from America that the United States government had not authorized Wilkes's exploit, "the war fever" remained unaffected. The Confederate flag flew side by side with the Stars and Stripes at the Adelphi Theatre in the Strand, "while ragged boys" sold small rebel banners at a penny each on the very steps of the British antislavery headquarters, Exeter Hall. Members of the British ministry, the senior Adams wrote home, "though believed not to be desirous of pressing matters to a violent issue, are powerless" in the face of the popular storm.[34]

Adams could not remember a period of greater strain in his entire life. Anxiously, he scanned the newspapers for hints of what the British government would do. John Bright visited the American legation on the evening of November 29, determined to use all of the influence in his possession to preserve peace with America. He pumped Adams for facts which he might use to this end in a speeech planned for December 4 at Rochdale.[35]

However, no one as realistic as the American minister could have seen much hope for peace in the London newspapers on November 30. They made it seem only too clear that "the dogs are all let loose." It now appeared that the British government intended to base a demand for an apology and the restitution of the Southern commissioners on the argument that Captain Wilkes had usurped for himself the functions of a prize court—that his failure to take the *Trent* into New York for adjudication there as a prize made the seizure an intolerable insult to Great Britain. Adams thought of "the frail sister, whose indignation at the attempt on her honor was tremendous the moment she discovered that her pursuer was frightened off the chase. If he had been more daring there would have been no outcry."[36]

VII.

A Desperate Struggle for Peace Begins

What can be more monstrous than that we, . . . an educated, a moral, and a Christian nation, . . . when an accident of this kind occurs, . . . should be all up in arms, every sword leaping from its scabbard, and every man looking about for his pistols and his blunderbusses? . . . let us be calm.

JOHN BRIGHT,
Speech at Rochdale, December 4, 1861.

The month of December, 1861, was for Charles Adams the cruelest of his entire English mission. According to his son Henry, the atmosphere in the American Legation "would have gorged a glutton of gloom." Less given to melodramatic alliteration, the minister, too, found little that was encouraging in the prospect. Convinced that the *Trent* incident would result in his departure from London, he could "hardly conceive the madness" which could have prompted officers of the United States "for so paltry a prize as these two men to hazard a difficulty with any foreign nation whatever." He could scarcely "bear to think of it." Writing Seward the morning after he had rushed back to London on hearing the *Trent* news, Adams said: "There is little reason to doubt that the same steamer which bears this will carry out a demand for an apology and the restoration of the men. . . . I shall await with resignation the instructions which will probably close my mission."[1]

"This house is not cheerful," Henry Adams wrote his brother Charles. Their mother was "in a state." The minds of all the Adamses had been for so long "kept in the stretch," that Henry, like his father, felt "a sort of permanent lowness and wretchedness" that took all the zest out of life. "I am half mad with vexation and despair."[2]

From the vantage point of the American legation in London, the people of England seemed to have whipped themselves into an enormous rage. Second Secretary Moran concluded "that all the Fishwives of Billingsgate have been transferred to Printing House Square." Moran bridled at the "slatternly abuse of us and ours" in the *Times* and scorched the pages of his private journal with vehement denunciations of the "palpable lies" found daily in the London newspapers. He saw "something positively infernal in the way these assassins are goading the nation on. . . . If a war should follow this wicked conduct," he declared, "reflecting Englishmen will blush in after years at the bigotry and blindness which hurried them into the struggle.[3]

Caught up in the tide of patriotic indignation that washed over England, even the staunchest friends of the United States fell momentarily away. "I dined with a large English party on Friday," a prominent American visitor testified; "all were strong Northern sympathizers, and all, nevertheless, for war if S. & M. are not given up." Monckton Milnes privately expressed his belief that "the Americans must give in" to avert war, but he was not confident that this would happen. "The real difficulty," he feared, "will be to get Mason and Slidell away alive. Future Lord Chief Justice John Duke Coleridge, who heretofore had "most heartily," supported the Northern cause, thought it "highly probable that in a few weeks time we shall be at war" with the United States. And William Forster concluded that " struggling for peace is like the struggles of a drowning man."[4]

Meanwhile, Richard Cobden put his busy pen to work suggesting to correspondents on both sides of the Atlantic that the *Trent* difficulty be submitted to arbitration and that the occasion be used to get the voluntary adherence of the United States to the abolition of the blockade. The adoption of the first suggestion would have constituted, ipso facto, a recognition of the Confederacy as an independent nation, and the accomplishment of the second object would have removed the North's most effective weapon against the South. Adams heard of Cobden's epistolary crusade and wondered what kind of a friend America had in this "apostle of free trade" who advocated the abandonment of "our only real effective measure . . . because the Manchester spinners are making things uncomfortable here. . . . we might as well be asked to give up our struggle altogether."[5]

Only sturdy John Bright held fast. Shortly after the news of the seizure of Mason and Slidell had reached England, he had told a dinner gathering at Rugby that Englishmen should withhold judgment on the case until more facts were available. Before crying out for active measures against the Americans, Bright admonished his listeners, Englishmen should "Wait till it is quite clear that it was the purpose of the Northern States to offend your dignity and insult your flag."[6]

As he put the finishing touches on a speech scheduled to be delivered at Rochdale on December 4, Bright received a warning from his friend Charles Villiers, one of three Liberals in the cabinet (along with Thomas Milner Gibson and William E. Gladstone). The members of the ministry, Villiers wrote, had merely done what was necessary in dealing with the *Trent* incident. Had English officials borne it "meekly, every fellow in the command of a [U.S. government] vessel w^d have vied with the other in heaping fresh & further insults upon us—with a view to the glory & perhaps promotion it would get him." Although he was careful to ask Bright not to "be deterred from saying what you think right at your meeting by any thing I may say," Villiers added, nevertheless, that he had learned from a reliable source "that Adams *is packing up.*" The American minister had apparently decided that his government would reject the British demands; hence, he had "*not a hope left in his mind of peace.*" In view of the probability of war, Villiers hinted, Bright ought not to make futile gestures in behalf of the prospective enemy. "Do not," the president of the board of trade suggested, "for your own sake be anti-national in what you say at the meeting."[7]

Cobden, too, offered advice. Bright ought to tell his constituents, he wrote, that the future of America lay with the North, rather than with slavery, and that the "legal dispute" regarding the *Trent* incident should be referred to arbitration if it could not be settled by Anglo-American diplomatic intercourse. "Especially," Cobden added, Bright ought to

> expose the *self-evident* groundlessness of the accusation made by some of our journals that the North wish to pick a quarrel whilst fighting a life or death struggle at home. The accusation is so utterly irrational that

it would be regarded as a proof that we want to take advantage of their weakness and to force a quarrel on *them*.[8]

The next day found Bright in Rochdale. In a stirring two-hour speech, he ridiculed Englishmen who sought to use the *Trent* affair as a pretext to accomplish the dismemberment of the American Union. "There cannot be a meaner motive than this," he charged. "If a man had a great heart within him, he would rather look forward to the day when . . . the whole of that vast continent might become one great confederation of States . . . with freedom everywhere, equality everywhere, law everywhere, peace everywhere,—such a confederation would afford at least some hope that man is not forsaken of Heaven, and that the future of our race may be better than the past."[9]

The burly Lancashireman castigated the London *Times* as "an insidious enemy of both countries" for its repeated statements that the *Trent* seizure evidenced the determination of the Washington government to pick a quarrel with England. That influential journal had done "all that it could do to poison the minds of the people of England, and to irritate the minds of the people of America." Moreover, Bright added, the *Times* had seemed to ally itself with the queen's ministers in a perfidious project of bringing about a rift with the United States.[10]

"What," Bright thundered,

can be more monstrous than that we, . . . an educated, a moral, and a Christian nation—at a moment when an accident of this kind occurs, before we have heard a word from [the United States government] in reply—should be all up in arms, every sword leaping from its scabbard, and every man looking about for his pistols and his blunderbusses? I think the conduct pursued . . . is much more the conduct of savages than of Christian and civilized men.

. . . In a few years, a very few years, the twenty millions of freemen in the North will be thirty millions, or even fifty millions—a population equal to or exceeding that of this kingdom. When that time comes, I pray it may not be said amongst them, that, in the darkest hour of their country's trials, England, the land of their fathers, looked on with icy coldness and saw unmoved the perils and calamities of their children."[11]

Bright, however, seemed as yet a lone voice crying "Peace" in a wilderness of belligerency. His friend John Motley, American minister at

Vienna, wrote to thank him for his speech. "I honor you more than I can tell," the American minister to Austria wrote, "for your courage in thus standing up in the midst of a tempest of unreasoning wrath now sweeping over England, to defend not an unpopular but apparently a hated cause." Cassius Clay, the volatile Kentuckian whom Lincoln had sent to represent the United States in St. Petersburg, wrote that Bright's words would "never be forgotten by the great nation" across the sea, and the English Liberal leader's name would survive in history along with that of George Washington and the other "great ones which belong not to a nation but to all mankind."[12]

United States consuls also sent plaudits. John Bigelow wrote from Paris: "God bless you for your noble speech at Rochdale. . . . you have exhibited no less wisdom than magnanimity." And Thomas Dudley wrote from Liverpool: "I have sent a copy of your speech to the President, Vice President, all the members of the Cabinet, the leading members of the Senate & House of Representatives, & to all the principal newspapers of the United States; also a copy to each of the ministers of the U. S. on the Continent of Europe." Whatever the issue of the current crisis, Dudley added, "the name of John Bright will ever be borne in grateful remembrance by the people of the United States for his efforts [to assist them] . . . to maintain their government and to uphold republican institutions, thereby to demonstrate to the world man's capacity to govern himself."[13]

Some of Bright's English Liberal friends were almost awed by the bluntness of his pro-Yankee declarations. Louis Mallet, one of Milner Gibson's assistants at the board of trade, wrote of "the profound admiration and gratitude with which I have just read your magnificent speech." And Richard Cobden wrote his friend: "Your admirable address cannot fail to do good—but tis a mad world we live in." To another correspondent, however, Cobden revealed his conviction that the North and South could never "lie in the same bed again." Bright, alone among the Liberals, he thought, would not "hear anything against the claims of the North." Cobden admired "his pluck," if not his good sense.[14]

Not content with courageous oratory as a means of tempering the English war cry against the North, Bright attempted to use every whit of political influence available to him to pressure the ministry in favor of conciliation. "Can you tell me," he wrote Milner Gibson, "whether the govt. has acted in a moderate & reasonable manner, so as to give the American govt. a way of escape from the difficulty which has arisen?" Were press accounts of the cabinet's position on the *Trent* affair true? Bright hoped the Americans would ask for arbitration of that question, "which England could not refuse," unless Palmerston desired an Anglo-American war.[15]

Should Milner Gibson, an old political and personal friend, retain his seat in a cabinet that declared war because of the *Trent* incident, Bright predicted that he would "regret it hereafter. Magnanimity and not meanness should be our course in regard to a country in such extreme difficulty. I don't expect this quality," he declared,

> in the English *chief ministers*, or in the services, or in the oligarchy which hates the greatness of America, or in the rich flunkies who follow them— but I do expect it in you and some others of the cabinet, should an opportunity arise for a display of it. As a minister I would not consent to any step which may make war inevitable, as for example, an *ultimatum* which it may be impossible, from the state of feeling & affairs in America, for the Washington govt. to accept. *I should leave the govt. before consenting to such a step.*
>
> Now, my dear Gibson, you will forgive me if I write thus plainly. War is the ruin of govts. as well as of people. Your govt. rests on the life of a man of 77. . . . Don't think of the present only—but of the future . . . & have no part in the devilish policy which would involve us in a war to ruin freedom in the North, & to set up slavedom in the South.
>
> I write to you as I would to my own Brother, & urge you by all that is sacred that you have a watchful care over your course in this perilous time. . . . I see you are sending troops to Canada, putting ships into commission, & exciting alarm in the seaports & offers of service from sailors—& thus by assuming a tone & manner of war, are placing increasing difficulties in the way of peace. . . . I am compelled to fear that there is a resolution in the *secret* Cabinet of which you are not a member, to have a war if possible out of this unfortunate difficulty.[16]

Bright also wrote Cobden to suggest that he get in touch with Gladstone to advise "moderation," for the chancellor of the exchequer had opposed the Crimean War, "and yet went into it," to his later regret; hence, he might be extra wary of a similar episode. Do not, Bright admonished, "be afraid of intruding when so much is at stake. There is a point at which war may be avoided—go beyond that and it becomes inevitable. He is open to reason and will accept your suggestions in a friendly spirit."[17]

Bright's frantic efforts to stem the tide of war preparations had little effect on his countrymen, other than to bring down upon him general ridicule. The *Times* printed long editorials in two separate issues chiding the radical Liberal leader for his lonely worship of Yankee democracy, in which, the *Times* writer declared, he was "a voice without an echo." And *Punch* retorted

> "Let us be calm," say you, JOHN BRIGHT?
> Oh yes, we will be calm;
> But that we may not have to fight,
> We'll show that we can arm. . . .
> We wait their answer calmly, but
> With hand upon the hilt:
> If they the gate of peace would shut
> Be theirs alone the guilt.[18]

To see the ill-concealed satisfaction of the South's partisans in England only made matters worse for the Union's adherents. From Switzerland came a plea for sanity from the great European Liberal, Count Agenor de Gasparin. "Messrs. Mason and Slideyl," he warned, "are a hundred-fold more dangerous within the walls of Fort Warren than in the streets of London or Paris; that which their diplomacy could not have obtained in many months, Captain Wilkes has procured for them in one hour. . . . At one blow the whole face of things is changed; recognition has become possible; the blockade is threatened; and the United States are likely to be forced to turn their arms from the South, to repel a more redoubtable foe." Further to the East, John L. Motley visualized a thousand horrors if England, "with the largest fleet which the world has ever seen," whose assistance all the South's generals and diplomats could not have equalled in twenty years, should become allied with the slaveholding rebels. Thoughts of Boston bombarded, the Federal navy destroyed, "occupation of Washington and New York by the Confederates and their English allies," were "too much to bear."[19]

Charles Francis Adams, though badly upset himself, tried to cheer up his fellow diplomats. Should war actually break out, he wrote, Americans could at least console themselves with the thought that the British would suffer more than they in the long run. As a belligerent, England would be throwing away the war profits that balanced off her economic losses from lack of cotton. She might injure the United States along the eastern seaboard, "but she cannot subject us. And the end will be that changes will take place in the course of trade as well as of political sympathies," for the United States would thenceforth be England's most bitter enemy. Treaties with a Southern slaveholding nation "must be made only as that of Faust was made, exchanging present enjoyment for eternal condemnation."[20]

Many friends of the Union looked to France for salvation from the *Trent* trouble. Only a few Americans actually thought the French would side with them against the English; more of them apparently longed for Gallic mediation of the *Trent* affair; but the most promising thought of all was based on the widespread fear in England that Napoleon III might take advantage of an Anglo-American conflict to carry out anti-British projects in Europe or elsewhere in the world. Such an apprehension might hold the English back from rushing into a war which otherwise they might welcome. It was because of France that a British diplomat as experienced as the earl of Clarendon dreaded the apparent desire of the Yankee "villains" to pick a quarrel with England. To the extent that "it w^d complete their everlasting & irretrievable ruin," he wrote, "I sh^d be glad of it, if I did not feel sure that N[apoleon] w^d instantly leave us in the lurch and do something in Europe w^h we can't stand."[21]

Napoleon, a notorious international busybody, might indeed be tempted by the *Trent* affair to tender his "good offices," which might enhance his prestige at the expense of France's cross-channel rival, by allowing him to serve, in effect, as England's judge. It would be awkward to refuse an offer by the emperor to preserve peace through mediation or arbitration, especially when the law seemed so clearly in England's favor. Visualizing Napoleon's intervention as a means of preventing a humiliating capitulation to the British ultimatum, while also avoiding war, many Americans in Europe expressed a strong desire for imperial intercession. One of Seward's close friends wrote him from Paris that, "if other things fail, is not this, ultimately, a fit question for referral to a Friendly Power?" And another former political associate of the secretary of state, also in Paris, added "that the Emperor of the French should act as arbitrator in the dispute." Acting on his own responsibility, but knowing full well his reputation in Europe as a person deeply in Seward's confidence, Roman Catholic Archbishop John Hughes intended to urge the emperor in person "to step in as arbitrator between England and America." From the United States legation at Berne, meanwhile, George Fogg wrote Adams to suggest "a *prompt* offer on the part of our government to submit the *entire* question to the arbitration of the Emperor Napoleon. The British government dare not reject the offer: and there can [be] no dishonor in our government making it. . . . It is certain that we are not now prepared for a *foreign* war with a great naval power." According to Fogg, the American representative at Berlin "entirely concurs in the suggestion foregoing." Whether that was in fact the case, Norman Judd did later seek an interview with the Prussian foreign minister, in the course of which he asked Bernstorff: "Why dont [*sic*] your government keep the Peace?" Should the United States government decide to debate the *Trent* question before responding positively to the British ultimatum, Judd suggested, the great continental European powers might then "lift their voices" to prevent war.[22]

Meanwhile, the American minister at Brussels, Henry Sanford, asked Napoleon's representative in Belgium to inquire whether his imperial master would agree to mediate or arbitrate the *Trent* dispute. Seward could help ensure French mediation, Sanford wrote the secretary of state, if he would attempt to evade the British demand without rejecting it entirely. The longer the United States could stall, Sanford suggested, the more time there would be for an antiwar movement to spring up in England, which might in due course force the British to ask Napoleon to arbitrate the affair. According to Sanford, "M. de Tallyrand seemed to Entertain this view favorably," and he would write French Foreign Minister Edouard Thouvenel that if the United States sought "to prolong the discussion," France should consider whether to intervene. In the meantime, Sanford wrote, European diplomatic sentiment, as well as public opinion, was veering toward French mediation as the best way to avert an Anglo-American war.[23]

77

In order for the French emperor to mediate the *Trent* controversy, however, his government would have to remain uncommitted on that question until a suitable invitation was extended. Within twenty-four hours of receiving the first news of the *Trent* seizure, Thouvenel realized that the British ultimatum that would be sent to Washington allowed no room for evasion or delay. Hence it was unlikely that French mediation or arbitration would be possible. Indeed, the only way the emperor could play a notable role in the affair was to proclaim at once, in time for his announcement to reach Washington prior to official action on the British demands, either that he would actively support the United States on the question, which would involve risking war with England over an interpretation of international law which the French had always rejected (and which they could not be sure the *Americans* would depart from *their* precedents to support)—or, alternatively, the French government might take the easy road by siding with England on the *Trent* issue.[24]

What the French ought to do was obvious. Press opinion throughout Europe, as Americans there testified, was spontaneously and virtually unanimous against the United States on the *Trent* question.[25] The Wilkes seizure was viewed, with hardly an exception, as a gross violation of international law. If the English went to war against the United States, they could be expected soon to smash the blockade that was preventing Southern cotton from reaching French textile mills. French cotton importers had only to wait until the American fleet was swept away by Britannia, and then they could once more share in the Southern cotton trade.

The French had little desire to help avert an Anglo-American conflict. Had they wished to act as peacemakers, they might have remained noncommittal on the *Trent* question, sacrificing political opportunism in favor of constructive statesmanship by announcing that, in all fairness, they ought to hear the American side of the case before making any official pronouncement. This would have permitted the longstanding English suspicions of French designs, as an astute American diplomat wrote Seward, gradually to cool "the hostile ardor of the British people." Some Americans hoped this "English jealousy of France" would in the end prove the principal preventive of war. Adams, for example, wrote from London that he considered "the awe in which this country stands of France" might aid his country to ride out the crisis. The French, however, hardly hesitated before flinging themselves into the controversy on the side of England.[26]

Thouvenel and Napoleon did not even wait to confirm the first sketchy intelligence of the *Trent* seizure, which they had received only from Count Charles de Flahault in London and from British journalistic sources. Without knowing precisely what the English were prepared to do about the case, and without any word from Henri Mercier at Washington, the French emperor, meeting with his cabinet on November 28, decided to endorse whatever demands might be sent to Washington by the British. That evening, Thouvenel wrote Flahault that Wilkes's seizure of the Confederate envoys was "wrong," and that the French minister in Washington would be told to express this opinion, and to give Lyons, whatever the latter's instructions, strong "moral support."[27]

When Thouvenel later learned the details of the British ultimatum from Flahault, he remarked to Henry Wellesley, Earl Cowley, the British ambassador at Paris, that the demand had his complete approbation. In the meantime, he had prepared his own dispatch to Mercier at Washington. He read it to the British ambassador on December 3, the emperor approved it on December 4, and a courier left Paris on the following day to take it to Mercier.[28]

The document began by declaring that the arrest of Mason and Slidell had appeared to be, in France as in England, an act far outside "the ordinary rules of international law." The French would deeply regret it if the members of the Washington cabinet "were inclined to approve the conduct of the *San Jacinto*'s commander." For to do so would be to strike a blow at the principles of neutral maritime rights which the United States government itself had long endorsed. Thouvenel recommended, therefore, that the United States government, "inspired by a just and upright feeling," yield to the British demands for the release of the Southern prisoners and for "explanations which may take from this act its offensive character toward the British flag."[29]

When Flahault gave Russell a copy of Thouvenel's dispatch to Mercier, the British foreign minister found it "very satisfactory," an appraisal echoed by Palmerston when he learned about it. Russell immediately sent Lyons a lengthy summary of its contents. He praised Thouvenel for having treated the *Trent* question with "great ability" while giving England moral support at the point of greatest danger, Washington. Palmerston, meanwhile, observed that the dispatch showed that the English might rely for the foreseeable future upon French backing against the Americans, because such was "in keeping with the interest of France & the Feelings of the Emperor against the Northerns."[30]

Lewis, too, anticipated Napoleon's support for England in the *Trent* affair, because it seemed "quite certain that the French Government wish for war between England and America. The blockade of the South would be raised and they would get the cotton which they want." And Cowley, who was in the best position to know, wrote a diplomat friend that the French, "behaving well and backing us up nobly," did so "not for our beaux yeux or for the righteousness of our cause, but because they hope that we shall go to war, open the Southern ports, and give them cotton." Cowley, convinced that the French hated the English "cordially & systematically," was nevertheless sure that "at the present moment they hate the Americans more, because they cannot get more cotton. . . . As to any real sentiments of upholding the rights of neutrals," the French only expressed them because it was temporarily expedient to do so. Undercurrents in the Paris journals, Cowley reported, indicated that French officials were "very insidiously" attempting to play "on the state of our relations with America," in the hope of benefiting France at British expense. Russell endorsed on the back of Cowley's letter that he was "quite sick" of French political "intrigues" against England.[31]

The crusty old earl of Clarendon had written Cowley, when first he heard of the *Trent* incident, that Napoleon would "like to take this occasion to make us feel that he is necessary to us and to avenge his griefs against us by causing us to eat dirt or go to war with the North with France against us or in a state of doubtful and ill-humoured neutrality." It was "altogether . . . a most serious look-out," for if the Americans had "the shadow of a shade of a hope" that Napoleon might "be with them or even perfectly neutral," their "insolence" would burst out again, and in that contingency Clarendon "would not give a sixpence for the chance of maintaining peace." Cowley would have to watch carefully for signs of duplicity by French officials, as the *Trent* crisis burgeoned in the weeks ahead.[32]

Cowley needed no such admonition to alert him to Gallic trickery. When he read in the newspapers that General Winfield Scott, only a few weeks retired as the commanding general of all the Union armies, had arrived in Paris, he was curious why this personage had come to France, especially since he seemed to be accompanied by two close political associates of the American secretary of state, and also since their appearance in Europe closely coincided with the receipt there of the first intelligence of the *Trent* "outrage." Cowley set to work to discover whether there was a connection between these events.[33]

Actually, there was no connection at all. During October, in response to many requests from United States citizens in Europe to send special agents there to counteract Confederate propaganda, the American secretary of state had requested a few elderly, political conservative Northern politicians to embark on such a venture. Two eminent churchmen, Episcopalian Bishop Charles P. McIlvaine of Ohio, and Roman Catholic Archbishop John Hughes of New York, agreed to make the trip to Europe, and Hughes insisted, against Seward's wishes, on taking as a traveling companion one of the secretary's oldest personal and political associates, the editor of the *Albany Evening Journal*, Thurlow Weed. Hughes and Weed sailed from New York on board the steamer *Arago* on November 6, amid a flutter of newspaper speculations about their supposed "diplomatic mission." McIlvaine was to follow about two weeks later. Also on board the *Arago* was Winfield Scott, who at the age of seventy-five was journeying to France for the sake of his health, which had practically broken under the strain of organizing the Union war effort.[34]

In the same issue of the London *Times* in which startled Englishmen first learned of Captain Wilkes's audacious abduction, they also might have read that the venerable Scott had stepped ashore at a French port into the shade of an "immense American flag" held high over him by fellow countrymen, who comprised a waving, cheering crowd that escorted him to a hotel "profusely decorated with American and French flags." Weed and Hughes were almost ignored during the general's triumphal journey from Le Havre to Paris.[35]

Hardly had the Yankee trio settled in their hotel rooms in the French capital city than they were asked by the American consul there, fresh from an editorial position on the *New York Evening Post*, to join with William L. Dayton, the American minister, and himself in promoting a peaceful settlement of the *Trent* affair. On the morning of their first strategy session the Paris newspapers were full of hostile comments toward the United States. The local correspondent of the *New York Times* could not "perceive one spark of sympathy" for those who had captured Mason and Slidell, and if France found it impossible to stay neutral in an Anglo-American war growing out of the *Trent* crisis, "Malakoff" warned that it was probable that Napoleon would enter the fray on England's side.[36]

The French had received all their information about the *Trent* affair from British sources. It was time for Americans to give their version of the incident. Moreover, a story was being whispered throughout the city that, as the British ambassador reported, "General Scott tells who chooses to listen to him that the Resolution to catch the Southern Commissioners was adoped on the proposition of Seward & the rest of the Cabinet—that the President was against it but was forced to give in," with the warmongering secretary of state, who "prepared" the plan to kidnap the Southern emissaries, "carrying the day." Another communicant, who had told Cowley he was "very well informed of what is passing at Washington," had provided a variation of this story. He had assured the ambassador "that he knows it to a certainty that Lincoln and Seward have imagined this *Trent* affair, in order to enable them to get with credit out of a war in which they find they have not the slightest chance of success." The Northern public, discontented with the Lincoln administration's policies, threatened "a complete change of government," and the president therefore ordered up "the popular cry against England, and Canada will now be the lure held out. An attempt will be made to come to terms with the South, when Mexico will probably become the object of the latter." Cowley did not know what credit to attach to these tidbits of information, but he wondered whether, indeed, "the North and South will not shake hands over a war with us."[37]

Insidious imputations about General Scott's business in Europe soon elicited strong denials from the old soldier of any conspiracies against England on the part of high administration officials in America. Scott told Percy Doyle, a British diplomat who had known him in Washington and in Mexico, that he was aware of the newspaper stories which quoted him as saying the seizure of the Southern commissioners

> wherever they were found had been decided upon before I left Washington. I beg you will, as a friend of mine, deny, as I shall publicly, this statement: so far from such being the case I did not know that Captain Wilks [*sic*] had left the African coast. . . .
>
> What did take place before I left Washington was that orders were given to send the "James Adger" and two or three other vessels of war to seize the comm^{rs}, dead or alive, if they were found on board the "Nashville" or any other Confederate vessel, but certainly no orders were given to seize them on board of any English or other Foreign vessel, and I cannot help feeling confident that Captain Wilks [*sic*] has acted on his own responsibility.

As for himself, Scott added, it was equally untrue that he had come to Paris on a special mission. Rather was he merely en route "to Italy on account of his health."[38]

Other prominent Americans in Europe quickly issued disclaimers of the alleged bellicosity of Lincoln's advisers, especially as rumored to have been depicted by Scott. At a hurriedly called meeting on December 2, Scott's traveling companions on the *Arago* joined the American minister and the American consul in drafting a letter for the general's signature, denying that the United States government had ever had the capture of Mason and Slidell under consideration, and asserting that "every instinct of prudence as well as of good neighborhood prompts our government to regard no honorable sacrifice too great for the preservation of the friendship of Great Britain." Published in the Paris *Constitutionnel* on the morning of December 4, and soon reprinted throughout Europe, this was hardly a warlike pronouncement from the foremost military man in America.[39]

In response to Scott's letter the pro-Northern London *Daily News* editorialized that "every paragraph . . . breathes an earnest desire for peace," and suggested that the queen's ministers show similar temperance in receiving the representations of the United States government in reply to the British claim for reparation. And Richard Cobden found the missive signed by "the Duke of Wellington of the States, . . . a very superior man in every way," most "admirable." It seemed odd that English "Bishops and Archbishops [should] leave an old warrior to perform the part of peacemaker." As an American in Paris wrote a British friend, if Scott's letter did "not convince your Cabinet & people how grossly they have been duped by *somebody* as to the attitude of the Washington government, nothing can."[40]

As soon as Scott's letter was published in Paris, Weed carried a copy of it to London to get it printed there. Bemoaning the current anti-Americanism of British journalists, generally, he had determined "to do something for the press" in England. Although Seward had opposed his going to Europe at all, and, as Weed complained, "did not tell me what to do or say" there, the Albany editor nevertheless procured some letters of introduction from Americans in Paris and soon materialized in London.[41]

The London newspapers did not require Weed's presence in that city to cause their editors to reprint Scott's letter from the Paris journals. Even the *Times* copied it unabridged. With a copy of the "Thunderer" under his arm, Weed went, on the evening of December 6, to see the American minister. He was pleased that Adams treated him kindly and did not dissuade him from setting about his self-appointed task of winning the confidence of prominent Englishmen, whom he planned to fill with pro-Union ideas, and with whose help he hoped to promote the cause of Anglo-American rapprochement. Despite deprecations by Liberals like Cobden, who dismissed him contemptuously as "Seward's wire-puller and . . . simply a politician," Weed soon established confidential relations with many English friends of the North, some of whom supplied the influence that enabled him to plant pro-Northern articles in British newspapers. John Bright liked Weed from the start. He described the New York journalist in his diary as "an old man, rather heavy and quiet in appearance, but giving evidence of strength and thought." The shrewd Rochdale Liberal vowed to value Weed's "information and judgment much."[42]

VIII.

The "Bête Noire"

The impression is general that Mr. Seward is resolved to insult England until she makes a war. He is the bête noire, that frightens them out of all their proprieties. It is of no use to deny it. . . . And if war finally happens, it will trace to this source one of its most prominent causes.

CHARLES FRANCIS ADAMS TO HIS SON,
Dec. 20, 1861.[1]

Thurlow Weed's quick trip to London was caused by more than a desire to dissassociate General Scott from rumors that the *Trent* abduction had been planned by the American cabinet. The journey was precipitated primarily by a disturbing remark in the London *Times* "City Intelligence" column that Lincoln and Seward might "have determined to hide the spectacle of their internal condition by a foreign war." Amazed by this report, the Methodist minister of the "American Church" in Paris, John M'Clintock, wrote a British acquaintance:

Does the British Cabinet *really* believe that Mr. Seward wishes to have war with England, & that his measures are intended to provoke it?

If you can, through any of your friends, get an answer to this that may be relied on, . . . it will go a great way, perhaps, towards preventing things from rushing on to war between America and England—a war which would thrill the master of evil with satanic joy.[2]

M'Clintock's London correspondent had already notified him, in a letter that crossed his in the mail, that "in the highest quarters" in England a strong desire prevailed "to avoid a fight *if possible*," but an equally strong fear existed "that Seward wants to force England into it." Why such an apprehension should be so universally held by British statesmen, the Reverend William Arthur did not know, but he guessed that the feeling might have resulted from some hiatus in "the personal relations between Lord Lyons & Seward," perhaps because a jaundiced view was taken "at Washington of Lyons's *proclivities*."[3]

M'Clintock took this disheartening intelligence to Thurlow Weed and Archbishop John Hughes. He then reported:

I have inquired of parties just from Washington, & knowing all Seward's heart & mind, & answer your questions thus:

1. So far as is known, the personal relations of Seward & Lyons are friendly—entirely so—six week ago.

2. Lord Lyons is believed in Washington to favour the South. The company at his house is largely of that side. His despatch case from Southern cities is called "the rebels' mail bag. . . ."

3. The notion that Seward, or the American government, *can* wish to add war with England to their war with the South, is so absurd that I can hardly imagine sensible men to entertain it. I told Thurlow Weed that your Cabinet really *did* entertain it; & he raised hands & eyes in wonder. Seward himself has not the slightest idea that you really believe any such thing.[4]

Weed, like other Americans in Paris, was "surprised and annoyed at the distrust and ill-will" exhibited in England toward his friend Seward. From Sidney Brooks, who had recently been visiting his sister, the wife of the American minister in London, Weed heard that everywhere in the British capital Brooks had "found people fortified with evidences of [Seward's] hostility to England." It was then that, after being shown Arthur's letter, the New Yorker decided to go to London and, as he told M'Clintock, "strain every nerve" to persuade English statesmen "of their error about Seward & our government."[5]

Weed had been in London only a few days when he discerned that "Strong, active and subtle influences" were at work there to render his friend Seward obnoxious to all Englishmen. The feeling against Seward was "almost infernal." So successful had been the secretary of state's slanderers that he was "everywhere regarded, not only as an enemy of England, but as one who, from personal hostility, or political consideration, really desires a collision between the two nations." In a letter to Seward praying that he had foreseen "the wisdom of concession to Eng-

lish tenacity about the honor of its flag," Weed warned of the general
English

> distrust of and hostility to yourself; how created or why, I know not. It
> has been skillfully worked. . . . I was told yesterday, repeatedly, that I
> ought to write the President demanding your dismissal. . . .
> It is said in high places that you seek war with England, because the
> Rebel war will ruin you. . . .[6]

There was nothing secret about the anti-Seward stories. British newspapers had printed them. No sooner had the news of the *Trent* incident
reached London, in fact, than an editorial writer for the London *Morning
Chronicle* informed his readers that Lincoln, "a feeble, confused, and
little-minded mediocrity," had been influenced by "Mr. Seward, the
firebrand at his elbow, . . . to provoke a quarrel with all Europe."
Meanwhile, a writer in the *London Daily News* declared: "Beneath
everything there exists an undercurrent of apprehension lest the American Government really contemplate the desperate policy of seeking to
fasten a quarrel on Great Britain, in order to gain a standing ground
for abandoning its design of subjugating" the South. And a spokesman
for the London *Times* had asserted that, although a majority of the
American cabinet membership probably favored preserving peace with
England, the "splenetic mind of Mr. SEWARD [had] been continually in-
fusing into his colleagues a feeling of enmity to this country." Having
"already despaired of reconquering the long tributary South," the American secretary of state had resolved "to retire from the contest amid the
conflagration of a European war, . . . seeking an indemnity for the loss
of the Southern States by absorbing the British possessions" in North
America.[7]

"Wild as are the words written and spoken by Secretary Seward," a
commentator wrote in the London *Morning Post*, "and reckless as the
American policy not infrequently is," it was yet improbable that the
Northern *people* were "seriously disposed to accept a war with England."
One solution, an editorial in the usually sensible Edinburgh *Scotsman*
suggested, was for the members of the United States Senate to "overthrow" Seward and "declare for redress and conciliation." This delusion
—that both the wish and the will to remove Seward from office existed at

that time among a majority of United States senators—was derived, perhaps, from a statement of Sir James Fergusson, who, after traveling in the Northern States during 1861, had returned to Edinburgh and declared: "The unpopularity of some of the leading members of the [Federal] government is extreme. Northern bankers of great influence and moderate views repeatedly in conversation with me expressed a strong desire for their removal and a belief that it would shortly be forced upon the President." A strong suspicion existed in the North, according to Fergusson, that some members of the Lincoln administration might even try "to plunge the country into a foreign war from selfish & personal considerations."[8]

Such stories reached receptive ears among the English aristocracy. Clarendon, for example, no sooner learned of the *Trent* "outrage" than he wrote Cowley that he had "no doubt" it was "a deliberate and premeditated insult. Ever since the Civil War began, Mr. Seward had been trying to provoke us into a quarrel and finding that it could not be effected at Washington he has determined to compass it at sea."[9]

Soon a private letter came from Lyons, written "in utmost haste," to confirm the fears of the Whig inner circle about Seward. For the British envoy at Washington wrote that he had been "told confidentially that orders were given from Washington, which led to the capture on board the 'Trent,' and that they were signed by Mr. Seward without the knowledge of the President." Lyons would not "vouch for the truth" of this piece of intelligence, but he did affirm that the secretary of state was "not sorry to have a question with us like this, in which it is difficult for France to take a part." Lyons's remarks were quickly whispered around London, there to merge with other tales of collusion between Wilkes and Fairfax, on one side, and Mason and Slidell on the other. As Weed put it, "the Females of the Caged Traitors," once they arrived in London, had "left the impression here that the catching was voluntary. The Secessionists in Paris were certainly jubilant over it." Although the thought might "be farfetched," Weed admitted; still, "why, it is asked, were not Despatches searched for [on board the Trent], as evidence on which to justify the Seizure?" Adams, on his part, heard "many people" in London persistently maintaining that the alleged collusion was probable, for "not long since" Wilkes, Fairfax, Mason, and Slidell were all "very fishy in regard to the justice of the government cause." John Bright heard substantially the same rumors. And a fellow country-man observed that "as to Wilkes, all was the most studious insult, his shotted gun, his live shell, his armed men, his bare cutlasses convinced every sailor I have heard speak that he deliberately meant to provoke war," and "that he must be at heart a secessionist."[10]

Whether Wilkes and Fairfax had acted as his instruments or not, few Englishmen doubted that Seward, in some manner, had arranged the *Trent* affair. The duke of Argyll, for example, took it for granted that the American secretary of state had ordered the *Trent* abduction. And the duke of Newcastle, after reading Lyons's latest letters, wrote the governor general of Canada that war was only "too likely" to result from the crisis, for "with Mr. Seward at the helm of the United States, and the Mob and the Press manning the vessel," it was probable that the "atonement" demanded by England would be refused. Meanwhile, an-other member of the ministry "heard . . . a man well entitled to credit say" that Seward and certain followers were "known to have a policy of making foreign war, to cover their retreat in acknowledging the inde-pendence of the South." This, the informant asserted, had been "openly spoken of at Boston in his hearing some weeks ago!"[11]

The "word" about Seward had been spread by British diplomacy throughout Europe. From Rome a high official at the Foreign Office received a note in which the writer supposed there was "not a chance left of avoiding war with America,—and if I am not much mistaken Seward wishes for war with England to save his own skin before it becomes evident to the North that it *cannot* reconquer the South. My acquaintance with Seward did not leave a favourable impression. I think him capable of any amount of dirty work." In Turin an American dip-lomat complained of "the insidious efforts of the British government," apparent even in Northern Italy, "to create a belief that the United States are seeking a quarrel with England." And Motley, through his "constant private correspondence with influential persons of various parties in England," had heard, over and over, the idea, carefully "nurtured in England—that our government desired to force that country into a war, in order to escape from a dilemma at home, & to cover our incapacity to deal with the Southern insurrection." This idea, Motley wrote, "has taken possession of a considerable portion of the English population." The reverberations of this "weak delusion of a sick man's brain," reached all the way to the Southern Confederacy, where high-ranking officers attributed the seizure of Mason and Slidell from the *Trent* to Seward's realization "that he cannot conquer a Union;" whereupon he had apparently decided "to provoke a foreign war as a good pretext for making a general peace." Secessionists in Paris were "in great glee" at Seward's "imbecility," certain that he was indeed resolved to "fight John Bull." [12]

Henry Adams, who had been acting in London as "Our Own Correspondent" of the *New York Times,* had informed his readers, several weeks before he learned of the *Trent* incident, that "for some reason or other" the American secretary of state was "much disliked" in England. The minister's son speculated that the aversion to Seward was partly owing "to the fact that commercial classes in this country receive their ideas on our affairs from the commercial classes at home, among whom Mr. SEWARD has never been a favorite." But there were also certain men, "high in position among the nominal supporters of the [Lincoln] Administration, and of large acquaintance and influence among the governing classes here, who seem to have made it their object to excite in this country distrust and suspicion of our whole foreign policy." These perfidious politicians, for whatever purposes, had apparently helped to influence the American correspondents of London newspapers, who echoed their sentiments. [13]

Once the news of the *Trent* adventure had shattered the serenity of the London legation, even Henry Adams, who had long admired Seward as a statesman, lashed out in rage and perplexity at his father's friend. If the Lincoln administration had "ordered the capture of those men," he vociferated, "I am satisfied that our present authorities are very unsuitable persons to conduct a war like this or to remain in the direction of our affairs. It is our ruin." Seward had left his London representative "in the most awkward and unfair position" by providing "no warning that such an act was thought of." Indeed, young Adams complained, the state department seemed "almost to have purposely encouraged us to waste our strength in trying to maintain the relations which it was itself intending to destroy. . . . What Seward means is more than I can guess. But if he means war . . . , or to run as close as he can without touching, then I say that Mr. Seward is the greatest criminal we've had yet."[14]

Such doubts about Seward, expressed by some of the secretary of state's friends as well as by those who did not know him personally, led Thurlow Weed to send a letter of protest to the London *Times*, which in several editorials had depicted the *Trent* affair as the logical culmination of Seward's relentless pursuit of a pretext for war with England. Admitting that Wilkes's abduction of Mason and Slidell could probably not be justified under international law, Weed declared that, nevertheless, he had been surprised at the impression seemingly widespread among the "English Government, its press, and its people," that Seward had "actually designed" to disrupt relations between the two countries. He felt "quite authorized" in disclaiming, "for Mr. SEWARD, unfriendly intentions and feelings towards England," and he begged

> to refer such English gentlemen as have acquaintance with, or opportunities for consulting, Mr. ADAMS, our resident Minister, for a true reflex of American sentiment and sympathies. That distinguished statesman . . . enjoys . . . the confidence of his Government; and, resigning his seat in Congress to assume diplomatic responsibilities, he is also familiar with the views and feelings of our public men.[15]

When Weed brought Adams his letter to the *Times* to see if the minister objected to its submission, the latter, although finding it "a little too smooth and deprecating" of the American position, did not attempt to enjoin its publication. He warned Weed, however, that "it would conciliate no favor" from the *Times*. Weed's hopes were raised when editor John T. Delane promptly accepted the letter, and even sent a proof sheet to Weed's hotel room for correction, but when the letter was published the next day it was accompanied by a long editorial reiterating the "facts" that allegedly illustrated a year-long campaign by Seward to force England into war against the United States. Weed's "quasi-diplomatic . . . defence of Mr. SEWARD," the *Times* editor proclaimed, had only "made the case of his client and his country considerably worse than he found it." For the American journalist had merely referred Englishmen to the American minister in London, "the misfortune being that Mr. ADAMS, who has the good will, has not the power, and Mr. SEWARD, who has the power, has not the good will." Disappointed at this sarcastic rebuff of his peace overture, Weed was still pleased to see his letter reprinted elsewhere in England and on the continent of Europe. For this wide republication, he wrote Seward, it was worth having "ventured into the Lion's Den," in which he "of course got scratched."[16]

In his rejoinder to Weed's letter, Delane had summarized the "evidence" that "the present Prime Minister of the United States of America" had long cherished "a deliberate . . . intention to do us an injury." First of all, the readers of the "Thunderer" learned that

during the visit of the Prince of WALES to the United States, Mr. SEWARD took advantage of an entertainment which was given to the Prince and his suite to tell the Duke of NEWCASTLE that he was likely to occupy high office, that when he did so it would become his duty to insult England, and that he should insult her accordingly.

A few months after this sally Mr. SEWARD found himself in the position he had anticipated, a quarrel between North and South was imminent, and the advice which Mr. SEWARD had tendered to the hostile parties was to abandon their dispute, and to combine their forces in a wholly unprovoked attack upon the British colony of Canada.

The next step of Mr. SEWARD was to publish a circular, calling upon the States to fortify the sea and lake frontier—a circular which was understood by everybody to refer to Great Britain, and was, indeed, capable of no other construction.

An English packet is then boarded by an American ship of war; four passengers are removed from the packet by violence, and placed at the disposal of the American Secretary of State. He orders them into strict confinement, without any diplomatic communication with the English Minister at Washington, and by so doing appears to adopt and ratify the action of the American commander.

This is all we know at present of the feelings, intentions, and proceedings of Mr. SEWARD. But it is quite enough to lead to a general persuasion that upon his ability to involve the United States in a war with England

Mr. SEWARD has staked his official, and, most probably, also his political existence, and that whatever may be the advantage to America of a war with this country, to him it has become an article of the very first necessity.[17]

No one in England knew better than Thurlow Weed how improbable were the remarks attributed to Seward by Newcastle. The London *Chronicle* had quoted them as follows: "'My Lord Duke, *either Mr. Lincoln or myself will be next President of the United States.* If Mr. Lincoln be chosen, I shall be Secretary, and *we are determined to take* the first opportunity that presents itself to insult your country.' 'If you do,' was the Duke of Newcastle's answer, 'you will bring a war between the two countries.' 'Oh no, there will be no war,' was Mr. Seward's rejoinder; 'but we will—we *must* insult you.'" It was this version of the story that was essentially repeated in the *Times* and elsewhere. Although it might not have been, as a writer in the *New York Times* later described it, entirely "a shameless and disgraceful" falsehood; neither could it have been wholly true. For the meeting between Seward and Newcastle had come after it had been decided that Lincoln, not Seward, would be the Republican nominee for president, but well before any hint had come from Lincoln or anyone else that the New York senator would occupy a high position in the next administration. Moreover, Seward himself had strongly urged the prince of Wales's visit to the United States, for the purpose of "maintaining and increasing friendly feeling between the people of the two countries," and it seems unlikely that he would have seized the occasion instead to threaten or insult England; nor, surely, had he really contemplated a provocation leading to a quarrel, would he have warned Englishmen in advance, thus putting them on guard.[18]

In his letter to the London *Times*, Weed, in the mildest terms, had contradicted Newcastle's interpretation of what Seward had told him, asserting that the spirit of the conversation "was misapprehended," and that Seward's remark had doubtless been "an attempted pleasantry, . . . certainly to be regretted," but easily understood by an American as mere "badinage." Privately, however, Weed was far less charitable to the duke, referring to his gossip as "an impeachment of the commonest sense." Warning Seward that he had been "infernally abused" in England, where "general distrust" of him had "been skillfully worked," Weed set diligently to work, soon after his arrival in London, to trace down every rumor of the American secretary of state's alleged hostility to England. Having heard the Newcastle story from many quarters, and having read it repeatedly in the newspapers, he finally got it, substantially unchanged, from the duke himself. In conversations with prominent English officials, he deprecated all the rumors, saying Seward was "utterly ignorant" of them, and that American political leaders, including the secretary of state, "had no more idea or intention of provoking a war with England than the government of the Moon."[19]

In the course of his conversations, Weed was often told that he ought to write Lincoln to demand the dismissal of the secretary of state. He was also informed by a member of parliament that Lady Napier, wife of the former British minister at Washington, was telling people that she had personally heard Seward talk, "in company," of going to war with England, and that when she had asked him why, he had replied "that it was the best thing that could happen for America." Every idle word Seward had spoken during a trip to England in 1859 had been "treasured up and a bad meaning given to it. For example he made enemies of a Noble Household for laughing at the enormous sums of money paid for Paintings. At another Dinner Table he gave offense by insisting that English books were absurdly expensive." All over England, Weed reported to Seward, "men are ransacking your Three Volumes [of published speeches] for every word against England." What was extracted from the secretary of state's past pronouncements was, of course, "tinged by the new impression that you want a war."[20]

A lead writer in the London *Daily Telegraph*, for example, claimed that a good illustration "of the spirit in which the present Foreign Minister of the Federal Government has acted" in dealing with England, was to be found in "an incident which occurred, we think, in 1849, when he was Governor of New York State. He was a guest at a public dinner, and in proposing one of the toasts remarked, . . . something to this effect—Prosperity to the British Empire until her American colonies shall obtain more liberal institutions!" Weed fired off a letter to the editor of the *Daily Telegraph* protesting that Seward, who was not governor of

New York, but rather a United States senator in 1849, might indeed "have referred, in some dinner speech, to Canada." But such references had never been hostile in spirit to England.

> Mr. Seward is speculative and sanguine . . . , a statesman . . . in advance of the age. He has believed in the possibility during his own lifetime of seeing that continent consolidated under one Government; and this less by conquest than from natural causes and by general consent. His course as a public man has heretofore been influenced more by considerations of this nature than by present and passing events.[21]

Also cited as an example of Seward's warlike propensities was a circular of October 14 addressed to the Northern governors of the seaboard and Great Lakes states, recommending that they improve their military defenses as a "precaution" against the possibility of European intervention in the current domestic conflict. A London *Times* editorial writer had claimed that "Europe read the circular with great surprise. . . . The wildest insanity of the other side of the Atlantic could scarcely dream that England was about to take advantage of a civil disorder to invade Maine or New York or Michigan . . . . Yet it would now appear that Mr. SEWARD's warning was not necessarily so absurd as it then appeared." For the American secretary of state had apparently "despaired of reconquering the long tributary South, and . . . had conceived the policy of seeking an indemnity for the loss of the Southern States by absorbing the British possessions" in North America. Hence, there was "method in his madness. . . . He knew that he was about to force a quarrel with England, and he could therefore already indicate where the struggle would necessarily be hottest."[22]

"We may be wrong," the *Times* spokesman continued,

> in attributing a coherent policy to so incoherent a personage as Mr. SEWARD. [But] . . . if the Government of the Federal States had conceived the design of abandoning the South and seeking an indemnity in the conquest of Canada, they would have acted just as they have hitherto acted. They would have strengthened their Northern frontier, they would have used every effort to excite their population against England, they would have sown seeds of jealousy and hostility between the two countries, they would have commenced a series of aggressions which no

country can endure without losing its self-respect and its consideration among its equals, and they would have chosen for their aggressions a period of the year when the coveted territory is cut off by climate from the assistance of the mother country.[23]

Accusations against Seward floated in the London air like wisps of poison smog. The third and most serious of the British charges against Seward was that, as a London *Times* editorial asserted, he had advised Northerners and Southerners to abandon their differences and join instead "in a wholly unprovoked attack upon the British colony of Canada." It was well known, a writer for the *Saturday Review* maintained, that this "piece of folly" had long been in Seward's mind; "yet in his most eccentric dreams" it was difficult to suppose that even the "wildly extravagant" American secretary of state could imagine the Southern Confederacy joining "the North in a war with Great Britain provoked by the capture of its own commissioners."[24]

The British sometimes seemed confused, however, about what it was that really motivated Seward's alleged designs on Canada. Russell, for example, accused the secretary of state, in a conversation with Adams, not of scheming to reunite North and South by war with England, but rather of advocating, in an electioneering speech, "the acquisition of Canada as an off-set to the possible loss of the slaveholding States." And the London *Times*, too, had repeated this indictment—suggesting that, as Lyons had written Russell and others the previous May, Seward had spoken openly on the hustings of absorbing Canada as territorial compensation for the permanent detachment of the Confederate States from the Union.[25]

In condemning the issuance of Seward's fortification circular as a deliberate act of enmity to Great Britain, his many English critics overlooked the prior British order of several regiments of troops to Canada and an increase of British warships in American waters earlier in the year, nor was it made clear how Yankee *defensive* measures could be taken as sure signs of *offensive* intent. As for the secretary of state's supposed scheme to seize Canada in the course of a war with England, Adams attempted to alleviate English suspicions on this point in an interview with Russell. He could not, he asserted, "precisely recollect" what speech of his chief's was referred to, but from my personal knowledge of the tenor of most of them, I would confidently affirm that any such reasoning was in its essence speculative, and had reference to the probable course of future events without in any way involving the adoption of a distinct line of aggressive policy to bring them about either now or hereafter. I knew that I had entertained similar notions, but I was very sure that a war to effect any artificial result was never in my contemplation. A conquest either as against Great Britain or the people of the Colonies was the very last way to realize it. It was wholly inconsistent with our doctrines.[26]

When Russell broke in at this point to express disagreement with Adams's last statement, instancing the case of the Mexican War, Adams reminded his lordship that this had been an episode in conflict with traditional American foreign policy, brought about under the aegis "of the very power now in arms against our authority. It was one of the causes which had brought on the present difficulties." The Republican administration of Abraham Lincoln, who had himself bitterly opposed the Mexican War in Congress, wanted no part of such policies.[27]

Adams's explanation of Seward's past remarks on the subject of Canada seems historically correct. In September of 1860, Seward had told a cheering throng at Lawrence, Kansas, that the United States would, sooner or later, come into possession of the entire continent of North America. The European powers with interests or colonies in America were gradually retiring, growing weaker every year. It was "only a question of fifty or one hundred years, before we shall be masters . . . over all this." Nowhere did this speech contain a hint of aggression toward Canada or any other European possession; in three or four generations more, Seward believed, the ripe pear would drop of its own volition into the ready hand. As Seward told a group of fellow New Yorkers on October 31, 1860, Canada would enter the Union voluntarily; indeed, "it would require the sword to prevent" the Canadian people eventually from joining the United States.[28]

But the speech which was most cited by Englishmen to show that Seward had aggressive designs on Canada was one delivered on December 22, 1860. The senator had arrived in New York City, on his way to Washington from his Auburn home to resume work in the Senate. One forthcoming item of business was the admission of Kansas to the Union.

as a free state. Friends dragged Seward from his hotel room, weary and dirty, to join them at a nearby dinner meeting of the New England Society, where he was of course asked to "sing for his supper." Foremost in the news at this time was the recently announced secession of South Carolina from the Union. Referring to this event, and contrasting it with the prospective statehood of Kansas, Seward said

> that for every State on this continent which will go out of the Union there stand ready at least two States on this continent of North America who will be glad to come in, and take their places with us. . . .
>
> No Republican State on this continent, or on any other, can stand alone; and the reason is a simple one. So much liberty, so much personal independence, so much scope for rivalry and emulation, are too much for any one State, standing singly, to maintain. . . . No gentlemen; . . . let South Carolina, Alabama, Louisiana, any other State, go out, and while she is rushing out, you will see Canada and all the Mexican States rushing in.

Here, too, Seward held to his invariable premise that the impetus for American absorption of Canada and other portions of North America would have to come from the foreign state or colony itself; at no time during the 1860 presidential election campaign or thereafter did he advocate conquest or coercion to secure Canada or any other territory.[29]

Some words uttered in the same speech, taken out of context, had been interpreted in England as "evidence" to indicate that even before he entered Lincoln's cabinet, Seward had schemed to reunite North and South by a war against British Canada. But that was by no means what Seward had said. Rather had he remarked, with his vast confidence in the centripetal power of the American Union, that if any foreign forces should "make a descent upon the City of New-York tomorrow—I believe all the hills of South Carolina would pour forth their population to the rescue of New-York [loud and prolonged cheers]. . . . If any of these powers were to make a descent upon Charleston and South Carolina, I know who would go to their rescue, [cries of 'Good, good,' and loud cheers]—we all know." The central idea underlying these statements was not the reunification of North and South for purposes of foreign conquest. Rather was it that unquenchable American patriotism, which knew no sectional boundaries, that would in the end restore the old Union without the necessity of coercion. To suggest that it was Seward who inspired editorials in the *New York Herald*, "putting forward," as the British governor general of Canada had written home in February, the notion of annexing Canada to the Free States (if separated)," was simply to ignore both Seward's public record and the notorious fact that the proprietor of the *Herald* was a longstanding political opponent of the New York senator's. The few editorials commending Seward which appeared in the *Herald* during 1861 were based on the false hypothesis that he had adopted James G. Bennett's own militant anglophobia as part of his foreign policy.[30]

Well before he suddenly began extolling the "statesmanship" of Seward, his long-time political opponent, Bennett had been frenetic in his espousal of "the conquest of Canada, of Cuba, and of Mexico" as soon as the South had been brought back into the Union. The slaveholders, he had written, would like nothing "better than the annexation of the last two, and the feeling at the North is strongly in favor of wresting Canada from the power of England." By such conquests would a united American people "largely extend our territory, add to our national wealth and greatness, and give a formidable blow to both England and Spain, in return for their treachery in taking advantage of our present troubles to aid in the destruction of the Union and carry out their own designs on this continent." Not until the British *Trent* ultimatum reached America, however, did Bennett try to tie Seward's "speeches made before the present administration came into office" to his own advocacy of "the annexation of the British North American possessions." Obviously, he had obtained most of his information about Seward's supposed designs on Canada from British newspaper commentary just then reaching the United States. Since these rumors suited his own purposes, the *Herald's* proprietor was quick to reinforce them and to discover that Seward was, after all, "a clear-minded" and "sagacious" statesman.[31]

"For twenty odd years," asserted a writer in the *New York Daily Tribune*, the columns of the *Herald* had "defamed and reviled" Seward "beyond precedent as the chief of demagogues, imposters, charlatans, and hypocrites—as the nucleus of corrupt combinations to enrich individuals at public cost, the champion of boundless extravagance, taxation, and debt—the high priest of fanaticism, sedition, and disunion, &c., &c.; under all which Gov. S. was steadily rising in position and in public appreciation." Suddenly, however, Bennett had begun to praise Seward for allegedly adopting a bellicose policy toward England, and the editor's favor, ladled on as immoderately as his abuse had been in former years, now threatened to prove the secretary of state's "ruin." For "Gov. Seward never proposed any such foray on Canada"; his critics in both England and America had "been misled by his blatant and hypocritical eulogist, *The Herald*, which is always preaching up a crusade for Canada or Cuba, or anything else which promises to effect a division in favor of Jeff Davis & Co."[32]

The fiction of Seward's diabolical ferocity[33] had simmered in English minds too long to be dispelled by the denials of Americans like Weed and Adams. For one thing, other Americans, perhaps equally entitled to credit, tended to reinforce the predominating image of Seward as bellicosity personified. During December, for example, a Northern promoter, the flamboyant George Train, gave several widely publicized speeches in England in which he defended the seizure of the Southern envoys from beneath the protection of the British ensign. Such expostulations only tended to corroborate the feeling, becoming more widespread than ever in England, that Americans were, as a group, pugnacious and irrational. Meanwhile, reports reached the British Foreign Office that American officials in Europe were, as in the case of Henry Sanford, assuming a "tone of indifference & boasting . . . in regard to . . . a war with Gt. Britain." Sanford was hinting broadly, both in Brussels and in Paris, "that the Federal Govt. as well as he himself calculated on the probability of France gladly ranging herself against Gt. Britain in the event of a war." The absurdity of these declarations, the British representative in Belgium was delighted to report, excited the "unqualified ridicule" of Old World diplomats; yet the fact that Sanford was "supposed to enjoy the confidence of President Lincoln as well as of Mr. Seward to a very great extent, as an authority on European matters," and the fact that he was "also considered as essentially one of their most active and devoted agents," gave his unconciliatory words great weight.[34]

Later, the English novelist Anthony Trollope recalled:

From the 1st of November, 1861, till the day [in March 1862] on which I left the States, I do not think that I heard a good word spoken of Mr. Seward as a Minister even by one of his own party. The radical or abolitionist Republicans all abused him. The Conservative or anti-abolition Republicans . . . spoke of him as a mistake. He had . . . none of the aptitudes of a statesman. He was there, and it was a pity. . . .

As to the Democrats, their language respecting him was as harsh as any that I have heard used towards the Southern leaders. He seemed to have no friend, no one who trusted him—and yet he was the President's chief minister.[35]

In large Northern newspapers like the *New York Daily Tribune,* Trollope might have read during 1861 numerous criticisms of Seward. Even though the *Tribune,* because of Greeley's intense journalistic rivalry with Bennett, sometimes carried columns defending the secretary of state against the *Herald's* misrepresentations of his policies, Greeley also wrote, shortly after the *Trent* affair began, that he had "regretted that Secretary Seward has not always evinced in his official and personal intercourse with the British and French Ambassadors, that earnest and frank desire to maintain the best understanding with them and their Governments that is the obvious dictate of National interest if not of National safety." Statements like this one tended to substantiate Lyons's oft-asserted contention that Seward pandered to American mass opinion. And "the popular view of the . . . capture on board the 'Trent,' " reported Lyons to his chief in London, was illustrated by an editorial printed in the Boston *Sunday Evening Transcript,* which proclaimed that the incident had given Great Britain

> the chance to do manfully what for thirty years she has been trying to do by stealth—aid in the civil war against the institutions and government of free men. . . .
>
> Let her now do something beyond drivelling—let her fight. If she has a particle of pluck, if she is not sunk to the very depth of debasement, if she is not as cowardly as she has been treacherous—she will meet the American people on the land and on the sea, as they long to meet her, once again, not only to lower the red banner of St. George as it never was lowered before, but to consolidate Canada with the Union of freemen, and extend the blessings of liberty over every inch of British soil on the broad continent of America.[36]

Meanwhile, the year-long slanders of Charles Sumner had continued to reverberate in London wherever political gossip was whispered. The Massachusetts senator's enmity toward Seward had been vented both through his close association with Lyons and directly by means of letters to English correspondents. Bright, for one, passed Sumner's statements around among his friends, almost as soon as he received them. They caused the Rochdale Radical to fear that between the American secretary of state "and Lord Lyons great difficulties may arise—the one acting not with good temper, and the other incompetent for the delicate business of his profession." When Weed, having heard the rumors in America, and having discovered that they had spread all over London as well, hinted to Adams that Seward's friends at home "had fixed the calumny on Charles Sumner," this did not surprise the minister. "Alas," he lamented, thinking of his many years of close friendship with the Boston abolitionist, "that I should have been so deceived in the disinterestedness of a man." In his campaign to remove Seward from the office that he apparently desired for himself, Sumner appeared to have abandoned all his scruples. And he had "done, by his Letters" attempting to excite prejudice against Seward, great harm to his country abroad, as Weed wrote the secretary of state. Indeed, Sumner had even gone so far as to write English correspondents not to give credit to Weed's comments on either American domestic politics or foreign policy.[37]

Adams was both angry and frustrated, he revealed in a "private and confidential" note to Seward, when he encountered

> the numerous charges which I have found circulating to the injury of your public and private character. And when such stories have been sent out from America by persons friendly to you, but half inclined to yield to the pressure of the authority under which they were uttered, I have uniformly replied by affirming my conviction that they were pure calumnies, and only a part of a system which I saw had originated immediately on your accession to office, and persevered in with a ferocity beyond belief. The effect of this I had occasion to feel here from the moment of my arrival, and it vexed me the more that I had no means of counteracting it beyond a bare denial.[38]

With so much adverse commentary about Seward appearing in the American press and crossing the Atlantic Ocean in letters from leading public men in the North, it was natural for foreigners to feel pessimistic, as did Edward Twisleton, an influential British barrister, about "the possibility of the President's taking a reasonable view" of the *Trent* affair. "Unfortunately," Lincoln was "said to be very much under the influence of Seward." Twisleton had "the lowest possible opinion both of the statesmanship and honesty of Seward." He was only too apt to reflect the Northern mob "temper," which would "refuse to recede" before the English ultimatum. Mrs. Twisleton, an American who had access to the views of Senator Sumner through her father, Professor Theodore Dwight, had become "intensely disgusted with Seward," and she told her husband that she hoped the secretary of state's "conduct," in bringing about the *Trent* crisis, would "lead to an effort to get rid of him."[39]

The receipt in Great Britain of the published diplomatic correspondence of the United States for the first ten months of 1861, which included most of the important dispatches from Lincoln's ministers abroad, as well as the instructions from the secretary of state, provided Englishmen with an opportunity to form judgments about Seward founded upon his own statements, rather than upon declarations about him by people whose own impressions were often based on prejudice, on misunderstanding, or on idle gossip. Printed in the form of a massive appendix to accompany the president's "state of the union" address, presented to Congress early in December, these diplomatic documents were soon subjected to excited editorial analyses in journals all over Europe, particularly in England. Lyons had reported from Washington, in forwarding copies of the papers, that their "spontaneous publication" at the very moment of the *Trent* crisis had "not a little increased the general uneasiness" among those people who feared Anglo-American war. For the act of printing several of Seward's spirited remonstrances against England, coupled with Lincoln's endorsement of the secretary of state's earlier recommendation "to erect fortifications and make deposits of arms and ammunition at well selected points upon the Great Lakes and Rivers," Lyons warned, had not only excited "no little alarm" among persons worried about the security of Canada, but it had also "caused no small degree of disquietude" in the American capital city. Foreign diplomats, Lyons declared, detected in Lincoln's message "suspicion and irritation on the part of this government." And the event was believed, on the whole, to signify "a return to the policy of endeavouring rather to appeal to the fears of foreign nations by menaces, than to conciliate their good will by frank and friendly language, and by a fair consideration of the injury they are suffering, and the difficult position in which they are placed by the Civil War which is raging here."[40]

Perhaps the British minister was still smarting from the preview his countrymen had obtained, several weeks previously, of the American diplomatic correspondence, when Seward's publication of an exchange of official notes with Lyons regarding certain imprisoned Englishmen had compelled many journalists in the Old Country to admit admiration for the secretary of state's cleverness and to express chagrin at Lyons's inability to debate him on equal terms. According to the London correspondent of the *New York Times*, it was "now acknowledged" there that Seward was "a 'doosed able fellah,'" and it was being suggested that the Foreign Office "ought to send one of its sharpest men to look after him." As one of Seward's friends wrote him from London: "Your correspondence with Lord Lyons is the topic of the Day here; it is a great Diplomatic triumph under which they *wince*." Inevitably, an attempt would be made by the English "to cover their mortification with abuse . . . & scurrilous attacks on yourself."[41]

Such attacks were soon resumed, based on carefully selected extracts from Seward's published diplomatic instructions. An editorial writer for the London *Saturday Review*, for example, found "a great want of ease and dignity in all that Mr. SEWARD writes, and his hasty and ill-considered opinions are reflected in a style which the most indulgent reader must pronounce one of the worst ever written." As for President Lincoln, he appeared to have "a meaning, although his education has not enabled him to express it." It was

> impossible to ascertain from the Presidential Message whether Mr. LINCOLN himself is aware of the gravity of the crisis with which he has to deal. He may possibly not even have been aware that he was engaged in a serious dispute with England. . . . Some of his advisers are more cunning and more mischievous, and there is much reason to fear that, with the aid of vulgar clamour, they will force their country into a wanton and unnecessary war.[42]

In Washington, Lyons, whose dispatches and private letters had influenced the frame of mind that had produced such inflammatory commentaries in England, was joined by other resident Englishmen in prognosticating inevitable war if Mason and Slidell were not released at once on receipt of the British ultimatum—not because Captain Wilkes had perpetrated an isolated outrage, but primarily because it was the latest in a long succession of grievances. According to statements given to the special correspondent of the *New York Daily Tribune* in Washington by Englishmen residing there, Great Britain had already "endured too much" from the United States, for many additional causes of offense had appeared "in some of the earlier dispatches of our Secretary of State, which are not included in the recently printed volume."[43]

Such pronouncements perplexed one of Charles Sumner's friends, who wrote him "to ask an explanation, how it is that you mention again the aggressive spirit of the Sec. of State, when the published instructions of the department sent to the ministers abroad seem to breathe no such spirit." Likewise were the editors of the *Tribune* puzzled to find that the "bullying, hectoring, menacing, insulting treatment of European Powers, &c., &c.," cited by leading British journals, especially the *Times* and the *Saturday Review*, simply could not be found in the printed volume containing Seward's diplomatic instructions. These epistles were, in fact, "eminently conciliatory as well as firm." The *Tribune* writer hoped that the publication of the documents would "disabuse the general minds of Christendom of many false and injurious impressions." The difficulty would be "to secure for these documents a European circulation" in the face of the inveterate injustice and determined hostility of the leading British newspapers.[44]

Some Englishmen also found the published diplomatic documents able and conciliatory. Charles Villiers, for example, told Weed that they were "models in taste and tone." And other prominent citizens of Great Britain, after reading some of Seward's instructions published in newspapers, admitted "his great ability." The British foreign minister, however, wrote Lyons near the end of the year that the "despatches which Seward has laid before Congress," and which "Adams never read to me," had impressed him as overly "long, vainglorious & insolent."[45]

By December 1861, most English statesmen had been well persuaded by Lyons and Sumner that Seward was a vapid braggart who pandered to public passions for his own political advantage. Then, soon after news of the capture of Mason and Slidell reached England, the London *Times* printed an admonition from its special correspondent in Washington that there was "popular passion and vengeance to be gratified" by the imprisonment of the Southern commissioners, "and I believe the Government will retain them at all risks, because it dare not give them up, not being strong enough to do what is right in the face of popular sentiment." There was, wrote William H. Russell, "so much violence of spirit among the lower order of the people, and they are so ignorant of everything except their own politics and passions, so saturated with pride and vanity, that any honourable concession, even in this hour of extremity, would prove fatal to its authors."[46]

The editors of the *Times* had already asserted that "the maxim of thousands of American politicians" was " 'Our country, right or wrong,' " and they had concluded that Wilkes's feat, having won him "a storm of popularity" in the United States, would compel the weak American government to "court, rather than disown, the hero of the hour." Hence the British demand for the release of the Southern commissioners would be "contemptuously rejected" in Washington. After all, was not "the foreign policy of America in the hands of a reckless adventurer," who could "evoke at will all the wild passions of a sovereign mob?" If England was "dragged into a war," a spokesman for the *Times* asserted,

> it will be the democracy who will force us into it. It will not be the rich or the educated, but the ignorant and the penniless, who will make a war in which they have nothing to lose, and of the events of which they have no power of perception.

The British would never "submit to have our nose tweaked in solemn form by Mr. SEWARD or his underlings."[47]

"The one topic of the day" in England, proclaimed the editors of the *Illustrated London News*, was "the great question whether American democracy will permit American statesmanship to do right." Even as-

suming that the president of the United States was capable of statesmanship, however, a writer in the *New Monthly Magazine* questioned
whether "the wisdom of the government and of reflecting men in America [could possibly] be backed by sufficient power to master a senseless
and rabid mob, which has no regard to consequences, domestic or foreign." The "Voice from Washington," according to *Mr. Punch*, would
probably take the following form:

> We've twice afore whipped all creation,
>   We've now got to whip it again.
> We air a remarkable nation
>   Of modest, but resolute men.
> John Bull, then, allow us to lick you,
>   And don't go resenting the act,
> Or into a cocked hat we'll kick you,
>   Yes, Sir-ee, you old hoss, that's a fact.[48]

The earl of Clarendon spoke for the traditional Whig "elite" when he
wrote Cowley that "the abstracted Southerners" would never be released
by Lincoln and Seward—"the humiliation would be too public and too
much at variance with the popular bitterness against the South. I don't
think it would be allowed by the mob which as it never reasons and is
not responsible would probably prefer the alternative of war." Argyll,
less anti-American, nevertheless condemned the seizure of Mason and
Slidell as an act "of inconceivable arrogance & folly" typical "of a purely
Democratic govt.," which probably would not "*dare* to acknowledge
itself in the wrong." The duke was therefore "very low as to the prospect—even—of Peace."[49]

Another cabinet member, Lord Stanley of Alderley, thought it certain
that "the mob of America" would prevent the Lincoln administration
from restoring the Southern envoys to British protection, in spite of the
wishes of "the merchants & more respectable people . . . to do so. . . .
Then the chances are we cannot escape a conflict." Even if the American
masses would permit an "apology as to neglect of form," Edward Twisleton wrote George Cornewall Lewis, they would also "submit to almost
anything rather than surrender their prisoners. Their false point of
honor would not be so much towards England as towards the South; as

they would feel humiliated and mortified beyond expression, if having had two of the Arch-rebels in their keeping three weeks and more, they should be afterwards constrained to release them." [50]

The prime minister of England had absolutely no confidence in the reasonableness of "republican nations." For, he stated, societies

in which the masses influence or direct the Destinies of the Country are ravaged much more by Passion than [guided] by Interest and for this Plain Reason namely that Passion is a single Feeling which aims directly at its object, while Interest is a calculation of relative Good and Evil, and is liable to Hesitation and Doubt; moreover Passion sways the masses, while Interest acts comparatively on the few.

When one considered that the Lincoln administration was "not guided by reasonable men," Palmerston informed the queen, it was impossible to "form any reasonable guess as to the answer which the Federal Government will make to the British demands." But it was unlikely that the Northern reply would make it possible to avoid war. [51]

IX.

Challenged by an Angry Lion

The temper of our people will not submit to dictation from England alone of what is and what is not international law.

New York Daily Tribune EDITORIAL,
December 17, 1861.

Many Americans were mystified to learn of the widespread conviction in England that high officials of the United States government, under Seward's inspiration, had planned the *Trent* seizure in order to force a war upon Great Britain. The apparent paranoia of the English seemed no more than the natural result of a longstanding jealous hatred, which had finally driven many of Queen Victoria's subjects to seek even the poorest pretext for a fight with the United States. Not only were English manufacturers, needing American cotton and tariff-free markets, pressuring the Palmerston ministry to make war by smashing the Federal blockade, but the precarious ministerial majority in the House of Commons was being threatened by those whom Adams described as

> beef-headed country squires, in whose breasts still rankle their grandfathers' hate of the tinkers and cobblers who conquered their mercenaries at Saratoga and Yorktown. . . . The Tories have been some years out of power; they want to get in; and they mean to turn out Palmerston & Co. either by crowding them into an unjust foray upon this country, or by accusing them of a lack of vigilance and of spirit in upholding British rights against our blockade and our naval operations generally.[1]

The situation thus seemed desperate when, on December 9, most major Northern morning newspapers carried a story extracted from the Edinburgh *Scotsman*, attributing to the British crown law officers the statement "that there might have been fair legal grounds" to justify an

American warship's seizing a British mail steamer as a prize of war, "even in British waters, if it could have been shown that she knowingly harboured the persons and property of enemies of the United States, in the shape of the delegates and their despatches." Eagerly most Northern journalists grasped at this frail hope. The opinion of the law officers completely settled "the Mason and Slidell difficulty," according to a writer for the *New York Herald*. There appeared to be a connection between this concession and contemporaneous news that the Confederate raider *Nashville* had been welcomed in Southampton after burning the American merchant vessel *Harvey Birch*. British press commentary, a *New York Times* writer declared, indicated a widespread conviction in England that the *Nashville* affair afforded the United States government a "just ground of complaint, if it does not present a *casus belli* even; so that it is not at all unlikely the British government will be very willing to quietly make the one case an offset to the other." Encouraged by a London *Star* editorial calling the "wanton" destruction of the *Harvey Birch* "a hideous blemish upon our nineteenth century civilization," an editorial writer for the *New York Daily Tribune* suggested that Americans might "dismiss all anxiety as to any trouble arising from the act of Captain Wilkes," for "the supposition, which seems general in England, that we have a grievance in this matter" of the *Harvey Birch*, was "excellent preparation" for the news that Mason and Slidell had been taken from a British vessel.[2]

None of these hopeful declarations mentioned that the British law officers had also held that an American commanding officer would have no right to remove the Confederate commissioners from a British ship and allow the vessel to continue its journey without submitting the capture to the jurisdiction of a prize court. Nor did many American press accounts refer to a segment of the Edinburgh *Scotsman*'s commentary in which "the wanton offensiveness and danger of the course understood to have been adopted . . . by the United States Government" was strongly condemned, and a desire attributed to members of the Lincoln administration "to insult and provoke the Government and people of Great Britain. As one dissenting New York journalist pointed out, it was "at least premature" to suggest that an opinion of the British crown law officers, reported in only one minor British newspaper, and rendered (if at all) well before any news of the *Trent* affair had reached England, had definitely upheld the legality of Wilkes's abduction of Mason and Slidell from the British mail packet. Northerners, fearful of a ruinous trans-Atlantic war, were grasping at straws.[3]

The momentary Yankee euphoria was soon shaken by the first telegraphic reports, received on December 12, of the wrathful explosion in Great Britain when the *Trent* abduction became known there. Although the *New York Times* published a hopeful editorial stating that when Englishmen eventually learned "that the seizure was characterized by every possible mark of courtesy and forbearance," they would regret their "first hasty expressions of ill temper," most Northern newspapers seemed to reflect apprehension of a serious international crisis.[4]

This atmosphere of alarm was intensified when news from England several days later reached North America. In every large Eastern city, newsboys shouted the message of the heavy black headlines they carried:

STARTLING NEWS FROM ENGLAND—
IMMINENT PROSPECT OF WAR.
DEMAND FOR REPARATION AND THE RETURN
OF THE REBEL COMMISSIONERS.
WAR SPIRIT RAMPANT IN ENGLAND—
FRANCE ACTS WITH ENGLAND—
BRITISH PRESS FULL OF THREATS AND BLUSTER—
ACTIVE NAVAL PREPARATIONS.
THE EXPORTATION OF GUNPOWDER, SALTPETRE,
&C., PROHIBITED.
ARMS AND ARTILLERY SHIPPED TO CANADA.
IMMENSE EXCITEMENT IN ENGLAND AND FRANCE.[5]

It was news "of the most bellicose character," one editorial writer conceded, and the chances of a diplomatic adjustment of the *Trent* affair were thereby greatly diminished. "We are on the brink of war with England," another writer warned, "and nothing but the highest and steadiest statesmanship at the helm . . . can save us from that direst of calamities." England was "making vigorous preparations" for war. And similar martial activity was reported taking place in Canada, with forts being filled with armaments and soldiers, and the militia "being stirred up after long inaction." The war scare caused stocks on the New York exchange to plummet. And in Washington, where tumultuous crowds thronged the streets and packed the hotel lobbies, the universal sentiment among Americans seemed to be a determination never to relinquish the rebel emissaries. Among foreign diplomats, consequently, the impression seemed almost unanimous that an Anglo-American war was imminent, for John Bull had apparently demanded "the return of Mason and Slidell in terms so peremptory as to preclude negotiation and prevent . . . offsetting the treatment of the Nashville against that of the Trent." [6]

The watchword of the *New York Herald* was defiance. If the English demands were actually as reported, the queen's ministers must "assume all the responsibilities of a war between the two nations." For no patriotic American would consider "for a moment" surrendering Mason and Slidell to the British government. The noise from London was merely a "bluff." Englishmen could not "afford to go to war with us." They would lose Canada, the British West Indies, and even Ireland as a result of such a conflict, as well as enough cotton to complete the ruin of their textile industries, enough wheat to starve their "population in three months," and two or three hundreds of millions of dollars which they had invested in American "properties." Would "England incur this tremendous loss for a mere abstraction?" The answer, obviously, was no. [7]

In the rival *New York Daily Tribune*, however, Horace Greeley asserted that the *Trent* affair was "a question for diplomacy, not for war." The dispute ought to be submitted to the arbitration of "a court of international publicists, and not to settlement by hostile declarations." The response of the United States government to the British ultimatum, if one should actually be on its way, should be "that it disclaims any intentional offense, and that while it thinks its act perfectly justifiable by the law of nations and the circumstances of the case, yet it will cheerfully submit it to arbitration and abide by the result." Such a course of action should be taken to "avert a foreign war," which "at this moment," Greeley wrote, "would be a terrible calamity. We must do all we can to avert it, except to sacrifice our honor." [8]

Other Northern journalists joined in the call for "a clear perception of truth and a calm determination to do whatever it dictates—be it the retracting of our position or the summoning for war of all the energies of a nation richer in men and resources than was England in her war against Napoleon." If the high officials of the Union decided "that we are not right," a Boston journalist asserted, "interest and national honor both demand prompt reparation, altogether irrespective of any outcry which may arise from a portion of the people and the press."[9]

If the British, in regard to the *Trent* question, would "avoid the menace of war," declared a New York editor, and if the British demand should be courteous, wrote Henry Raymond, and if it should be based on the *irregularity* of Wilkes's proceeding against the *Trent*, the United States government might *"concur at once"* in the opinion of the crown law officers that the seizure of Mason and Slidell was invalid because the American captain had failed to take the captured vessel into port for regular adjudication in a prize court. Indeed, the British view of the case seemed "essentially just. . . . A police-officer arrests a suspected thief, —but he does not try the question of his guilt,—still less does he execute sentence on the spot. He hands him over to the Courts of law." So perhaps Mason and Slidell could be released to the British government on parole, until a judicial or arbitrator's tribunal decided the question of the legality or illegality of their presence on board the *Trent*.[10]

"One point," the editor of the *New York Times* continued, "is noticeable in our foreign dispatches." All such reports were

> colored by the assumption that the United States are seeking a war with England as a means of closing their internal strife; and that Mr. Seward has pursued a policy and held a tone indicative of such a purpose. *Nothing could possibly be more preposterous than such an opinion. . . .* The Government and the people know perfectly well that to plunge into a war with England now, would be simply to give the army and navy of England to the support of the rebel cause. . . . Nor do we believe it will be possible for any candid man in England or America to read the diplomatic correspondence of Mr. *SEWARD . . .*, without conceding the utter groundlessness of the reproaches and suspicions to which he has been subjected.
>
> In our opinion, . . . if the act of Capt. *WILKES* was not in conformity with public law, it will be disavowed.[11]

More reports from across the Atlantic Ocean filled the pages of Northern newspapers as mail steamers arrived within reach of telegraph lines from Newfoundland to New York. Bold black headlines told of *"WAR FEVER STILL HIGH IN ENGLAND.... MORE TROOPS COMING TO CANADA,"* and *"CONTINUED WAR EXCITEMENT IN ENGLAND. AN IMMENSE ARMAMENT IN COURSE OF PREPARATION."*

Even more ominously, perhaps, dispatches from the European continent indicated that "bad feeling" prevailed against the United States in France and that the French government, although it would probably remain neutral in the event of an Anglo-American war, clearly supported the British position in regard to the capture of the Southern commissioners. Yet many Americans, journalists and statesmen included, eagerly snatched at reports from Paris that Napoleon would gladly mediate the *Trent* question. How the French emperor could act as an impartial umpire of a dispute in regard to which he had already taken a decided position was never explained.[12]

Nor did the most authoritative news and editorial columns reveal the intentions of Washington officialdom. The opinion prevailing among members of the president's cabinet was reported by one source "to be, that the most that will be required [by the British government] will be, that the United States Government apologize for the act, which it will do and hold on to the prisoners." On the strength of such sanguine reports from the Federal capital, the New York stock market stabilized and a peaceful solution of the *Trent* affair was confidently awaited. Yet how this could be logically assumed in the face of fresh intelligence received almost daily of assiduous British and Canadian war preparations, and in view of the detailed descriptions of the British ultimatum that had arrived from England, must have puzzled *some* anxious Americans. Certainly no solace was to be gained from the announcement of Bennett's Washington correspondent that the *Trent* question had been discussed in a cabinet meeting "for several hours" on December 16, after which it had been revealed that—"Whatever the demands from England may be—and the English newspaper bluster is not taken as any true indication of the intention of that government—our government have resolved that Mason and Slidell shall never be given up. This may be relied upon as a fixed fact."[13]

At Fort Warren the Lincoln administration's prize prisoners followed the newspaper debates relating to their disposition with great interest. They lived well in custody. Servants brought them teas and toddies and cleaned their rooms daily; and card games, regular mail deliveries, and much visiting about with fellow prisoners made the days pass pleasantly. Mason wrote: "We all prayed earnestly that the Yankees would refuse to surrender us . . . , knowing as we did that the war with England to follow such a refusal would speedily terminate the war with the South."[14]

Yet this comfortable confinement had its unpleasant moments. Mason was unable to fathom, for example, why Seward, whose name "would go with infamy to posterity," would not allow a "State Prisoner" in Fort Warren freely to consult legal counsel in order to bring a *habeas corpus* action for his release. Nor did the Southern envoys appreciate the secretary of state's refusal to allow them to mail letters transferring their extensive bank credits in Europe to the accounts of other Southerners already there. Their personal mail, both incoming and outgoing, was opened and read by Colonel Dimick. They were denied visits from relatives living in the North. And they were forced, when outside their own quarters, to take the air in close proximity to their social inferiors, many of whom were in the process of becoming infected with the mumps, as an epidemic of that disease reached the crowded prison from the mainland.[15]

There were, however, many delightful aspects to incarceration as a political offender under the benevolent jurisdiction of the amiable Dimick. Gifts and letters of condolence from Yankee admirers were showered on the rebel emissaries; indeed, one indignant Boston lady complained that every boat to Fort Warren carried "champagne, fruit, cigars, English papers and letters of sympathy and friendship." A New York editorial writer contrasted the lot of Union officers, forced to "lie in cold, small, and damp cells" at Richmond, isolated from visitors and from each other, while the people of Boston heaped "luxuries" upon the rebel prisoners at Fort Warren. "Grapes; fruits of the hot-house and the tropics; wines, sparkling and still, sweet and dry . . . ; flowers in fragrant variety, with most bewitching taste arranged; softest blankets," it had been discovered, flowed "in a full stream to the confined but not disagreeable abode of the arch traitors in Fort Warren."[16]

Yankee indignation was beneath the notice of the Southern emissaries, who considered their many privileges as prisoners merely a matter of prerogative. In a letter to his wife, Mason told how he and his fellow envoys were "allowed to get from Boston anything we want." A captured Confederate soldier had been assigned as his body servant; he was "very attentive and valuable." "Frequent letters" addressed to the distinguished captives were forwarded by such influential Northern friends as the former American minister to England, George M. Dallas. "We have," Mason wrote, "all the newspapers daily, and any books we want are tendered us from Boston." The prisoners were "at entire liberty" indoors, "no espionage, and allowed to walk at pleasure within ample limits in the enclosure." The Federal officers were "always courteous and kind." Warm clothing had been "abundantly" provided. The *food*, Mason gloated, furnished "a better daily table than any hotel affords; and whatever wine and other luxuries we choose." From Baltimore and Boston came "fine hams by the dozen, turkeys, saddles of mutton, and canvasbacks." And the Southern officers and Maryland secessionist officials who shared this fine fare were excellent company.[17]

Confidently, Mason and Slidell awaited an ultimatum from Great Britain demanding their release. When they learned in mid-December from newspapers that a queen's messenger was on his way to Washington with a set of special dispatches to Lyons, they apparently assumed that either an Anglo-American war or their release would promptly follow. Mason claimed in a later autobiographical statement that he had bet "fifty barrels of corn with my fellow-prisoner, Charles J. Faulkner, Esq., of Berkeley County, Virginia," that the British would demand that the prisoners be returned at once to the protection of the British flag. Faulkner, Buchanan's last minister at Paris, had been arrested for treason when he returned to the United States early in 1861. When he was eventually exchanged for a Northern congressman captured by Confederate soldiers at the battle of Bull Run, he was greeted at the Richmond train depot by the governor of Virginia, the mayor of the Confederate capital, and an "immense" crowd of cheering citizens, who paraded him through the streets, accompanied by a band, to the city hall. There he delivered a fiery speech, in which he declared that should Lincoln release Mason and Slidell the abolition sentiment of the North would "overwhelm him, and if he does not they will be involved in a war with England."[18]

Such sentiments were already the rule in Dixie, where the initial reaction to the removal of the envoys from the *Trent* was one of ill-concealed satisfaction. As one eyewitness affirmed, most Southerners "rejoiced in the prospect of retaliation by England" for the *Trent* capture. A clerk in the office of the Confederate secretary of war, on being informed of the seizure, told his chief that, ultimately, the event "would bring the Eagle cowering to the feet of the Lion;" whereupon Judah Benjamin "smiled and said it was, perhaps, the best thing that could have happened." Meanwhile, most Confederate journalists, particularly those writing for newspapers published in the Southern capital, took their respective cues from Jefferson Davis, who maintained that Wilkes had "violated the rights of embassy," long "held sacred, even among barbarians." To abduct the Southern envoys from a British ship, Davis said, was the same as "to seize them in the streets of London." Therefore, declared a writer in the *Richmond Enquirer*, it would be "impossible for the English Government, without disgrace, to fail to exact the fullest reparation." If Lincoln refused to apologize and release the Southern emissaries, the English would fight. Indeed, "immediate naval hostilities" between Great Britain and the United States were "almost certain," wrote a commentator in the *Richmond Examiner*. And it would probably be discovered that Mason and Slidell were "more useful to the Confederacy within the walls of their prison than they could have hoped to be . . . either at St. James or in the Tuileries."[19]

Some Southerners, however, suspected that Lincoln's secretary of state was "too smart a Yankee to undertake the British Lion, with us on his hands." And England, "after all . . . not dying" yet from the lack of slaveholder's cotton, would "magnanimously accept any apology for the Mason and Slidell affair that smart Yankee Seward tenders her." As the editor of the Richmond *Whig* proclaimed: Seward could be relied upon "to disavow the act of the United States officer, promise to break him, and express great regret for the indignity." As for the Yankee president, a Richmond columnist for a Charleston newspaper thought that Lincoln, too, would desire to nullify Wilkes's act, despite "the fact that the officer in command of the *San Jacinto* must have acted under special imperative orders." The Illinois lawyer would not hesitate to lie to "save a war with England." And, although "John Bull will know it is a lie and grumble a little, . . . his selfishness will teach him to join SEWARD in chuckling over his excellent Yankee trick, rather than go to fighting about it." Mason and Slidell could therefore be expected to reappear at Richmond "at an early day." According to James D. Bulloch, a recent arrival in the Confederate capital after having guided the *Fingal* from England through the blockade, the British prime minister would probably prove "indifferent . . . to the question involved in the seizure by the Yankees . . . of Messrs. Mason and Slidell." Hence the British government would hardly be likely to make war over the incident.[20]

The great question, as a writer for a small town Virginia newspaper phrased it, was whether the British would uphold their "dignity" by punishing the Northerners for having committed "such an insolent and lawless act." Or, as an editorial writer indicated in the Savannah *Republican*, England's honor having been wounded, would "she stand it"? The British leaders had exhibited little sympathy for the South so far, grumbled one of the editors of the New Orleans *Crescent*; hence it was idle to expect war over the *Trent* question, unless John Bull was "forced to it, or sees that he can make a great deal of money by it." Perhaps a growing shortage of Southern cotton would "stir up the old fellow to do a good act once in his life." But it was quite likely, according to an editorial in the New Orleans *Delta*, that the queen's government would "do nothing."[21]

At first the proprietor of a Nashville newspaper agreed that the British "Lion will do but little more than growl for the present," but after reflecting upon the matter for a few days, the same gentleman was more hopeful that the British might react forcibly. For Mr. Bull was after all "a presumptuous old rip, and when he thinks he can do so with a show of impunity, does not fail to make his power felt." Still, a New Orleans journalist cautioned, an "enormous debt" was owed to British citizens by Northerners—a debt that would be repudiated in case of war. With "the misery and ruin of thousands of English families" at stake, the British governmental leaders would find a face-saving way to avoid a war.[22]

The news of the ferocious English outburst over the *Trent* incident eventually arrived, however, and sent "a thrill of joy" pulsing throughout the Confederacy. Should Palmerston submit to the Yankee insult, he would soon "be overthrown," after which the supposedly pro-Southern earl of Derby would "vindicate the honor and interests of England." The only escape for the bumbling Lincoln was "a clean back out." In Nashville, "everyone" looked for the English soon to join the fight against the North. Meanwhile, a writer for the Richmond *Dispatch* gloated that England would never miss her one chance permanently to curb "the aspirations of her Yankee rival." In New Orleans, too, a spokesman welcomed the "glorious" news of *"THE BRITISH LION AROUSED."* The "arrogant and besotted leaders of Lincolnism" had supposed "they could offer an insult to the British flag with absolute impunity." Her Majesty's ministers could be expected at once to grasp the "fair and justifiable pretext" presented by the *Trent* incident "for raising the blockade and reopening trade with the Southern ports."[23]

Desperate for British aid, but unwilling to beg for it, Confederate officials in Richmond assured each other that an Anglo-American conflict over the *Trent* affair was "inevitable." A writer for the Richmond *Examiner* exhibited the same fervent hope when he wrote that Lincoln could "do absolutely nothing but refuse the demands of Great Britain, and abide the consequences of that refusal." First there would be a diplomatic rupture; then would come British recognition of Confederate independence; next would come British military aid against the hated Yankees; and, finally, would follow full-scale trans-Atlantic war to complete the permanent destruction of the Union. Southerners cheered the reports of "bold defiance" at Washington, which indicated that an Anglo-American War was imminent.[24]

That the attitude of official Washington was indeed defiant was also testified to by foreign diplomats there. Soon after news reached that city of the abduction of Mason and Slidell, the Belgian minister wrote home that the act had "been carried out by the express order of Mr. Seward," and the Lincoln administration appeared *"determined* to uphold what it believes to be its rights in this question." The Russian envoy, too, reported that Seward had expressly commanded Wilkes "to seize the two commissioners without respecting the British flag." Even the French representative in Washington, who seemed to believe Seward's assurance that he was "ignorant of the circumstances" of the *Trent* incident, still found it strange "that about the same time that the commander of the San Jacinto received his orders, Mr. Seward . . . decided to withdraw the exequatur of the English Consul at Charleston, and published the circular regarding the coastal fortifications." People among those "best placed to follow the workings of the Washington Cabinet," Henri Mercier added, had concluded from all this that the secretary of state "had decided to provoke England," perhaps into a war.[25]

The president's advisers, wrote Mercier, were greatly at odds about how to deal with the *Trent* question. Some energetically insisted that England would swallow the affront, "as she has done so many times before in her relations with America." Others among Lincoln's counselors, however; led by General McClellan, maintained that it was "folly, at a moment when England might perhaps seek a pretext for a rupture, to furnish it." In the end, the Frenchman judged, *public opinion* would rule over Lincoln and his cabinet—and public opinion was currently belligerent toward England, with the press "almost unanimous in sustaining the right of the Federal government in arresting Messrs. Slidell and Mason." Lincoln, according to the Russian minister, had not known about the order which Seward had issued for the seizure of the Southern emissaries. He seemed initially "disposed to disavow Captain Wilkes' act, restore the prisoners, and apologize to England." But he had encountered "strong opposition from part of his Cabinet and from the demagogues among his advisers who . . . believe that they . . . could permit themselves to do anything against England." Consequently, "the little movement which had coalesced around the President in favor of offering satisfaction to England" seemed to be moribund.[26]

Such early reports were based largely on unsubstantiated rumors, wishful thinking, and conflicting press accounts. As several weeks passed, foreign diplomats residing in Washington began to portray the *Trent* crisis in more accurate terms for their chiefs at home. What the Belgian minister termed initially "an immense sensation" among the envoys, which had nearly all of them apparently in "a furious flutter about the capture of Slidell and Mason" as almost sure to result in war, gradually took shape as a question capable of diplomatic resolution. Fearing conflict with England, the Americans had greeted the first news of the event with spasms of extreme nervousness, which had only been calmed by the growing conviction, hammered home by the newspapers, that the crisis "could only have a peaceful solution." For, Mercier suggested, Captain Wilkes's act seemed to Americans "sufficiently authorized" by British precedents of international law to prevent serious objections from being offered to it in London; moreover, many Northerners believed "that in the present state of Europe, the jealousy of England towards France, will prevent her from risking alone a hazardous war against the United States." But once these two delusions were dispelled, Mercier thought it would "be difficult to say what sentiments will take the place of the confidence which prevails today." Although the leading Northern officials would still "not shrink from the prospect of a war with England," they "would certainly have to struggle against internal complications" that might force them after all to adopt a pacific policy.[27]

By early December the Belgian minister was convinced that the Americans had "begun to regret" the seizure of Mason and Slidell. Seward had reportedly expressed both doubt about the legal right to commit the act and a fear of its consequences. Although public opinion was generally bellicose, Blondeel von Cuelebrouck thought that if the English asked "restitution in some very gentle way, I still believe that their request will be acceded to." Mercier, too, noticed that finally the Americans "begin to consider the price to be paid and understand that a great mistake has been committed." But how could that mistake be corrected? Perhaps the secretary of state would furnish the answer. "Some remarks of Mr. Seward to me," Mercier related,

> cause me to think that he is ready to offer as much reparation as popular opinion would sustain. But will he go so far as to return the prisoners? Such will be without doubt the question, and such a sacrifice of self-esteem will appear very difficult to American pride, especially after so many demonstrations. Nevertheless I see some persons who do not hold this to be impossible.[28]

One of these persons was Lyons. All eyes in Washington were on the British minister, who from the outset of the crisis had made no secret of his opinion, according to the Belgian envoy, that he viewed Wilkes's "deed as very serious." Indeed, the Englishman had denounced the act to Russian representative Edouard de Stoeckl "as the gravest insult ever perpetrated against the British flag." And to Mercier he asserted that he profoundly regretted an incident which presented "his government with the alternative either of finding itself engaged [in war] without France, ... or by yielding, of seeing its prestige undergo a new and serious blow." Lyons hoped his superiors in the British cabinet would "not be too demanding"; he preferred that they should make it as easy as possible for the Americans to give way. But in any case, he told Mercier early in December, he fervently hoped that "there will be no rupture."[29]

Lyons's private letters and official dispatches were pessimistic. Repeatedly he assured his superiors in London that he would take no "decided step without orders" in regard to the *Trent* crisis. It was, he recognized, natural for the Northern press to welcome the seizure of Mason and Slidell with "great exultation"; he was, however, "afraid that . . . the joy is not lessened by the consideration that the capture was effected by a high-handed proceeding towards a British vessel." Without the means of interviewing British eyewitnesses to the incident, Lyons could safely express "no opinion on the questions of international law involved," nor could he "hazard a conjecture as to the course which will be taken by Her Majesty's Government." Hence, he believed that it was "only proper and prudent" for him to await orders from London before taking any action or making any statement whatever in regard to the case. Confidentially, he wrote Russell that he feared "many of the men high in office" in the Lincoln administration were unwilling to sacrifice their political popularity by recommending spontaneous reparation for Wilkes's act. The American "people at large" were convinced that England had been insulted, and they were "much pleased" at the transaction. Further "insults and unpardonable acts of violence would only too probably follow." Preparations should be made in London at once for war. Meanwhile, Lyons would "maintain the most complete reserve" on the *Trent* question.[30]

Despite Lyons's oft-reiterated resolutions of reticence, Northern newspapers carried reports of private statements allegedly made by him which he found distressing. According to stories filed by the Washington correspondents of two rival New York journals, the British minister, although "silent in his official capacity," had been "unofficially almost impertinent in his conversation," having declared, only three or four days after he received word of the abduction, that the Lincoln administration must "disavow the act of Captain Wilkes and must return Mason and Slidell" to English custody. Lyons's whole tone had been one of "menace," and he had been vigorously supported by Don Gabriel Garcia y Tassara, the Spanish minister, who had openly declared that if Mason and Slidell had been taken from a Spanish vessel "he would immediately have demanded his passports." [31]

Such "assertions concerning language stated to have been held by me in private conversation," Lyons protested in a dispatch to Russell, were "wholly without foundation." He had avoided the subject of the *Trent* incident "as much as possible, and have said no more than that it is an untoward event which I very much regret." He had expressed no opinion to anyone, either on the legal aspects of the case or regarding "the course likely to be taken by Her Majesty's Government." And he had avoided all communication whatever "on the subject, verbal or written, official or private, with any member of the Government of the United States." Afraid to deny the reports publicly because "contradiction from me would [be] . . . almost as dangerous as affirmation," Lyons was enormously relieved that the newspapers soon began to carry "more correct accounts of my language (or rather silence)." He suspected "that this must have been done on a hint from Mr. Seward." [32]

Believing that Washington officials were "certainly frightened about the capture on board the 'Trent,'" Lyons was pleased to notice "the moderation of the newspapers, which is (for them) wonderful." Although the Yankee Public, "with their usual silliness," had made heroes of Wilkes and Fairfax, "giving them dinners, serenades, and so forth," the Northern press had taken a very defensive position, principally through "a tremendous outpouring of learning on international law," most of which was designed to justify the capture. The British minister had heard that officials in the Lincoln administration had information that, "in a recent hypothetical case, the Law Officers of the Crown decided in favour of the right of the United States to take Mason and Slidell out of a British Ship or Postal Packet." Having received a copy of the law officers' opinion from the Foreign Office, Lyons noted that, although they had ruled that the Americans might have a right to seize the *Trent* for carrying the Confederate emissaries and their dispatches, they had *not* "decided that Mason and Slidell might be taken out of the packet." So the legal issue was still unresolved, as far as Lyons knew. To avoid being drawn into a discussion of it, he secluded himself from officials of the United States government, including Seward.[33]

One reason for Lyons's reticence regarding the *Trent* question was his fear that the slightest complaint from him would provoke a counterblast from Seward over another, somewhat embarrassing, issue. For the secretary of state, Lyons apprehended, had recently come into possession of damaging evidence of British assistance to the Confederates. On the same day on which the British minister forwarded the first news of the *Trent* incident to Russell, he also reported that a prominent Southerner, Ruston Maury, had been imprisoned at Fort Lafayette for allegedly carrying a large bundle of letters out of the Confederate States while traveling under the protection of a British passport furnished by Her Majesty's consul at New Orleans. There seemed "little doubt" that the charges were well-founded and that Consul William Mure had actively assisted in the scheme, in violation of regulations previously sent him by Lyons. The British minister warned his consular representative at New York to be sure, while interviewing the captives claiming British protection at Fort Lafayette, "not to elicit awkward disclosures from Mr. Maury on this subject in the hearing of other prisoners." But there was always a chance that the Southerner would volunteer to confess his misdeeds and in the process implicate British officials. Such a confession would not improve the chances of reaching a peaceable settlement of the *Trent* crisis.[34]

The occasion of the president's annual message, opening a new session of Congress, came and passed; and Lyons was relieved to report that Lincoln had not mentioned the *Trent* case at all—"the wisest course," he thought, for Lincoln remained thereby "free to act when the views of Her Majesty's government are known." The usual bombast, however, had been vented in the House of Representatives, where Wilkes was commended by resolution. And the portion of the president's message relating to foreign affairs, supposedly authored by Seward, seemed to Lyons to signify a return to the policy of menacing foreign nations, rather than conciliating their good will "by frank and friendly language."[35]

The nearest thing to an official American pronouncement on the *Trent* affair was an attachment to the presidential message, in which the secretary of the navy commended Wilkes for his role in the abduction of Mason and Slidell. This, taken with Lincoln's own recommendation to Congress to erect fortifications and establish munitions depots in the area of the Great Lakes, seemed ominous to Lyons. He had been "frightened" to learn from the Canadian minister of finance, who was in Washington to confer with American treasury officials, that Canada was virtually defenseless at the moment, and he wrote Russell that he hoped "these people are not fully aware of it—or we shall have 'rebels' seized on our soil as well as on our decks." The British minister's apprehensions were hardly relieved when his Canadian visitor told him that the president himself, on the evening of December 4, had "abjured for himself and the Cabinet all thoughts of aggression upon Canada." Lincoln's explanation for the recommendation to construct fortifications and to establish supplies of arms along the coasts of the Great Lakes was that "We must say something to satisfy the people." With "the people" in a state of dangerous unrest over the *Trent* and *Nashville* questions, that was little solace to the British envoy. Moreover, the president had admitted that he had been himself "opposed to Mr. Seward's Circular for putting the Coasts in a state of defence, but had been overruled" by his secretary of state. Hence, although Lincoln might well be "honest & sincere in what he said, . . . he was very far from being Master of his Cabinet," which was led by an advocate of "braggadocio" diplomacy—a gentleman well known (via Lyons's reports of the previous spring) to have advocated a policy of provocation toward England.[36]

"The general uneasiness" had been increased by "the spontaneous publication at this moment of the strong Despatches to the U. S. Ministers abroad," which showed Seward "in his first and worst manner." Perhaps "the vanity of authorship," as Lyons put it, was responsible for the secretary of state's having published "his own interminable Despatches." But the timing of the volume's release to the press might also have been calculated to stir the emotions of Americans against England at a moment of acute crisis. As for Seward's instructions to his ministers at

London and Paris, any person who took the time to read them all in sequence would soon notice "the curious manner in which, under cover of a cloud of words," Seward retreated "from all the strong pretensions he has put forward, whenever they are seriously resisted or paid no attention to. . . . The worst of it is," Lyons complained, that the secretary of state "always tries violence in language first, and thus runs the risk of pledging himself and the Nation to violent courses, if he be taken at once at his word." The British minister had not seen Seward since receiving the news of the *Trent* seizure. He was "thoroughly convinced that I could only make the matter worse, by talking to him about it."[37]

Although Lyons wrote that he thought it unlikely that the Americans would take the initiative in declaring war against England, "on no other ground than that *they* have taken men out of *our* Steamer," he still feared than an explosion of Yankee wrath might follow delivery of a British remonstrance concerning the *Trent* question. "It cannot end well," he predicted. "If the storm should blow over this time our [Yankee] friends will be encouraged to new aggressions." And sooner or later trans-Atlantic war would erupt. Laboring week after week to stave off such a conflict, Lyons had (he claimed) been engaged in "a constant wearisome effort" to avoid a contingency wherein England would either have to fight or to yield "to unreasonable pretensions or violent language" on the part of the Americans. Nobody, he complained, could "form an idea of the pains, the labours, and the minute attention" which he had "applied to dealing with the perplexing and disagreeable questions which have arisen almost daily." Now, in making plans hurriedly to evacuate the British legation in case diplomatic relations were severed over the *Trent* incident, he wondered whether it would even be safe to chance the "fierce excitement" almost certain to prevail at a major American port. "But after all," he half-heartedly reassured himself, "I am not living among savages."[38]

As the time drew near for receipt of the expected British ultimatum regarding the *Trent* seizure, both Lincoln and Seward issued repeated denials that any instructions had been sent to Wilkes to abduct the Confederate emissaries from the British mail packet. The minister from Bremen was inclined to agree with the postmaster general, who termed the secretary of state "a tricky politician who believes only in the meanest arts." But the president, he declared, was "incapable of an intentional un-truth." The Belgian minister had no doubt whatever "that the President and Mr. Seward, if they retain freedom of action, will restore Slidell and Mason at once and avoid a war at all cost." But the intense anglophobia of the American public made it "impossible to say" what would eventu-ally ensue. Much would depend "on the tone of the note which Lord Lyons will be ordered to deliver." If the British demand was not discour-teous, a British journalist in Washington asserted, the leading men there were disposed "to back out if they can and give up the men sooner than have a foreign war on their hands."[39]

X.

What Will They Do?

We rejoice at the dilemma in which the Yankees are placed. What will they do? . . . Let them surrender SLIDELL and MASON and their Secretaries, . . . and they will breed a schism among themselves which will end in their destruction. . . . Let them refuse, and brave the waked wrath of England if they can. . . . Let them decide as they may, the South will be largely the gainer.

The New Orleans Bee,
December 19, 1861, p. 1.

During the month following the delivery of Mason and Slidell to Fort Warren, President Abraham Lincoln maintained a cautious silence on the *Trent* question.[1] The first indication of his views on that subject appeared in a New York newspaper story telegraphed from Washington on the evening of November 18. Bearing the headline "THE PRESIDENT'S POSITION RESPECTING THE ARREST OF SLIDELL AND MASON," it asserted that Lincoln, on receiving reports of the capture, "declared emphatically" that the Southern emissaries "should not be surrendered by this government, even if their detention should cost a war with Great Britain." All the "legal advisers" of the Federal government maintained "that a careful examination of the opinions and decisions of the most distinguished writers upon international law, and their application to the facts in the case, as well as to all the precedents in modern history, [completely justified] . . . the proceeding of Captain Wilkes." Hence the same journalist reiterated the next day, foreign diplomats in Washington, infected with the poison disseminated by the proslavery Buchanan administration, might "rave in vain." Lincoln's administration was "determined not to be moved from its conviction of right by all the menaces they can possibly utter." Wilkes's act would be sustained "at all cost, even if it should involve the government in war with Great Britain."[2]

It appears likely, however, that the Washington correspondent of the *New York Herald* drew an unwarranted conclusion from nearly correct information. An apparently authoritative story in the *Daily National Intelligencer*, supported several days later by a statement from the assistant secretary of state, indicated satisfaction among the high officials in the Lincoln administration that, as Frederick Seward declared on November 22, the capture of Mason and Slidell "was entirely in accordance with the principles of international law as laid down by the best and most authoritative writers on the subject, and more especially was it in strict conformity with English practice and the opinions of the most eminent English judges." Adam Gurowski, a State Department clerk-translator, reflected this early impression in his diary, when he argued (probably no more than echoing some remarks contained in a dispatch from the United States consul in Havana reporting Wilkes's intention to abduct the rebel envoys from the *Trent*) that Mason and Slidell were "travelling commissioners of war, of bloodshed and rebellion," who could legally be seized "in any neutral vessel" sailing from any seaport whatever.[3]

An initial conviction that the *Trent* abduction was legal was, however, not quite the same thing as a willingness to fight a war with England in order to retain the captives. Following the examples of President Lincoln and Secretary of State Seward, the members of the Federal cabinet maintained, on the whole, a remarkable silence on the subject of the *Trent* affair. Occasionally, rumors of some cabinet member's position on the question leaked into the newspapers; but such stories, viewed in retrospect, are conflicting and unreliable. On November 19, for example, W. H. Russell reported from Washington to his English readers that Lincoln, Postmaster General Montgomery Blair, and Treasury Secretary Salmon Chase were "said to be in favour of giving the captives up." On the previous day, however, the capital correspondent for a generally reliable American newspaper testified that Chase sustained the *Trent* abduction and regretted that Wilkes did not seize the vessel as a prize of war. "Mr. Seward and others" in the cabinet were reported, meanwhile, "to sustain the capture," but who those "others" were was not divulged.

Perhaps Navy Secretary Gideon Welles was one of them, for he had not hesitated publicly to give his "emphatic approval" of Wilkes's act, and he had privately opposed relinquishing the captives to England. Nor had the American attorney general disavowed the seizure. Rather had he recorded in his diary his conviction that there was "no danger" that "great Britain should take offence at the violation of her Flag." For he was positive that the capture was lawful according to British precedents. No reliable record appears to exist of the opinions, if any, expressed on the *Trent* question prior to Christmas Day by the secretaries of war and of the interior. As for statements attributed to Seward prior to the receipt of the British ultimatum, their exact meaning is difficult to determine. If, for example, the secretary of state was as pleased with Wilkes's act as some of his bitter political opponents later asserted (waiting until after his death to do so), why, then, did he in his first communication to his London representative dealing with the *Trent* affair, make a point of saying that Wilkes had acted without instruction from Washington and that the United States government was prepared to consider any British objections to the step with "the best disposition" towards Great Britain, and as "a civilized and humane nation—a Christian people"?[4]

"The Mason and Slidell affair," Seward wrote his wife, "will try the British temper." In helping the president draft his annual message to Congress, the secretary of state inserted a passage ostensibly relating to the payment of compensation to Great Britain for illegal acts against the English ship *Perthshire*, but capable of being applied to the *Trent* question as well. "Justice," the passage read, "requires that we should commit no belligerent act not founded in strict right, as sanctioned by public law." Otherwise, the presidential address made no allusion whatever to the current Anglo-American crisis, which inspired suggestions in newspapers that Lincoln must have regarded the imbroglio as a matter of little importance. This was an impression that Lincoln and Seward may have intended to create, in order to help alleviate public agitation on the subject. Meanwhile, Lincoln told a visiting Canadian official that the *Trent* question "could be arranged" without a quarrel. And two days later declared to an Illinois senator that "there would probably be no trouble" with England about the matter, for he understood that the seizure of Mason and Slidell was justified by international law. About the same time he assured Wilkes in person, so the latter testified, that although the captain "had kicked up a breeze . . . he intended to stand by me and rejoiced over the boldness as he said of my act."[5]

The messenger bearing the ultimatum of Her Majesty's government reached Lyons at 11:30 P.M. on December 18. Earlier that evening a Washington writer for the *New York Herald* had telegraphed his editor that Lincoln and Seward were not worried in the least over what the British might say about the case of Mason and Slidell. "I have the highest authority," he declared, "for saying that *the possibility of their surrender under any circumstances, does not now exist.* The President is firm and immovable on this point." Another reporter, however, received a contrary impression from the secretary of state, whom he quoted as asserting "that everything consistent with the honour of the U.S. would be done to make England feel the U.S. did not mean to hurt her feelings or injure her *prestige*."[6]

On the morning of Thursday, December 19, Seward told the French minister that he would endeavor with all his ability to avoid a rupture with England. "We will not have war," he declared; "great nations like England and the United States do not make war from mere emotion." Mercier left the interview believing the secretary of state "very much disposed . . . to release his prisoners if England demands them." Others, too, in the Lincoln administration appeared "to be preparing for this concession." Still the question in the minds of many onlookers was whether "public opinion," revealed in Congress and in the Northern press as hostile to the idea of relinquishing the Confederate captives, would "permit" Lincoln and Seward to hand them over to the British.[7]

Later that day, the British minister, following instructions to the letter, made an oral delivery of his government's *Trent* ultimatum to the American secretary of state. Lyons told Seward that, in order to permit the United States government "of its own accord [to] offer this reparation," he "had come to him without any written demand or even any written paper at all in my hand." He "was willing to be guided" by Seward in making American compliance with the British requisition "most easy."[8]

Seward asked whether the British ultimatum had a time limit. Lyons said that although he "wished to avoid . . . the slightest appearance of a

menace," he would tell the secretary of state "privately and confidentially
. . . that the term was seven days." Seward then asked for a copy of the
ultimatum, "unofficially and informally," so that he and Lincoln could
study it carefully before the seven-day time period began to run. Lyons
"was very glad [to] . . . give Mr. Seward (who is now on the peace side
of the Cabinet) time to work with the President before the affair comes
before the Cabinet itself." Two extra days would also allow more time
for the French remonstrance supporting England on the *Trent* matter
to reach Mercier and be transmitted to the American authorities prior
to their reaching a decision about an official response.[9]

No sooner had Seward received a copy of the crucial dispatch, sent to
him by messenger in an envelope marked "Private and Confidential,"
than he went to Lyons's house to make further inquiries. Saying he was
pleased that the British demand was expressed in language "courteous
and friendly, and not dictatorial or menacing," he asked, "in strict confidence," what Lyons would do if within the seven-day time limit Seward
sent him "a refusal, or a proposal to discuss the question?" His instructions were positive, Lyons replied;

> If the answer was not satisfactory—& particularly if it did not include the
> immediate surrender of the Prisoners—I could not accept it.
>   I was not sorry to tell him this in the way I did. . . . I did the only
> thing which will make them yield if they ever do, let them know that
> we were really in earnest.

Promising to allow Lyons to make official delivery of the British ultimatum on Saturday, December 21, Seward returned to the State Department.[10]

"Mr. Seward has taken up all my time," Lyons complained to Russell.
He had scarcely had time to dash off a hurried summary of their conversation in time to catch the Cunard steamer for England, which he
had already detained at New York for several days in order to carry
home his dispatches. He intended to make the official delivery of the
ultimatum on Saturday, at which time "the seven days would begin to
run." But he would "be in some degree guided by what Mr. Seward
would say" on that occasion, for the secretary of state seemed "inclined

to surrender the Prisoners, if he can manage to do so without injury to his personal position in the Country." After leaving Seward, the British minister wrote: "I don't think it likely the Americans will yield, but I don't think it quite impossible; particularly if they see preparations for war on our side."[11]

On Saturday, December 21, Lyons appeared at Seward's office to read him the British ultimatum. The secretary of state, however, suggested that since the press of business had interfered with his study of the *Trent* question,[12] he would be obliged to the English envoy if the latter would consent to defer official delivery of Russell's crucial dispatch until Monday. Lyons hesitated, then he agreed; hence the formal presentation of the British *Trent* demand did not actually take place until the morning of December 23. At that time the British envoy, after handing the document to Seward, said that, "in order that this grave and painful matter should be deliberately considered" by the highest officials of the United States government, he would "consent to a delay of seven days" and no more, before declaring "that the time for an answer had gone by." According to Lyons, Seward desired to be allowed "not to consider this announcement of a fixed time as a part of the official communication." For "it would very much increase his difficulties in dealing with the question to be obliged to announce that a certain time was peremptorily fixed. It was quite enough, he said, that he was himself aware of it. He would take care that I should receive an answer within the time." Lyons answered

> that he was at liberty to make what use he pleased of the announcement; but that it must be distinctly understood between him and me, that it had been made. . . . All that I required of him was to take care that neither Her M's. govt. nor I should be accused of acting without giving due warning. There must be no mistake on the point. At noon on Monday next the thirtieth the time fixed by my instructions would be expired.[13]

Meanwhile, Mercier, still lacking instructions from Paris, but anxious in every possible way to support his British colleague, had gone of his own volition to see Seward. In the course of the ensuing interview the Frenchman received the distinct impression that Seward was using every

means available to him to postpone as long as possible consideration by
the president and his cabinet of the British *Trent* demand, both in the
hope that public opinion might become less bellicose on the question, and
also in order to discover definitively how the French government viewed
the matter. "Do you think," the secretary of state asked Mercier, "that
Lord Lyons's departure would necessarily mean war?" The Frenchman
replied "that it was difficult to doubt it, in view of the immense preparations which were being made in England." He thought he detected a
hope on Seward's part that if diplomatic relations were severed by
Lyons's departure, the actual initiation of hostilities might be postponed
until the French emperor could mediate a compromise. Anxious to destroy this hope, he told Seward bluntly that to him delay seemed "impossible," for the English had evidently set a definite time limit for
compliance with their demands; and the French could not blame them
for doing what they probably would have felt necessary to do themselves. However, Mercier continued, since he assumed from what Seward
had previously told him that the secretary of state was disposed to go
as far in the direction of reparations as necessary to avoid a war, he
believed he was safe in saying that he "could count on the Emperor's
government to do everything it could to make that decision less painful."
Mercier himself would be ready at any time "to explain and justify any
decision favorable to a peaceful arrangement." Thanking the French
minister for his offer of aid, Seward suggested, nevertheless, that they
both wait for Thouvenel's instructions relating to the *Trent* question, in
case they should turn out to be other than what Mercier supposed they
would be.[14]

Thankful for "the moral support given to my demands by M. Mercier,"
the British minister prepared to endure the suspense of awaiting the
American reply. "What it will be," he wrote Russell,

> depends very much upon the news which will be brought by the packet
> tomorrow [from Europe]. If it convinces the people here that it is sur-
> render or war without any hope of a diversion in their favour by France,
> our terms will perhaps be complied with. If there is any hope left that
> there will only be a rupture of diplomatic relations, or that we shall ac-
> cept the mediation of France, no concession will be made. There is no
> doubt that both government and people are very much frightened, but

still I do not think anything but the first shot will convince the bulk of the population that England will ever really go to war.

. . . Unless I receive an announcement that the Prisoners will be surrendered to *us*, and at least not a refusal to make an apology before noon on this day [next] week, no other course will be open to me than to demand my passports, . . . and go away at once. [Any] delay will be dangerous. I am so convinced that unless we give our friends here a good lesson this time, we shall have the same trouble with them again very soon, under less advantageous circumstances. . . . Surrender or war will have a very good effect on them, but anything less will make them more self-confident than ever, & lead them on to their ruin. . . .

You will perhaps be surprised to find Mr. Seward on the side of peace. He does not like the look of the spirit he has called up. Ten months of office have dispelled many of his illusions. I presume that he no longer believes in . . . the return of the South to the arms of the North in case of a foreign war; in his power to frighten the nations of Europe by great words; in the ease with which the U. S. could crush rebellion with one hand and chastise Europe with the other; in the notion that the relations with England in particular are safe playthings to be used for the amusement of the American people.

Seward, the British minister reported, was "in a very painful dilemma." He was faced with a choice of having to justify to his countrymen "the humiliation of yielding to England," which might abruptly end his own political career, or of becoming "the author of a disastrous Foreign War." Lyons thought that if the president and the other members of the cabinet thrust the whole burden of responsibility for surrendering the Southern captives on Seward's shoulders, "he may refuse to bear it."[15]

Soon Lyons's communication of the British ultimatum to Seward was whispered all over Washington; but neither Lyons nor Mercier would divulge, even to their friends in the diplomatic corps, what had been said during their conferences with the secretary of state. The Belgian minister, however, noted that since Lyons had seen Seward "the principal newspapers of New York have completely altered their tone. . . . They advise restitution, and that sudden conversion is generally attributed to the inspiration of the secretary of state." Hence, although the "most influential members of the Senate" vigorously opposed yielding to England, and Congress as a whole unquestionably agreed, Cuelebrouck wrote his foreign minister in Brussels that he believed "that the President and Mr. Seward, left to their own inspirations," would relinquish the prisoners.[16]

The changed tone of certain newspapers was indeed significant. The *Daily National Intelligencer*, for example, had previously exhibited only defiance of Great Britain. Yet, on the morning after Lyons had received the British ultimatum, that influential journal carried an editorial suggesting that the United States government might tackle the *Trent* problem by proposing "a grand international . . . arbitrament" of the entire field of neutral maritime rights under international law. Meanwhile, the *New York Times* printed a series of articles, extending over a period of several days, asserting, on "the best authority" in Washington, that "the demands of England will be met in a spirit of conciliation," extending even to the restoration of "the rebel Ministers" to British jurisdiction; while an editorial writer in the *New York Daily Tribune* suggested "that several members of the cabinet" favored surrendering Mason and Slidell to England, if that could be honorably done. The president and the secretary of the treasury were both said to predict "a peaceful solution" of the *Trent* affair.[17]

Even the proprietor of the *New York Herald* adjusted his commentaries upon the crisis to conform to the new pacific line. On December 19 he had printed an authoritative story from Washington proclaiming that the prisoners would *never* be surrendered, accompanied by an editorial saying, in effect, that if the English were determined to have a war over Mason and Slidell, the Americans would use their very large army and navy against vulnerable British territory in the Western Hemisphere; meanwhile, Ireland would revolt; and the contagion of war would race around the world until it brought an end to British maritime supremacy. Then, on December 21, Bennett wrote that:

> From the information that reaches us from Washington, there is reason to believe that on the *Trent* difficulty with England the government will assume an attitude of sublime moderation, even to yielding up the traitors, Mason and Slidell, should it prove necessary. . . .
>
> . . . all apprehensions of a rupture with England . . . may be dismissed. Our Cabinet . . . will yield to the present demands of England . . . , even if these demands involve the restoration of Mason and Slidell to the

protection of the British flag, and a disavowal of or an apology for their seizure by Captain Wilkes. . . .[18]

Edward Everett inferred from the unofficial newspaper "expressions of opinion from Washington, inspired I imagine from the Department of State, . . . that if the surrender of Mason & Slidell is demanded, they will be given up." And the British "Special Correspondent" in Washington noted how the New York newspapers had "backed down at once" following Lyons's first meeting with Seward subsequent to the arrival of the English ultimatum. Yet Her Majesty's representative was "very mysterious" about the situation. William Howard Russell had inquired at the British legation about the progress of the *Trent* case, and he complained: "They won't tell me a thing about it." With the temper of Congress and the attitude of the American people still apparently bellicose, Russell, who had earlier predicted that the release of the Southern emissaries would bring about the overthrow of the Lincoln administration, still did not "think these fellows will give up Mason & Slidell—in which case God help the World." If an Anglo-American conflict were begun, "Old Nick will be unchained for some time to come."[19]

XI.

Poised upon the Brink

If the Americans are determined upon [war], and if, as I believe, they have been looking for an opportunity to quarrel with us, the sooner it comes, the better, as we are not likely to have a better case to go to war about, nor shall we ever be better, or they worse, prepared for war.

EARL OF CLARENDON TO DUCHESS OF MANCHESTER,
December 14, 1861.[1]

While W. H. Russell and Lyons were sending reports to London forecasting an unsatisfactory response in Washington to the *Trent* crisis, the feeling in London remained "very strong" against the United States, according to young Mary Adams. The newspapers, she wrote, were "perfectly vile. Just consider yourself happy that you are not living among a people that you hate & that hate you, and never however you may be situated expect sympathy from an Englishman." One week later, Henry Adams perceived that "the spirit of hostility to the United States still continues as deep and as strong as ever. . . . The streets are still echoing threats and insults. . . . There is no sign of slackening energy at the arsenals and the dockyards."[2]

For his part, the head of the Adams family was surprised to find out that his old friend Richard H. Dana, Jr., now attorney general of Massachusetts, had publicly clothed himself in Great Britain's "cast-off rags" regarding the seizure of enemy civilians at sea. "Our record on this question as against her," Adams wrote, "is like the Arch-angel Michael's as against Satan. And now we are trying to prove that she was right." Americans in London could not understand "the calm confidence" exhibited by legal luminaries like Dana that "Great Britain will abide by her former policy, merely because you can quote chapter and verse against her." Too many important Englishmen avidly sought to help split the great young oak of the American Union. In May, Adams asserted, they had driven "in the tip of the wedge, and now you can't imagine that a few spider's webs of half a century back will . . . be strong enough to hold [them back] from driving it home. Little do you understand of the fast-anchored isle." Now, he wrote Dana, the crisis had reached such a point that he expected to "have a chance before long to talk it over with you" in person.[3]

Adams's pessimism was caused by more than depressing missives from friends at home; it was stimulated also by British journalistic commentary "literally overflowing," as another American said regarding the London *Saturday Review* of December 7, "with malignant abuse of the United States." Many Americans, Adams included, read an article in the London *Times* which expressed the opinion that "the commencement of war would, by breaking up the blockade of the Southern ports, at once set free our industry from all the anxieties of a cotton famine, and insure prosperity to Lancashire throughout the winter. . . . At the same time, we should open our trade to the 8 millions in the Confederate States who desire nothing better than to be our customers." Such overt expressions of greed, M'Clintock wrote from Paris, were discouraging signs of a readiness to believe that, as the London *Chronicle* expressed it, " 'a war with the Northern remnant of the U.S. would be an event which not many Englishmen could pretend honestly to regret.' " The entire *Chronicle* article, M'Clintock averred, was "blood-thirsty, insulting and vulgar, to a savage extent. The *Herald* is little better; and the *Post* only a little."[4]

Eminent British citizens privately exuded anti-American animosity. Former Lord Chancellor Henry Brougham wrote Gladstone, for example, that "unhappily that vile fellow Seward and that imbecile Lincoln will have made their [state of the Union] address before our despatches arrive & so may have committed themselves in subserviency to their agent, the mob, which will make it more difficult for them to get right." But this situation was only another "flagrant illustration of the endless mischief of mob govern[men]t." The British, wrote John T. Delane, editor of the London *Times*, were possessed by a "real, downright, honest desire to avenge . . . the foul & incessant abuse of the American statesmen, orators & press, & if we are foiled by a surrender of the prisoners there will be an universal feeling of disappointment. We expect, however, that they will show fight—and *hope* it—for we trust that we will give them such a dusting this time that even Everett, Bancroft & Co. won't be able to coin victories out of their defeats. . . . the whole Army, Navy & Volunteers are of one mind & all mad for service in America."[5]

Lord Cowley, the British ambassador at Paris, wrote that he had "always apprehended that Lincoln & Co. would run a muck with us, in the hopes of obtaining Canada as a set off against their loss of territory in the South." Now, he asserted, "all hope of an amicable solution of the 'Trent' question [should be] considered at an end." Seward had "evidently determined on a desperate game." It was most unfortunate, Sir Henry Holland wrote, "that such a fool as Seward should have power to do such horrible mischief." And Gladstone declared: "The worst omens for the American answer [were] to be found in the multitude of follies . . . committed during the present year" by the Northern leaders.[6]

Yet Gladstone could not "yet despair of a favourable solution," as long as one was "even possible." Russell, too, despite another "sad account of Canada" from Lyons, inclined "more & more to the opinion that if the [American] answer is a reasoning & not a blunt offensive answer, we should send once more across the Atlantic to ask compliance. . . . I do not think the country would approve an immediate declaration of war." Edward Ellice, a powerful member of Parliament, had called on Russell to say he thought the Yankees would "allow Lyons to come away, & then give in." If so, the British objective would yet be attained.[7]

An editorial writer for a popular London weekly worried "whether bells or cannon will be the fittest ushers to announce the New Year." To Cobden the probable outcome was painfully obvious, for the hasty preparations for war in England signified that Palmerston, Russell, and a majority of their colleagues, "having got together . . . an enormous armed force" for defense against France, would now employ the *Trent* crisis as a pretext to initiate hostilities against the United States to avoid "ridicule" in the forthcoming session of Parliament because of wasteful military expenditures. Napoleon had been "too wise & cool to afford an excuse for attacking him." Hence the *Trent* difficulty provided the only "vent" for British militarists. After two or three days of discussions with

Englishmen other than Cobden, Weed reached the same conclusion. "Unless our friends at home in the Cabinet and in Congress are wiser than I dare hope," he added, "war is inevitable."[8]

A fellow M.P. from Leeds wrote Cobden that he was "deeply anxious ... and astonished at the prevailing pugnacity & resentment against the Yankees." Such reports from correspondents all over England moved Cobden, riding out an attack of bronchial asthma at his Midhurst home, to express his indignation at "the cowardice of our offering for the first time to pick a quarrel with the Americans because they are in the agony of a civil war." Readers of British newspapers, Cobden observed, learned "a good deal about the warlike *Mob* in America, but ... our swell mob in England will match them." With grim satisfaction he suggested that Englishmen "who are so eager for fighting forget that as a naval power the States are not weakened by the separation, for all the ships and sailors belong to the North."[9]

Cobden did not believe that "the old Dodger," Palmerston, wanted war. Rather did the premier scheme "to mount the British Lion and furnish an excuse for the present [military] establishments, and perhaps to justify further expenditure." Palmerston had been aided, it appeared, not only by "alarmist journals," but also by skittish dispatches from Her Majesty's representative in the United States. Cobden had "no faith" in Lyons. Such a delicate position required "a man of mature judgment and large experience instead of a Lord without any antecedents." Cobden had heard that Gibson, who had been "discontented" with dispatches from Washington that were made available to members of the cabinet, lacked confidence in Lyons's discretion and was very "ill at ease" about him. Bright, for his part, had written Cobden that he considered Lyons "stupid and mischievous." Unfortunately, Cobden asserted, it was too late to prevent the *Trent* trouble by sending Lyons "a dry nurse ... from the Foreign Office."[10]

Persistently during December, Cobden reiterated to his friends and acquaintances that, "in spite of all the bluster of the papers, ... there can be no war on such an issue as has been raised by the lawyers who drew up the case for the cabinet." The *Trent* dispute could easily be settled if the two governments could agree "what is to be done with Mason and Slidell. The wisest course would be to leave open their prison door by mistake and let them run." Bright, however, could not share his friend's expectation of a peaceful settlement. "Looking at the acts of the Government," he wrote, "and [at] the writing of the Press inspired by them, I think war almost inevitable—unless the States can accept some unbearable humiliation." He agreed that friends of peace should exert themselves to mobilize support for French arbitration or mediation, and he thought that in the British cabinet Gladstone, Villiers, and Gibson, at least, would "not go into the crime of war without warning." Bright had written Milner Gibson and Villiers and hoped soon to see Gladstone personally. In the meantime, he recommended that Cobden should write the chancellor of the exchequer, who had in 1853 allowed "*the Whig section of the Cabinet*" to plunge the British nation into the Russian War "before he suspected real danger." Currently, Gladstone might be again lost "in Homer, or in some equally remote realm of thought and study," while "the firebrands at the Foreign Office" prepared for another "conflagration." If so, Cobden should rouse him in the name of peace.[11]

Even should Gladstone be fully aware of the dangers at hand, however, Cobden feared he lacked "vigour or will in the Cabinet" effectively to oppose the militarism of the older members. He underestimated the chancellor of the exchequer, who was already struggling to arrest the ministerial thrust toward war. Gladstone was hard at work examining legal precedents relating to the *Trent* question. He wrote a letter urging Argyll, who was on vacation in France, to hurry back to London in time to join in cabinet consideration of the American reply to the British ultimatum. And he wrote anxiously to Gibson regarding the *Trent* question, and seems to have agreed with the president of the board of trade that "even though Lyons should come away, . . . the dispute may after all be settled without war."[12]

As Cobden, Gladstone, and their friends began to work assiduously for peace, the foreign minister's wife sensed the political undercurrents and wrote: "There can be no doubt that we have done deeds very like that of Captain Wilkes . . . but I wish we had not done them. . . . It is all terrible and awful, and I hope and pray war may be averted." Lady Russell's husband had told her that "not a word had been spoken, not a deed done by him, but what showed the friendliest feeling to the

United States and the strongest wish to remain at peace with them." Despite "the first natural burst of indignation" in England over the *Trent* "outrage," the Russells believed that the queen's subjects would nevertheless "be ready to execrate the Ministry if all right and honourable means were not taken to prevent so fearful a calamity" as an Anglo-American war.[13]

An important editorial printed in the London *Times* on Monday, December 9, pointed out that all notable East Coast newspapers in America, except the *Herald*, which represented only "the scum" of New York City, exhibited "a wholesome change in . . . public opinion," in the form of "a sudden hush, a rapid subsidence in the bluster of previous weeks." Apparently, the editors of these substantial journals had "been let into the secret that there is nothing to be said for Captain WILKES and his piratical frigate." Now they wrote "delicately of the affair of the Trent, and [were] even preparing the way for the restitution of the captive Commissioners." With great relief readers of the extracts from American newspapers published in the *Times* and in other British journals learned that Mason and Slidell *might* after all be released without a fight.[14]

The American minister in London was quick to notice the growing aversion to war. He reported home with satisfaction that antiwar sermons were being preached in churches all over the great city. Many Englishmen were beginning to hesitate at the thought of "making war upon a form." As the dissenters, reformers, and liberals seemed suddenly aroused to work for peace, public opinion was obviously "changing a good deal."[15]

Morse, also, noted that the war cry was slightly subsiding, as the "men of the 'middling' classes, men of republican proclivities, of the Bright and Cobden school, and many religious persons," began to exert "influence on the public mind of England." Palmerston had once observed, sagely, that in the end England always followed the consciences of her nonconformists. But much, Adams knew, still depended upon further accounts from America. The president had not yet delivered his annual message to Congress, which might greatly affect matters. "Let us hope," the American minister wrote a fellow diplomat, "that he understands the great solemnity of his responsibilities."[16]

"Just now," Adams wrote a Boston friend, "I feel as if I were perched on the top of a volcano, doubtful at every minute where I may find myself." He could only hope that "the expected explosion" would impel him "without broken bones as far as Boston." To his son Charles he wrote: "It has given us an indescribably sad feeling to witness the exultation in America over an event which bids fair to be the final calamity." And Henry probably reflected his father's frustration when he inserted in the same mail bag a letter declaring his inability to keep from "laughing and cursing at the same time as I see the accounts of the talk of our people. What a bloody set of fools they are! ... Good God, what's got into you all? You're mad, all of you."[17]

On December 13, Thurlow Weed managed to arrange an interview with the British foreign secretary. Although the American minister was well known to be sensitive to any infringement upon his prerogatives, Adams on this occasion seemed pleased at the prospect of assistance from another American. When Weed returned that evening for dinner, he told Adams that during his visit to Pembroke Lodge, Russell had offered but slight encouragement in response to the New Yorker's plea for peace. The best that Weed had been able to obtain from a rather formal and chilly discussion had been an inference that war would not immediately follow a refusal by the Americans to give up the Southern commissioners, although a temporary cessation of diplomatic relations would have to be assumed. The foreign minister's wife had, however, remarked privately that the queen was distressed over the possibility of war with America and was "deeply anxious for an amicable settlement." This was somewhat encouraging. Nevertheless, Weed was compelled to conclude from his visit that the purpose of the British cabinet, at least, was still "War, unless," he wrote Seward, "you give up S. & M.—or, in your reply, compel them to open the door—a door they intend to keep shut." As for Adams, he found Weed's story of his visit consistent with his own opinion "that the policy of Lord Palmerston is to terrify America into such terms as he will dictate, which he means to be consistent with the preservation of peace." Such brinksmanship might indeed be successful, the American minister thought, but the premier's strategy seemed "perilous" to the point of criminal irresponsibility.[18]

Toward bedtime on December 16, Adams's weekly dispatch bag arrived. In it was an important instruction from Seward that gave the American minister some encouragement. Wilkes's act, the secretary of state declared, had been committed "without instructions and even without the knowledge of the Government." Seward indicated that he and Lyons were both withholding official comment on the *Trent* affair "until we hear what the British Government may have to say on the subject." The secretary also broke off the correspondence on the Bunch case and that pertaining to other sources of tension between the two countries. He declared that the United States government placed the highest value on the friendship of Great Britain, but lamented the presence of three major grounds of complaint against that country: (1) the arrival in the southern Confederacy of vessels laden with arms and ammunition from Great Britain; (2) diplomatic communications with the Confederate authorities by British Consul Robert Bunch at Charleston; and (3) the supply of the Confederate warship *Sumter* at Trinidad with coal and provisions, an act unduplicated by any other European state. Even considering these complaints, however, Seward's instruction was phrased in the most friendly language. After discussing it with Adams, Weed thought that it afforded "him and me a gleam of hope." As Seward had invited his London representative to read the document to Palmerston or to Russell, if he judged it wise to do so, Adams decided to seize this opportunity to pass on evidence that Seward was not hostile to England.[19]

After ascertaining that the British prime minister was too ill with gout to transact official business, Adams made an appointment to take Seward's instruction to the Foreign Office on December 19. Russell listened intently as the American minister read the message. He then expressed his thorough disagreement with the secretary of state's accusations of unneutral activity by the British. The British attorney general, he declared, had ruled that the Foreign Enlistment Act prohibited the warlike equipping of a vessel belonging to a belligerent power but did not prohibit the shipment of arms and ammunition to such a power. Hence the British government could not legally stop such shipments to the Confederacy. But since much greater amounts of munitions had gone to the North where no blockade impeded shipments, the advantage was on the side of the United States. As for the coaling and provisioning of Southern cruisers in the British colonies, Russell added, this had all been done by private business concerns, never by the authorities, and here there was no difference between British policy and that of any other neutral country.[20]

When Russell had concluded his refutation of Seward's arguments, Adams ventured the opinion that all these petty irritations should not "make a moment's difficulty between countries really well disposed to one another." But the *Trent* case was another matter. Would Russell tell him the British position on that subject?[21]

Russell's response was to let Adams have the substance of the British ultimatum. The foreign secretary added that provided the imprisoned Southern envoys were restored to British protection, the explanation that Adams had just given him—that the United States government had not authorized the seizure—would constitute a sufficient apology. Adams immediately recognized that here Russell had, in effect, seized the first available pretext to withdraw one of the two British demands. All that now remained to be done was to release the four captives. Heartened, the American minister concluded from this that there was "nothing in the nature of the difference itself to produce a war," provided (he wrote Seward somewhat pointedly) that the leaders of both governments were *really* "bent on preserving the peace." If the American secretary of state wanted war he could have one; if, however, he desired peace, all he had to do was to release Mason and Slidell and their secretaries.[22]

Adams admitted to Russell that he personally believed that if his government should sustain Captain Wilkes's act, it would be abandoning its long-standing adherence to the doctrine of neutral rights and adopting the British point of view, which for half a century it had strongly opposed. When Russell pointed out that France stood with Great Britain in the *Trent* matter, Adams could not refrain from remarking that France had always been very consistent in its regard for neutral rights, but he regretted that he could not pay England the same compliment. Russell permitted himself a slight smile at this sally and rejoined, as he rose to say good-by, that he would be happy to dispense with compliments if the *Trent* matter could be amicably arranged. (Later, regarding this remark, Adams wrote Richard H. Dana, Jr., that it comprised, in a "nutshell, . . . the entire public policy of the country. It is English and nothing else. . . . They are content to forego the barren tribute of praise in consideration of their securing the solid pudding of national profit . . . thus has it ever been in the foreign dealings of our canny parent! . . . compliments are very well, but results are better.") At the door, Russell added that there had been many things said and done by the British government fifty or sixty years before which he could hardly defend, but that if all questions were left only to Adams and himself, he did not doubt that they should soon be able to resolve them. Adams nodded his acknowledgment of this friendly observation and returned home, while Russell hurried to Pembroke Lodge to inform his wife that the interview with the American representative had been "encouraging."[23]

Adams had now done all he could do to avert war. Within twenty-four hours after his conversation with Russell, stocks on the London exchange went up, and Consul Thomas Dudley at Liverpool joyously wrote Seward that the "war excitement here has subsided." Weed thought that Adams's delivery of Seward's instruction had "partly settled the English mind for Peace." But Adams himself could still feel little confidence in the favorable issue of the entanglement. The London *Morning Post*, generally supposed to be the mouthpiece of Palmerston, remained bellicose, making Adams lean to the belief that the prime minister was "laboring for war all the time that Lord Russell is talking peace. . . . If Mr. Seward is awkward enough to give the pretext, the result will be likely to follow."[24]

No British politician seemed to have the means to arrest the public storm. "The leading newspapers," Adams wrote, "roll out as much fiery lava as Vesuvius is doing, daily. The clubs and the army and the navy and the people in the streets generally are raving for war." The question was whether those on the side of peace—the "religious people and a large number of stock jobbers and traders, together with the radical following of Messrs. Cobden and Bright"—could gain the upper hand. The public chortle from across the Atlantic Ocean had only complicated matters: it seemed to the exasperated Adams that many of his countrymen regarded Mason and Slidell "as more precious than all their worldly possessions." As for himself, he "would part with them at a cent apiece."[25]

In Brussels, Henry Sanford was still intensely involved in the *Trent* question, but he had finally abandoned his earlier attitude of defiance toward England and had begun telling friends: "Candidly I hope we have given up the men. . . . We can't afford to fight [Great Britain] right now." The English seemed to have gone "mad on this 'Trent' question & Palmerston chuckles at the prospect of death." The British "governing class—represented by Palmerston"— thirsted for war with a nation which had "become too big & powerful & too great a commercial rival, & they have got the chance to hit us safely, with their enormous armament, meant for their French neighbor, & they will not easily give up the idea." Tempting to such men was the anticipated "double satisfaction of clipping our wings & showing France what they can do on the Seas." Hence, the "prodigious" preparations for war in London. "Still," Sanford hoped, "this eagerness to fight may overreach itself & Manchester & Birmingham take time to figure up its cost & results," after which a "reaction & failure of the war party" might occur. For "the spirit of calculation" was not by any means an exclusively Yankee characteristic. Sanford did "not know a more *close* reckoner than commercial John Bull." As "each day's discussion & calculation calms public sentiment & lets off superfluous British bile, & shows the costs & perils of a war," he thought, the chances for peace, though still meager, increased.[26]

When Adams took Seward's instruction to the British foreign minister on December 19, he greatly reduced the chance that England would make war over the *Trent* question. At once Russell addressed a "minute" to his cabinet colleagues to inform them of what Seward had written, and they were both surprised and relieved to learn, as Lewis put it, that the American secretary of state was in fact "conciliatory and friendly— & [did] not wish to provoke a war." Seward's communication, Louis Mallet wrote, was "most satisfactory . . . , containing everything that is conciliatory & moderate with regard to the exercise of belligerent rights by the Federal govt." Lincoln and Seward had both refrained from approving Wilkes's action. "Could anything show more clearly," Argyll wrote Gladstone, that the president and his secretary of state desired "to avoid collision, to keep open a door for their own retreat?" Gladstone thought Adams's language to Russell was "not capable of any decent or tolerable construction unless they intend to give up the commissioners." And Lady Palmerston was heard to declare: "We shall not have war with America." Meanwhile, on the morning of December 22, Weed reported that Edward Ellice, "the man nearest to the Ministry of any in England," had told him "emphatically" that the *Trent* matter would not result in war.[27]

Still, conditioned by many months of dire predictions from Lyons, the two elderly statesmen who ran British foreign relations gave Seward's message only cautious countenance. Russell wrote Palmerston, for example, that although "Adams's language yesterday was entirely in favour of yielding to us, if our tone is not too peremptory," it was possible that what was said in London was yet "but a slight indication of what may be evident at Washington. If the mob rules, our demand will be rejected." Argyll, too, thought that "the American *People* 'out-of-doors' " might have ended all chance of peace since Seward wrote; therefore the British could prudently heed only "ultimate decisions, not . . . half formed intentions."[28]

Meanwhile, the prime minister, abed with "a very sharp and disabling attack" of gout, wrote: "As to any Despatch written by Seward before he received our Demands, I attach very little value to it, and one cannot speculate on the nature of the answer we shall receive. We are doing all we can do on the assumption that we are to have a refusal and that is all we can be expected to do."[29]

Hence, despite Seward's assurances of peaceful intentions in Washington, the British continued their war preparations. Lewis and his assistant, George F. S. Robinson, earl de Grey, traded memoranda regarding troops, weapons, supplies, and barracks accommodations for Canada, while Somerset planned for, first, "an opening of the [Northern] blockade by a strong force driving away or if possible engaging all vessels of war of the U.S.; . . . next occupying & blockading the Chesapeake; 3rd to blockade the approach to New York." Somerset also wrote Newcastle to ask whether the colonial secretary could "send to the Governor of Canada or to some Hudson's Bay people that they might get some trappers or such other adventurous rogues as may be found," to cut an American telegraphic wire located near the Canadian border "in several places." Lewis discovered the duke of Wellington had laid down two precepts for "conducting a war on the frontiers of Canada:" (1) that it "should be solely defensive—and . . . (2) naval superiority on the [Great] Lakes a *sine qua non*." And the foreign secretary took down a volume of Sir Archibald Alison's *History*, to familiarize himself with the tactics of both belligerents during the Canadian campaigns of the War of 1812. By the day after Christmas, planners in the British War Department had made arrangements to reinforce the North American provinces with 28,400 additional troops.[30]

All of these preparations continued amid whispers of underhanded Yankee plots, such as those brought to the attention of the Foreign Office by William S. Lindsay, a strong parliamentary supporter of the Confederate cause, who pressed hard for "a treaty offensive & defensive with the South," to be obtained "before war is declared." This would prevent Seward from manipulating a quick "settlement with the South, so that he might have the whole military force of the North ready for an attack upon Canada." Moreover, Lindsay cautioned that he had "reason to know ... that letters of marque had already been sent" to England from the United States, "and that at the first notice of war, they would be distributed to vessels actually in English harbours, which merely would proceed to sea and inflict very great damage on English commerce." Russell took this ridiculous warning seriously enough to suggest that "the American vessels in our ports should be watched," and to order that inquiries be instituted based on "this information of Lindsay's (without question)."[31]

On December 26 Palmerston was bemused by

> a private letter from Lyons to Russell of the 6th Decr. It represents the Yankees to be in a Fool's Paradise about the Trent affair, which Lincoln told a Canadian, that the Federal govt. would have no difficulty in "getting along with." I take it that our summons, and the many communications they will at the same time receive from Europe, will come upon them like a thunderclap, and if one was to make a guess it would certainly be against compliance, but they may try to evade a direct refusal.[32]

Palmerston had been "shocked" by the death of Prince Albert, on December 14, more than some of his friends "supposed possible." According to Clarendon, he was "*very* far from well. He over-taxes his strength, and unless he makes some change in that respect, he cannot last long." Granville had never before seen the premier "so low" and wrote: "Lady Palmerston appeared to me for the first time to be a little anxious about him." Lewis thought that Palmerston looked "very ill" and "much distressed" by the prince's demise, while Clarendon wrote that Palmerston "never was so much affected by any event in his life." Hence, his "courage, his long experience, [and] his truly British character," as old Brougham admiringly wrote, were at a critical juncture at least partly neutralized by physical infirmity and emotional stress. Still, Palmerston was far from the only British statesman who, during the Christmas season, was "so taken up with the anxieties of Windsor that other matters, however grave, [were] almost forgotten."[33]

Since the leader of the Conservative opposition, the earl of Derby, had approved "all that has been done" by the ministry regarding the *Trent* affair, there was apparently no danger of a Conservative effort in the forthcoming Parliament to drive Palmerston from power by means of an attack upon his "American policy." Cobden continued, however, to snipe away from the political left. Calling Palmerston "the evil genius" of England, he bitterly asserted that the premier had accomplished "nothing in his career which can be remembered 20 years after his withdrawal from the scene, except it be an unequaled activity in promoting discord & alienation in quarters where the interests of the country demand conciliation." Now, at age seventy-seven, the premier seemed "bent on pursuing a similar policy towards America." Had Englishmen "no India, no Ireland, & no other great problems," Cobden asked, "to be solved by us or our children, that we should dye into the very blood of the future generations of the North an ineradicable desire for vengeance against our descendants in England?" Asking Gladstone "to forgive me this plainness," Cobden pleaded with him not to allow himself to be drawn by Palmerston into any position that might contribute to war with the United States.[34]

Gladstone replied:

I will not at present undertake to answer in detail for the wisdom of our warlike preparations. But, apart from particular character and amount, I think that they are obviously defensive . . . & that the Northerners cannot plead them as provocative of war.

151

As respects the cause of difference at this moment, I am entirely satisfied it is not due to instructions from the Govt. of the United States; and
on the whole I reject the supposition that that Govt. can be predisposed
to a quarrel with us: but I am not sure that it will have courage to do
right in the face of popular clamour....[35]

Milner Gibson, too, thought the British cabinet had adopted a "moderate and reasonable" course regarding the *Trent* incident, and the one
best calculated to "get through peacefully," provided Lincoln and Seward
responded in kind. In his opinion the British had not "menaced or ...
done more than asked the reparation in a calm tone." And Villiers, the
remaining Liberal in the cabinet, wrote Bright that he, "no less ... than
others in the Cabinet," looked with "horror & detestation" on any war,
"if by any honourable or pieced out means it can be possibly avoided."
Bright needed to know "the *whole truth*" about the cabinet action on the
Trent affair; namely, that no member present to deliberate what course
to pursue "had any desire to do anything but allay the feeling & even
mitigate the character of the act." Villiers rarely encountered Palmerston except at cabinet meetings, but he was compelled to bear witness
to the premier's "good temper & moderation on those occasions." He was
the last member of the cabinet to become "hastily committed to a serious
& senseless war." Rather had Palmerston and his ministerial colleagues
been faced with "only two courses ... when ... all Europe as well as all
England cried out for reparation for an act that foul.... They had either
to resign their places & run from the difficulty or to make the complaint
& seek the only reparation that all mankind would consider due in the
case, in the least offensive & quarrelsome manner possible. It was the last
that they preferred to do."[36]

Bright, nevertheless, continued to "*suspect* there is a section of our
Government disposed for war," perhaps not even consciously, but owing
to having been "steeped in the traditions of the last generation, when
to make war and to dabble in blood was as common a thing as for
leaves to fall in the autumn." Traditionalists in foreign policy like
Palmerston and Russell were "always wrong." They had refused to sign
a convention proposed by Seward for Northern acceptance of "the 'non
privateering' clause, ... because, doubtless, [they] rather wished to favor
the South," and now, should war occur, "our ships will have to run the

risk of the 500 privateers which the States can put upon the seas! Verily the wise men are not to be found in the seats of our rulers!"[37]

The prime minister, Bright wrote an American friend, had

> made his only reputation by the pretence that he is plucky and instant in the defense of English honour, and he is in that condition just now that a revival of popularity is very needful for him. If foreign affairs are tranquil, his Govt. must break up. Bluster and occasionally war even have been resorted to by ministers in past times to sustain a tottering statesman or a falling party, and I am not sure that some of our present ministers have a morality superior to that of their predecessors.[38]

Cobden agreed. All the war excitement about America stemmed from *"Palmerstonism,"* he wrote, which meant getting up "a row, to occupy the people's attention and find excuses for keeping up the [military] establishments." The prime minister's "bustle" had been accompanied by "atrocious" language in his personal "organ," the London *Morning Post*, which had "led the way for all the howling for war." But Palmerston did not himself intend war; he only sought "to justify the maintenance of the present expenditure." Cobden thought that the current ministry "ought to be called to account for the enormous expense we have been put to in preparing for a war, instead of waiting for an answer. There is no remedy for this costly game but in getting rid of Palmerston. He is costing us 10 millions a year at least."[39]

Influenced perhaps by Bright and Cobden, the American minister in Vienna agreed that behind the turmoil of war preparations in England lurked Palmerston's lust to continue in office. For "Pam's" political position had been getting progressively more precarious. Now he had raised "a good cry—'Insult to the flag'—'Outrage to English honor'—'Yankee insolence'—'Death before dishonor' and so on," and he hoped to make use of it to stem the Conservative reaction apparently underway in England. "Our people," Motley wrote, "are discussing the matter as a law point—not dreaming that an immense party in England had seized on the matter as a casus belli *because they were looking for one.*"[40]

In London, Adams had discerned by December 22 that "This great excitement has been gotten up in order to lift the ministry out of a ditch." Palmerston, the American minister thought, had cleverly created a national sentiment that would enable his ministry to "tide over the next session" of Parliament, for the English public would never turn to the Tories in preference to the doughty premier in time of war or threat of war. To Adams, however, this was "very dangerous meddling with edge tools," and as yet he dared not place much confidence in the long-term outcome. The English people were "now all lashed up into hostility, so that if we get over this, it will only be to fall into the next trap." Burdened by the strain of waiting for an uncertain issue, the American minister even allowed himself to ponder whether it would not be best to get on with the war that seemed almost inevitable. Such a dismal frame of mind signaled a need for a temporary separation from the worries of his official position. Moran agreed that his chief would benefit from "some relaxation from the cares of office."[41]

On December 24, therefore, Adams went with his family to spend Christmas at the country home of Russell Sturgis, a wealthy partner in the great banking house of Baring Brothers, but, perhaps remembering the circumstances of his last vacation less than one month before, he soon began to feel uneasy at his absence from London. On the day after Christmas, leaving the other Adamses ensconced in the luxuries of Walton estate, he returned alone to his London office, where he waited anxiously for the crucial tidings from overseas.[42]

XII.

Awaiting the American Response

We watch the progress of events in America by the lurid glare of the passions that burn on this side of the ocean.

CHARLES F. ADAMS TO HIS SON,
December 27, 1861.[1]

As the tension-ridden month of December drew to an inauspicious close, feeling was still high in England against America. Gladstone's well-informed niece wrote in her diary that she had "scarcely a doubt that there will be war," while the chancellor of the exchequer himself could offer correspondents "no more than hopes" for peace, and few of those. Brougham had "expected the greater fear of war to prevail [in Washington] over the lesser fear of the mob," but he had now abandoned "that hope." Newcastle wrote: "A few days will decide, whether we have peace or war. I fear the latter."[2]

A Southern arms agent wrote from London that he and his fellow Confederates were "all waiting with almost breathless anxiety for the arrival of the answer from the United States." A Confederate diplomat residing in the same city asserted in a private letter to the Confederate president that "The opinion now prevails here, in all circles, that there will be war. In that event, by the time it is proclaimed, Engd. will have a vast steam fleet upon the American coast & will sweep away the blockading squadrons from before our ports." Such elation stood in stark contrast to Sanford's wistful hopes for peace. He hoped, he wrote Weed, "for a reaction caused in part by the over eagerness of Palmerston & Co. & by the calculations of the cost & results of the war which Englishmen will in a cooler moment commence making." Nevertheless, "the anxiety

& apprehension I have had," he wrote, "makes me sleepless & half sick."[3]

During the latter part of December, however, almost unnoticed by men like Sanford, peace societies all over England had begun to petition the government for arbitration, for delay, for anything that might offer hope of averting war with the United States. Allied with them were the reformers—idealists and religious dissenters—led by the hard-hitting duo of Bright and Cobden. On December 13 a large meeting was held in the town hall of the industrial city of Birmingham, at which a resolution in favor of arbitration of "the American question," sponsored by the African Aid Society, was "unanimously" passed. Taking note of this development, Bright wrote Charles Sumner that he hoped the Americans, if they chose not to comply with the demands of the British government regarding the *Trent* case, would still "make some offer of negotiation and arbitration that will strengthen the hands of all moderate men here, and make it impossible for our 'religious public' to support a war." On the same day, Bright also wrote Cobden that all "indications of a movement for peace among the religious bodies" ought to be encouraged. He believed that resolutions similar to those passed at Birmingham "could be carried in every town in the Kingdom." Cobden agreed. He, too, began writing letters to promote the idea of arbitration. He recommended that a central committee, formed "to urge arbitration in the American difficulty," be established in London and that it be brought into close communication with similar committees in such outlying towns as Brighton. "It is deplorable," he added, "to see how the rich and influential people must always be led by the poor and illiterate. From the time of the Apostles it has always been so." By December 21, Cobden felt confident enough to write: "There will be no war on this Trent affair; that is certain. . . . The reaction against the incendiaries is complete. I am told now that at the Foreign Office they are (much against their will) hunting up precedents for arbitration, knowing they must come to that rather than war."[4]

Even at Liverpool, the great hotbed of pro-Confederate sentiment, the American consul observed that "the war excitement here has subsided into deep anxiety. All now earnestly desire that war may be avoided." At the Brighton protest meeting, members of Parliament endorsed a resolution asserting that "war with America under existing circumstances would be unjustifiable and deserving the condemnation of the English people." Simultaneously, a large public meeting at Islington gave a proposal for arbitration "hearty acceptance." At Leeds, Edward Gaines was publishing proarbitration articles in the *Mercury*, while William Forster told an assembly of his constituents at Bradford that if Mason and Slidell were not released "the dispute should be referred to arbitration." A resolution to this effect unanimously carried.[5]

Bright wrote an American friend that it was "a great mistake to imagine that our people are against your people." The leaders of the British government were mostly "men drawn from the aristocratic families," men "from a natural instinct" hostile to American democracy. These same men dominated the English press and the military services. "But," Bright attested, "we have other and better influences—the town populations, the nonconformist congregations, the quiet & religious people, and generally I believe the working men—these have done much to put down the war cry, and to make a very considerable demonstration in favour of moderation, & if needful of arbitration. . . . The feeling here is strongly in favour of peace."[6]

Americans in England did their part to support the efforts of the English pacifists. Weed, seeking out influential Londoners, coaxing, arguing, pleading for moderation and peace, and planting conciliatory articles in the daily press, did his part; likewise Bishop McIlvaine, off on a preaching tour in the British countryside, paying visits to fellow bishops and lower clergy, brought about, as Weed testified, "good wherever he goes." McIlvaine reported that sermons expressing a strong aversion to making war upon the United States over Mason and Slidell had been "preached all over the land" and prayer meetings with the same object were "very numerous. Indeed almost wherever you hear a prayer *that* comes in."[7]

In confirmation of McIlvaine's impressions was an assembly of about four thousand persons at Exeter Hall, gathered together by the English Evangelical Alliance to pray for peace; meanwhile, both the influential Peace Society and the almost identical Society of Friends swung into action. Members of the former organization sent letters to the leaders of many Christian churches urging application of religious principles to the *Trent* question, while adherents of the latter group sent a memorial favoring arbitration to the British prime minister. A large meeting of dissenting ministry in London adopted unanimously resolutions opposing war over the *Trent* question and urging arbitration, while the Congregational Union, the Baptists, and the Independents also acted similarly by themselves. A flurry of letters to the newspapers favoring arbitration provoked almost as many replies from those who opposed arbitrating questions of "honour" or feared that such a step would only result in American stalling while Seward prepared fresh insults. Cobden's letter to the Brighton workingmen was printed in the London *Times* in order that it might serve as the text for not one but two editorials in rebuttal. But Lord Ebury, a leading religious layman, immediately followed with an epistle so cogently phrased that the *Times*'s editorial writer was reduced to wondering why the recent publication of a diplomatic dispatch aligning the French government solidly behind Great Britain on the *Trent* question, being in effect a form of arbitration, had not "quieted the Peace Society for a day or two."[8]

The prime minister of England was impressed by all this agitation. Although he had long since learned to dismiss "Cobden's twaddle," he had nevertheless remarked to the Russian ambassador several months earlier that there were actually "two Powers in this Country, the government & public opinion, & that both must concur for any great & important steps." Now he was feeling pressure, not only from the "provinces," but even from members of the cabinet. As early as December 10, Gladstone had shown a disposition "to consider whether any such expedient [as arbitration] can be interposed." As Bright and Cobden were already ascertaining, their friends Villiers and Gibson were likewise at least open-minded on the question. Some of the most conservative members of the cabinet were worried, as Lewis put it, that Seward would "offer to refer the [*Trent*] matter to arbitration." They did not intend, in the words of an editorial writer for the London *Times*, to "be outwitted by fair words and a procrastinating policy, which they are pleased to call 'protracted negotiation.'" Gladstone had heard of some proposals made by Americans that "a general rearrangement . . . of the law of nations . . . be substituted for a direct reparation in the particular case." He forwarded one such proposal to Russell, along with the remark that he supposed "the Americans will probably have sense enough to avoid absolute refusal but not courage enough to do the right thing"; hence, they would probably propose "some form of arbitration," which, should they release or parole the captured Southern commissioners "to abide the issue," might give them "a fair case instead of a very bad one."[9]

"Our present course," Russell replied, "is a very plain one." Although the cabinet's decision might "become very embarrassing after receiving the American answer," he did not see any point in speculating about the nature of that response. What could not be evaded was that "our passengers" should be "placed under the British flag once more." He had heard that Dayton had declared " 'the U. States will undoubtedly be desirous of avoiding *under existing circumstances* a war with Great Britain.' Exactly so, & if this matter could be patched up & the South subdued, they would be very glad of a war of rancour, & of conquest. For this reason I am for having our full rights *now*."[10]

One "dodge" which might be tried by the unscrupulous "Federals," Palmerston apprehended, was to "take Mason & Slidell to the border of the Country and there let them loose." This had earlier been suggested as a possibility by Thouvenel at Paris. Should it actually happen, the prime minister wrote Russell, "I think we ought to send a ship of war to Charleston to bring Slidell & Mason to Europe according to their original destination." Russell had already warned Lyons about the "ingenuity of American lawyers" seeking "to entangle you in endless arguments" about the *Trent* case, in order to evade substantial compliance with the British demands. The British minister in Washington should beware of such traps, for Seward had "all the genius of a country attorney." The English should "be very cautious, as we are in the right, to keep in the right." Should there be any evasion of the British ultimatum, Lyons would have to leave Washington.[11]

A worried lord chancellor wrote Palmerston on December 30 to recommend preparing "for every evasive answer by the U. States." Suppose, he queried, Seward should say, in response to the British demand for the release of the Southern commissioners, that they had been transferred into the custody of the local authorities, who had exclusive criminal jurisdiction in the case and could not be interfered with from Washington? Or "suppose again" that Seward should say that an

American prize court should decide the question of the disposition of Mason and Slidell? Palmerston replied:

> My dear Lord Westbury, my answer to your first case would be, we know nothing and care nothing for your domestic laws. You as a nation have done us an injury and an affront and have violated our rights; you as a nation must forthwith make the only reparation which we can accept and it is for you to find the way of doing so. They would only have to march a Corporal's guard to the Prison to bring away the Prisoners, and as the Military Power now supersedes the authority of the Law they could have no practical difficulty in so dealing with the matter.
>
> As to your second case my answer would be what we demand is that the Prisoners shall be restored to the protection of the British Flag and shall be in the same condition in which they would have been if they had not been taken out of the Trent, & that it would be a bad joke on the part of the Americans to demand that we should send the Trent to be adjudicated upon by an American Prize Court as if she had been captured which she was not. Such a Demand would at least have the merit of novelty.
>
> It is however more likely that they will meet our demand by some evasive dodge, than that they will either simply yield or simply refuse.[12]

Thanking Palmerston for his letter, Westbury responded that he had "little doubt" that the Yankees would try to argue "International Law" to justify their action against the *Trent*. They would probably "offer to leave it to some Third Power or somebody to decide, *not however* offering to give up the prisoners." The lord chancellor was determined that such evasions should not avail. And he was supported by an editorial writer for the London *Times*, who declared that Englishmen would not be "content to be befooled and duped by such contrivances as can be invented by Mr. Seward." Until the Southern commissioners stood "once more under the flag which is pledged to protect them there can be no negotiation, either protracted or accelerated."[13]

Some Englishmen were so afraid of a negotiation that they decided "that a war *now* will be the best for us in the long run." Among "the mercantile classes" of Glasgow, the feeling had grown, according to one of Gladstone's correspondents there, that chastisement of the Americans for their "arrogance and presumption" was overdue. Although a minority desired peace, most residents of Glasgow, Gladstone was informed, were opposed to "anything like an arbitration or negotiation."[14]

Such comments, however, were apparently exceptional. For the telegraphic news from America that reached England on New Year's Day —indicating, as Bright put it, that "the storm seems blowing over for a time"—inspired many expressions of cautious optimism among prominent Englishmen. Argyll, for example, noticed that the American Congress virtually "declined to pledge itself to the legality of the act" of Captain Wilkes, even while commending him personally for his seizure of the Confederate envoys. It had been "monstrous" for Englishmen "to anticipate war as a necessity—with the courageous addition that now is a good time when our enemy has his hands full!"[15]

Referring to "Telegrams from New York giving a hope of compliance with our Demands," Palmerston wrote Russell that, nevertheless, he had been "told by a person not unlikely to be well informed that Cameron who I believe is War Secretary has written to the American Minister at Brussels [*sic*] that the Cabinet have determined *not* to give up the prisoners. We shall have some clue to guide us when we get Lyons's next Despatches." Russell replied that he expected to receive Lyons's dispatches later that night, but in the meantime he still retained "good hopes," for Cameron was "the most warlike of the ministers & Sanford at Brussels the most warlike of the diplomatists." Both were therefore unreliable.[16]

That night, Russell read Lyons's opinion that nothing "but the first shot" would convince most Americans "that England will really go to war." However, Seward, at least, was now "on the side of peace. He does not like the look of the spirit he has called up." The secretary of state knew "his countrymen well enough to believe that if he can convince them there is a real danger of war, they may forgive him for the humiliation of yielding to England, while it would be fatal to him to be the author of a disastrous foreign war." But what course Seward would eventually take Lyons could not predict. If Lincoln and the other members of the Washington cabinet threw upon him the entire burden of explaining to the aroused people why the Southern prisoners were released, Lyons thought, the secretary of state might be unwilling to bear it.[17]

Russell wrote Granville: "Lyons says it is not likely the govt. will yield—but his letters give hope. Seward is on the peace side of the Cabinet, and he has much influence with the President." Granville was delighted to see that "the news from America, although not decisive, looks favourable to peace." It would be for England "a great mercy to be spared the war." Within hours a summary of Lyons's encouraging dispatch was being passed among members of the British cabinet, and accounts of a less sanguine private letter from the British minister at Washington were also circulating. Palmerston, making a rapid recovery from his serious attack of gout, cautiously acknowledged that Lyons's reports did indeed "look peaceful," but "as to the question of peace or war the chances either way seem as yet . . . to be pretty nearly equal." Nothing concrete had been received from America; only news indicating, as Clarendon observed, that Northern journalists were "rather less blatant all through their bluster about not giving up the men," and also seeming to show "a sort of pacific aspect" through falling securities on the New York stock exchange. Lewis, for his part, thought that Lyons's dispatch showed Seward behaving "like a man who is preparing the way for concession, but whether he will ultimately yield is still uncertain."[18]

Forster wrote de Grey at the War Office that he now thought peace was probable, although he thought "the reaction in favour of peace yesterday was almost as unreasonable as the war depression before." He was thankful his friend would "not . . . be a great war minister just yet." The "hopeful" news from America, a regular correspondent wrote Gladstone, indicated that the Americans might "surrender their prisoners with a tolerably good grace"; if so, he thought, it would have been owing "to the energy & decision of your Cabinet that we have escaped a calamitous war." This, the earl of Derby agreed, had been "the only tone" to take with the Americans. The British, in his opinion, had "hitherto erred on the side of too great forebearance in *acts*—in words we cannot be too courteous and moderate; but if we are to have flung to the surface such scum as Seward and Co. it is just as well that they should understand that blustering is not always safe, and . . . will not in the end improve their 'personal position.' "[19]

To a request by Gladstone asking whether the members of the British cabinet ought to be called to meet in London on "the day by which the

American answer is pretty sure to arrive," Russell responded that he had "not summoned the Cabinet as I expect pretty confidently a compliance. . . ." Gladstone found these "sanguine expectations" an "agreeable surprise." But he feared the calm interval might only be "a trough between the waves."[20]

By reading the same newspapers and through hearing some of the same rumors as highly placed Englishmen, the American representative in London began likewise to see signs of "a considerable degree of reaction and a growing hope that the friendly relations between the two countries may be preserved." "The general tendency," he thought, appeared "favorable. . . . Though not decisive, the indications are peaceful." The responsible officials of the United States government seemed to have remained relatively calm in the face of the British demand and the American public, on the whole, appeared to retain confidence in its leadership.[21]

But Adams's hopeful frame of mind endured only until his private letters arrived, at which time he was revisited by depression. For many Northerners seemed to have greeted the British outcry over the *Trent* "outrage" with loud defiance. Hence, Adams apprehended that the "sensible amelioration" of the British temper might only prove to be a brief lull until the most recent American news was digested in England. His son Charles, in Boston, reflected the confusion and oscillating emotions that appeared to beset the American public generally. To a letter from Henry warning that England intended to make war, Charles had replied that "this nation doesn't. England may force us into a war, but the feeling here is eminently pacific." Less than one week later, however, Charles had added a fiery postscript: "We don't mean here to go to war, but as for those men we don't want to give them up." He would rather fight. "If England wants a war God-damn her, I think she ought to have it."[22]

According to the American newspapers, Adams's old political associate, John P. Hale, had announced in the Senate that he did not believe the Southern captives should be relinquished. Rather than allow the United States to be humiliated, it would be far better to fight the British to the death. "What a howl there is round the manger!" the Reverend Nathaniel Frothingham wrote Adams on Christmas Eve.[23]

Adams decided that it was time to set forth his own views about the *Trent* case for his son's guidance. Adjuring Charles to keep his letter "quite private," he began by reproaching his son for desiring to retain Mason and Slidell at Fort Warren, even at the cost of war with Great Britain. "Who are they," wrote Adams, "that the country should risk sacrificing itself for their sakes? What can they do in Europe that any two other men sent in their places could not do quite as well? Have we not got enough such cattle here already? Had not they done their worst in vain, when this new contrivance of our own came in to do for them what they never could have accomplished if they had spent their lives here?"[24]

Adams was "convinced that Captain Wilkes was wrong—and that it is for the good of the world that no sea captain have a right to make himself judge, jury and executioner among the crews or passengers of the ships of other nations than his own. Much less do I believe," he added, "that his caprice should be permitted to have the effect of staking the lives of thousands of the best and bravest innocent people of two great nations on a false point of honor." He did not wish, however, to be understood as taking the side of the English. For "to say that Captain Wilkes committed an outrage because he did not commit two"—because he did not seize the *Trent* as well as its rebel passengers—was "about as sound a proposition in morals as it is in logic." No more worthy was the argument that the reason Mason and Slidell could not be taken was because they were going to a neutral port. Adams had "no respect whatever for such quibbles, even should they be honored with the approbation of all the bench and bar of Great Britain." It was absurd to make war on "such frivolous pretenses."[25]

Adams would probably have been surprised that many prominent Englishmen agreed with him. Argyll, for example, wrote Gladstone that he was "in a disagreeable state of mind," largely because he felt the English "plea" was "most unsatisfactory." Indeed, the duke declared, he had, in any event,

> a profound distrust of what is called "International Law." The very name is essentially misleading. The general principles of right and reason which regulate the intercourse of nations are incapable of being embodied in a code of "Laws" in the same sense in which we speak of

"Laws" Municipal. The consequence is that governments are perpetually resting their case[s] on mere technical pleas which are really dishonest —because very often they do not represent the *real objection.* . . .

. . . It is perfectly true that forms & modes of procedure are of the essence of Justice. But such pleas [as those contained in the English *Trent* ultimatum] imply that if the proper forms had been complied with, there would have been no ground of complaint.

I cannot admit this in the case of the Trent. That a West India mail packet on her ordinary voyage *away from* both belligerent countries, and incapable therefore of carrying contraband of war to either of them, should be liable to be stopped & taken into a Yankee Port, and brought before a Yankee Court, is a doctrine which seems to be intolerable, and which I am satisfied we never should have admitted. . . . The rules quoted as those of "International Law" are utterly inapplicable to such a case: and no decision of any American Court would make such a Power tolerable by neutral States.

Then, again, these technical pleas are liable to so many counterarguments of the same attorney-like character. . . . For example. If we admit the right to stop & search this class of vessel, with such a destination, perfectly known & notorious, it would follow that the officer of the "San Jacinto" had a right to call for the passenger list to see whether there were soldiers on board. But this was refused. Such refusal was illegal, if the search itself was legal. But illegal resistance subjects vessels to forfeiture according to *Dicta* which I have seen quoted. Therefore, again we come to the point that the Yankees would have been justified in condemning the Trent!

Which seems to me *reductio ad absurdum.* New conditions require perpetual modifications of the "Law of Nations", and I do not think that mail packets plying between neutral ports are vessels which ought in any case to be liable to such seizure. . . .

All of which makes me desire that grounds *as broad as possible*—as little technical and attorney-like as possible—may be taken in our demands & reclamations.[26]

The lord privy seal was not the only member of the British cabinet worried whether his associates might not be on the verge of basing a declaration of war on a mere legal technicality. The president of the board of trade declared that international law appeared to him "often a great heap of nonsense," and that the real issue with the Americans was simply that Captain Wilkes had seized several passengers off a neutral British mail packet, bound from one neutral port to another. From Washington, W. H. Russell wrote the editor of the London *Times* that there was "too much of a legal subtlety in the points raised by the Government, and it would have been better at once to say, 'Precedent be damned! We won't take political offenders from neutral ships going from one neutral port to another, and we won't let them be taken from under our flag when as neutrals we are bearing them from one neutral port to another.' "[27]

After the British ultimatum had been sent to Washington, many British officials had begun an exhaustive search for precedents to justify their government's stand. Memoranda poured into the Foreign Office relating to legal aspects of the *Trent* question. Fearing "tricky Yankee pettifoggers," Russell was trying to overwhelm any quibbles directed against the British position with a huge pile of precedents. Yet, to Americans like M'Clintock at least, this emphasis on "punctilio" seemed only to indicate that the English sought a pretext "to join the slaveholders & to strike us in our time of weakness . . . for a *vice* of procedure, not for a substantial wrong." Sumner wrote that he was "shocked by the readiness with which the people and government of Great Britain have [set] . . . all these armaments and troops in motion . . . on a point of law which it needed lawyers to detect. There is bad blood in England; and I fear that the case of the 'Trent' was only the present opportunity for it, and that another will soon be found."[28]

As the days dragged by, the suspense in the American legation weighed heavily on those inside. Adams had received no information from Seward regarding the *Trent* affair since December 16, save two equivocal sentences dated December 20. Seward had written then only that he now had the British demands, and that he was "considering the subject calmly and with a disposition to avert new complications, but not with any fear or any disposition to accept humiliation." Paul Julius Reuter, proprietor of the first world-wide telegraphic news service, visited Adams on January 6 to beg the American minister for news. From all quarters of Europe, said Reuter, his subscribers were eagerly soliciting information about the progress of the *Trent* case. Reuter little imagined, Adams thought bitterly, "how entirely my government keeps me without information." On the morning of January 8 he wrote a Boston friend that the "state of complete suspense" in which he and his family had been living for over one month had become almost intolerable. Regarding whether to expect peace or war, he did "not know what to think." Meanwhile, Moran's anxiety about the intentions of the American government ment reached "fever heat." On January 7 he burst out: "This is cruel. Our suspense amounts to anguish."[29]

The tension had forced high British officials, too, close to the edge of endurance. Newspapers were eagerly scanned for the slightest hint of what the Americans might do. The news which arrived on January 6 was ambiguous, leading Layard to worry whether there was "still a hitch" that would justify Lyons's pessimism. Still he could not "believe the captives will not be given up." Weed had told him the previous evening that both Adams and himself shared Layard's expectation of a peaceful settlement.[30]

On the following day more dispatches arrived from Lyons, in one of which he expressed the opinion, Layard observed, "that the surrender of the captives would be 'a very improbable event,'" but he hoped that strong support for the English demands by Mercier, on instructions from Thouvenel, would help to persuade the Americans to yield to them. Russell, on reading the same dispatches, wrote the prime minister: "I am still inclined to think Lincoln will submit, but not till the clock is 59 minutes past 11." The editor of the London *Times* told Lord Stanley of Alderley that he did not expect the prisoners to be given up, and Lord Stanley feared "Seward & Lincoln are too far committed to [Wilkes's] venture to yield." According to one who had spoken with Lady Palmerston, her husband believed that the Americans would act defiantly and "let Lord Lyons go, but give up before fighting begins." Meanwhile, Newcastle thought the most recent news from America so "far from satisfactory [that] . . . I should not be surprised to see Lord Lyons on Monday." By the evening of January 8, as Lewis summarized the situation, it appeared "that the chances are equally balanced, but that the probability is slightly in favour of peace by some means or other."[31]

XIII.

A Decision at Last

Hitherto Mr. Seward has managed our foreign relations well. . . . But upon the course he may now take, and the ability with which he manages the case of the arrest of Mason and Slidell, his character as a minister and as a statesman will greatly depend.

New York Herald EDITORIAL,
December 18, 1861, p. 4.

Probably no American had a more intense personal interest in the disposition of the *Trent* affair than Captain Charles Wilkes. His seizure of the Southern emissaries had caused millions of loyal Americans to praise his name. He was lionized in the Northern press. Inasmuch as Wilkes's residence in Washington had been robbed the previous winter "of plate and other valuables to a considerable amount," it was widely suggested in New York that the Chamber of Commerce present him with a silver service. And the citizens of Boston, their mayor pledged, would in the meantime order a "suitably inscribed" silver sword to be manufactured especially for the captain. "Let the handsome thing be done," wrote a prominent New York journalist. A "happy inspiration" had brought Wilkes a notable victory. Now, the writer urged, the American people should "consecrate another *Fourth* of July to him. Load him down with services of plate and swords of the cunningest and costliest art."[1]

While visiting in New York City on his way to Washington to report to the Navy Department for reassignment, Wilkes was the center of attention wherever he went. When he was introduced to the audience at an evening meeting of the New York Historical Society, those present "cheered and shouted until compelled to desist from sheer physical exhaustion." The president of the Society finally brought the meeting to order—first to move that Wilkes be made an honorary member, a motion at once approved by loud acclamation—and then to heap upon Wilkes additional praise and expressions of admiration, concluding thus: "It is, Sir, your prerogative to make history; ours to commemorate it. In making up the record of yours, Sir, we may promise you, in advance, that we will reserve one of the fairest pages in the bright annals of American history." Amidst the applause that followed, Wilkes rose once more to thank the president for his kind words and to protest that he had merely done his duty—which statement was greeted with intensified cheering.[2]

On the morning of December 5, Wilkes was given a public reception by the mayor and city council of New York. After the usual lavish praise from Fernando Wood, who had recently been defeated for reelection as the city's chief magistrate, Wilkes again stated that his role in the *Trent* affair had been a small one, and that his officers deserved to share in the approbation that had followed the deed. Then, for approximately one hour, a long line of citizens filed past the tall, dignified captain to shake his hand and gaze admiringly at his "countenance expressive of benevolence, suavity, and firmness." The same expression was preserved for the ages two days later, when Wilkes appeared at Gurney's Photographic Gallery in full uniform to have "several imperial portraits" made, both for "*cartes de viste*" and for framing.[3]

It was during this pleasurable interlude at his place of birth, however, that Wilkes probably first became aware of an ominous absence of exuberance about his recent exploit among high officials in Washington. The secretary of the navy, for example, had written him a public letter of congratulation which, while declaring that the seizure of Mason and Slidell had his "emphatic approval," also pointedly remarked that the secretary refrained from expressing "an opinion on the course pursued in omitting to capture the vessel which had these public enemies on board further than to say that the forbearance exercised in this instance must not be permitted to constitute a precedent hereafter. . . ."[4] Meanwhile, a congressional resolution requesting the president to award Wilkes a gold medal as a reward for "his good conduct in promptly arresting the rebel ambassadors" was voted down and a substitute resolution passed giving the *San Jacinto*'s captain a vote of thanks only. Commenting on this event, an editorial spokesman for the *New York*

Times stated: "In thus putting on record a formal approval of an act which has called forth universal public satisfaction, there is, of course, no intention to prejudge a case on which neither our own nor the British Government has as yet pronounced an opinion, and which is now properly a matter of diplomacy alone." Thus was Wilkes informed that if his "bold deed" was subsequently disavowed by the Lincoln administration and the captives released, historians might not, after all, call him "hero."[5]

Such ruminations probably troubled the captain during his triumphal progress southward to Washington. Late on Saturday, December 14, he reached his Washington home. Given the usual "serenade" accorded to a returning hero, beginning with "Hail to the Chief" played by the Marine Band, Wilkes, introduced to the crowd by the mayor of Washington, "modestly said that a man who had merely done his duty did not deserve an ovation." Pleading "severe indisposition," he soon retired within his house. Before going to bed, perhaps Wilkes glanced out his window across Lafayette Square to the White House where resided the man who had the power abruptly to end his brief period of glory with a stroke of his pen.[6]

Soon Wilkes paid a call upon the president. Later he remembered Lincoln's observation that his visitor had certainly "kicked up a breeze," but that the "boldness" of the *Trent* seizure had caused the chief executive to rejoice. Had he not also heard rumors "that the Government had decided to give up Mason and Slidell," the president's words would probably have satisfied Wilkes. But for anyone who felt that the rebel captives had been justly caught and should be tightly held, there was little encouragement in an editorial in the usually anti-British *New York Herald*. A spokesman for that journal had urged "the wisdom of deferring a final settlement with England until we shall have made an end of this Southern rebellion." The authorities at Washington should restore Mason and Slidell to British protection, and they should acknowledge that

> while Captain Wilkes would have been right in seizing the *Trent* steamer and in bringing her before a prize court for adjudication, he was wrong in limiting his proceeding to the seizure of his prisoners; and that we regret that his controlling considerations of international

courtesy and leniency should have resulted in the very offense which it was his particular object to avoid.[7]

The president was an avid reader of newspapers. He was also a close student of legislative politics. He could not have overlooked the fate of a resolution presented to the House of Representatives on December 16 by Clement L. Vallandigham, an Ohio "Copperhead" Democrat, which called upon Lincoln to approve and support "the act of Captain Wilkes, in spite of any menace or demand of the British Government; and that this House pledges its full support to him in upholding now the honor and vindicating the courage of the Government and people of the United States against a foreign Power." This resolution, by a vote of 109 to 16, was sent to the Committee on Foreign Affairs in order to allow it gently to expire.[8]

Rudolf Schleiden, minister in Washington from Bremen, wrote his German superiors that the only chance of peace rested on the judgment of Lincoln. For Seward's assurances that the *Trent* affair would be peaceably resolved had been undermined, in the opinion of the minister from Bremen, by disagreements in the cabinet over what approach to take to the British ultimatum. Moreover, Schleiden's close friend, Senator Sumner, still had misgivings about the true intentions of the secretary of state. The Massachusetts senator had accused Seward, in a letter to John Bright, of having "been disposed to a course of much harshness" toward England. He had opposed this policy, he said, but the secretary's "fatal mismanagement" of foreign relations had ensured that, at a moment of crisis, there was "no quarter where we can find good will. Alas! for my country," Sumner wrote, for the English seemed bent on conflict. Two foreign envoys had told him on December 23 that the danger of war was imminent. And Seward, whose apparent bellicosity toward the British had appalled Sumner earlier in the year, had the fate of the country in his hands.[9]

Seward would not discuss the *Trent* case with Sumner, declaring only that Wilkes had committed an "unauthorized" act, and that he was "reserving himself in order to see what view England would take." So the Massachusetts senator concentrated his lobbying on Lincoln. To aid his cause, he was able to quote letters from his constituents, such as one reporting it to be the "almost universal opinion . . . among intelligent men" in Boston that the Southern envoys should be relinquished in order to avoid, at whatever cost in mortified pride, "a divided empire and a devastating war." Sumner also took Lincoln some letters which he had recently received from John Bright and Richard Cobden, pleading for peace and understanding. The president, who seemed to Sumner "astonished" at the references to British belligerence in these missives, protested that, as far as he had power to influence events, there would be "no war."[10]

Both Lincoln and Seward probably noted that Cobden's instantaneous reaction upon learning about the capture of Mason and Slidell had been to write the Massachusetts senator that although the act might "be right in point of law," it had been "wrong in point of policy." For many Englishmen were alert for a pretext to aid the Southern Confederacy. "Formerly," Cobden asserted, "England feared a war with the United States as much from the dependence on your cotton as from a dread of your power. *Now* the popular opinion (however erroneous) is that a war would give us cotton. And we, of course, consider your power weakened by your Civil War." The English press, Cobden predicted, would "as usual try to envenom the affair." The editors of the London *Morning Post*, said often to speak for the prime minister, had been quick to publish "a most incendiary article—quite worthy of the New York Herald." Other journals would probably contain similar bits of bellicosity.[11]

What was essentially a "trivial incident," Cobden declared, could easily be magnified by displays of "temper" on both sides of the Atlantic into a serious conflict. "It is for us," he wrote Sumner, "& all who care for the interests of humanity, to do our utmost to thwart these mischief-makers." Cobden had

> made a vow during the Crimean War that if another war broke out between England and any other Power I would not utter a word with a view of shortening its duration, for reason and argument are lost in the clash of armed men, whose struggle can only be concluded by the exhaustion of one or both parties. Did it ever occur to you in reading our history how utterly unavailing was the eloquence of Chatham and Burke to stay our War with the American Colonies, and how completely the

efforts of Fox and his friends were thrown away in attempting to put a stop to the war of the French Revolution?

The obvious futility, then, of such attempts at intervention had convinced Cobden never again "to utter a word about the merits of a war after it has begun." The real task of statesmanship was rather "to try to prevent hostilities occurring" in the first place. Cobden, Bright, and their handful of Radical friends would "stand in the breach, as usual, to stem the tide of passion."[12]

Such pleas as were made for restraint and understanding, Cobden believed, would have to be directed less to English public opinion than to the handful of men who supervised British political affairs. For events in America had provoked only "confusion in John Bull's poor head." Rather than independently to formulate opinions on trans-Atlantic issues, most Englishmen preferred to leave such matters to the members of the Palmerston ministry. "Which Government," Cobden added, ". . . is the most friendly to your Government, that could be found in England, for, although Palmerston is fond of hot water, he boasts that he never got us into serious war. As for his colleagues, they are all sedate, peaceable men."[13]

While offering sympathy and promising to work for peace in England, Cobden also sent Sumner a suggestion about how the Americans might deal with the British *Trent* ultimatum. A passage in "General Scott's admirable letter," he wrote, provided the basis for a satisfactory answer. For Scott had asserted he was "sure that the President and people of the United States would be but too happy" to liberate the Southern envoys, if by so doing "they could emancipate the commerce of the world." Cobden discerned "a great idea" in this statement. "If I were in the position of your Government," he wrote,

> I would act upon it, and thus, by a great strategic movement, turn the flank of the European Powers, *especially of the governing class of England*. I would propose to let Mason and Slidell go free, and stipulate at the same time for a complete abandonment of the old code of maritime law as upheld by England and the European Powers. I would propose that private property at sea should be exempt from capture by armed Government ships. On this condition I would give my adhesion to the

173

abolition of privateering. . . . I would propose to abolish blockades of purely commercial ports, excepting for articles contraband of war.

Such a course would avert war over the *Trent* question. By anticipating a probable European movement during 1862 to break the Southern blockade for cotton, it would also, through a voluntary removal of obstacles to the export of that article, tend to prevent a war from breaking out over that issue. And, finally, it would allow the Americans to "gain in moral power by leading old Europe in the path of civilization."[14]

Most members of the Palmerston ministry would tend, of course, to reject such a proposition. For the "governing class," Cobden wrote, would be "averse" to *any* such "revolution in maritime law, by which the pretence for vast armaments would be annihilated. . . . It would be useless, therefore, . . . to propose these changes through the channels of secret diplomacy. It must be done publicly." An appeal must be made directly to the "busy toiling multitude." For "when a sufficient motive is presented," Cobden declared, "to induce the busy millions to exert their power, they can always bring the aristocracy into subjection to their will." A public proclamation in Washington of the proposals suggested by Cobden could be followed by pressure on the English "mercantile and manufacturing community [to] compel this Ministry, or some other, to accept them." Thus not only would the *Trent* crisis be pacifically terminated, but also some of the fundamental problems of international relations would be solved.[15]

It must have been obvious both to Sumner and to Lincoln, upon reading Cobden's suggestions, that they were based on an erroneous understanding of the Northern position. For the Englishman had written that the great need of the North was merely "*time* to ensure its triumph over the South. . . . And the *only way in which you can have time is by abolishing the blockade.*" All very well—but what good would it do to gain additional time in which to fight the South, when the sale of Southern cotton to Europe during that time would be used, directly or indirectly, to pay for munitions and mercenary soldiers to aid the Southerners in their struggle? If the Northerners tried to stop the shipment of such assistance to Confederate ports, would not the maritime clashes that would ensue jeopardize the peace between America and

England as much as, or more than, the growing cotton shortage promised to do? As a war measure, the blockade was *working*; it was in fact one of the few obvious successes of the entire Northern military effort; and it would be next to impossible to persuade the American people to abandon it, to relinquish Mason and Slidell, and simultaneously to give up the cherished right of privateering, so intimately associated with past triumphs of American arms on the oceans of the world, all merely in order to avoid a *possible* clash with England over what was essentially a minor incident. So, although there was food for thought in Cobden's observations about the positions of the British government and people in regard to the *Trent* affair, there was little sense in his recommendation of how the Americans might best deal with the exigency.[16]

John Bright's advice was altogether more realistic than Cobden's.[17] After warning Sumner that the war spirit in England was very strong, fed by newspapers whose anti-American writers had found the *Trent* affair a "treasuretrove," Bright then offered this counsel. "If I were Minister or President in your country," he wrote,

> I would write the most complete answer the case is capable of, and in a friendly and courteous tone, send it to this country. I would say that if after this, your view of the case is not accepted, you are ready to refer the matter to any sovereign, or two sovereigns, or Governments of Europe, or to any other eligible tribunal, and to abide by their decision, and you will rejoice to join with the leading European Governments in amendments and modifications of international law in respect to the powers of belligerents and the rights of neutrals. . . .
>
> I need not tell you who are much better acquainted with modern history than I am, that nations drift into wars . . . often thro' the want of a resolute hand at some moment early in the quarrel. So now, a courageous stroke, not of arms, but of moral action, may save you and us.[18]

Bright's letter offered the perplexed president, always ill at ease when called upon to deal with questions of foreign relations, the guide he needed to formulate his reply to Lyons. He seems to have consulted it as he wrote.[19] Suggesting that the facts regarding the *Trent* case contained in the British communication seemed "to be only a partial record, in the making up of which, he [Lincoln] had been allowed no part," he went on to assert that the American people would allow their government to "undo the act complained of, only upon a fair showing that it was wrong, or, at least, very questionable." He inquired whether the British government would "hear the United States upon the matter in question," whether, in Bright's words, it would receive "the most complete answer the case is capable of." Once the United States had been given time to present its side of the case, Lincoln would then offer two alternatives: first, submission of the matter to international arbitration; or that, based upon the complete record of facts introduced by both parties, the British government might alone "determine whether any, and if any, what reparation is due from the United States; provided" (1) the reparation should not differ from that proposed in Lyons's note, and (2) "that the determination thus made shall be the law for all future analogous cases, between Great Brittain [*sic*] and the United States."[20]

The day after writing his draft note to Lyons, the president told a senator from his home state that he "feared trouble" over the *Trent* affair, and that to avert it he had already written a note to the British government. It is probable that Lincoln continued for the next two or three days to mull over the wording of his draft reply, for on Monday, December 23, the same day on which Lyons officially handed Seward the British ultimatum, Sumner wrote: "The President himself will apply his mind to every word of the answer, so that it will be essentially his; and he hopes for peace."[21]

Sumner "spoke with the President several times on arbitration, and proposed Prussia, or, better still, three leading publicists on the Continent to sit in judgment." He showed Lincoln another letter from Bright, advising the Americans once more to "state your case in all its completeness, and then to offer to leave the question to the decision of some tribunal—say the French Emperor, or the King of Holland, or the King of Prussia, or the Emperor of Russia, or any two of them—and at the same time to restate your willingness so to amend and define international law as to make such cases of difficulty impossible hereafter." The impact of such counsel upon the president's developing attitude is indicated in a journalist's Washington column, written late on December 23. Insiders in the capital, this writer asserted, "anticipated from Mr.

Lincoln an offer to leave this difficulty to the decision of an umpire to be selected by England herself, from one of the four great European Powers, if the opportunity to make this offer is allowed him." If the British refused arbitration, then Lincoln would probably yield the captives peaceably. For "surrender, in preference to war," was being "pressed upon Mr. Lincoln by both civilians and military men, high in position."[22]

Lincoln's cabinet assembled on Christmas morning to consider the *Trent* case. During this meeting the president apparently developed misgivings about the expediency of seeking arbitration. The advice of Sumner and others to do so had indeed helped to persuade Lincoln that the Southern prisoners ought to be relinquished, but arbitration was too slow a method of doing it. The Americans had been served with an ultimatum. They had been told to give up the imprisoned Confederate envoys or see the British minister withdrawn from Washington and face the possibility of a war to follow, with almost sure defeat a consequence of any conflict with the armed might of England, when allied with the forces of the Southern insurgents. In the inflamed state of public opinion on both sides of the Atlantic Ocean, such vacillation as Lincoln had contemplated was too dangerous. As an editorial writer for the *New York Herald* asserted, it was "better gracefully to yield to the exigencies of the crisis, and promptly relieve England of her convenient pretext for a quarrel, without the intervention of any third party."[23]

If decisive action was required, then, what form should it take? The president, temperamentally a procrastinator, looked now to Seward for a suggestion of some swift and certain action. For more than one month the secretary of state had maintained a most uncharacteristic reticence concerning the *Trent* affair. He had been engaged in gathering all available information bearing on the subject, especially in the form of diplomatic dispatches and private letters from Europe. In a report so accurate that it must have been based on inside information, the Washington correspondent of the *New York Times* related generally what had passed between Seward and Lyons at their meeting on Saturday, December 21, and added that "the English Government will demand a disavowal of the act of Captain WILKES by our Government, and a restoration of MASON AND SLIDELL to British custody; but this demand will be couched in respectful language, not shutting the door to an amicable adjustment." Seward, the *Times*'s reporter added, had told Lyons that he was not yet ready to give the *Trent* question "the immediate and careful attention which its importance demanded, but that he would be prepared without undue delay, and . . . would be pleased to notify his Lordship" when his answer was ready. What Seward was waiting for most of all appeared to be an analysis by Adams of the situation in London. As the *Tribune*'s Washington correspondent suggested, Seward was hoping soon to learn "whether the dispatches to Mr. Adams . . . , informing the British Government that Capt. Wilkes acted without specific instructions, will allay the popular excitement or abate the ministerial demands."[24]

According to the Washington correspondent of still a third New York newspaper, the *Herald*, it was also "of the utmost importance to know precisely the attitude of France." For it was "vain and silly for us to talk wildly about fighting the whole world on account of a couple of miserable renegade rebels." Press dispatches from Paris uniformly spoke of the French as backing, "with remarkable unanimity," the British position on the *Trent* question. But it was natural for Seward to wish also to hear directly from his own men in Europe. On December 24 a meeting of the cabinet, called to consider the British ultimatum, was postponed twenty-four hours, probably on Seward's request. The secretary of state, seeming to Sumner "tranquil and confident," still waited.[25]

Prior to Christmas Day, Seward had received very meager information from Europe. He had learned from Thurlow Weed at Paris that Americans there all maintained that the United States could "hope for nothing friendly from France." Dayton had written that "the almost universal impression" in Paris was that if the *Trent* abduction was supported in Washington, "war will follow." On "good authority" the American minister in France had learned that at a Council of State held by the emperor, "it was resolved to *recognize* the Confederate Government," should Anglo-American war ensue. Meanwhile, from Adams at London had come the gloomy report that the anti-American feeling there was "running very high . . . and little confidence is entertained of the possibility of preserving peaceful relations." The minister had decided to begin making "arrangements for the termination of my stay at this post." Weed, too, had learned that in England "the indignation is wild and permeates all classes." British governmental leaders were known to believe "that if the taking of the Rebels from under the Protection of the British Flag was intended and is avowed and maintained, *it means war*."[26]

Also in the secretary of state's hands several days before December 25 was a long letter from Charles Mackay of London, a "devoted friend" who had previously exchanged visits with Seward, both in England and in America. Mackay, a journalist, lecturer, poet, and songwriter, wrote of the excitement created in London by the news of the *Trent* incident. Never within his memory had he witnessed "such a burst of feeling." "The people," he wrote, were "frantic with rage, and were the country polled I fear that 999 men out of 1,000 would declare for immediate war." The prime minister could not "resist the impulse if he would." He had inevitably "decided to demand reparation" from the United States. And Mackay had been told by a normally "peaceful member of our Parliament . . . that if this insult were not atoned for he saw no use for a flag; that he would recommend the British colours to be torn into shreds and sent to Washington for the use of the Presidential water-closets." This sort of statement, Mackay asserted, was common among "the whole people" of London. Because he mixed "a great deal with people of all classes of society," he wrote, he had "the means of feeling the public pulse as thoroughly as any man in London." His admiration of and esteem for Seward had induced him hurriedly to send "openly the result of my observations."[27]

Such was the nature of the information from Europe in Seward's possession prior to Christmas Day, 1861.[28] Although all reports indicated great obstacles in the way of continued peace with England, they made up no more than a tentative case. Not until December 25 did intelligence arrive in Washington which could be considered conclusive. It was on this morning that Seward learned from Dayton that the French press remained "unanimous" in agreeing with British journals that Wilkes's act was an outrage; indeed, some of the French newspapers known to reflect the views of leading public men had gone "so far as to declare that it is the manifest duty and policy of the Emperor to make common cause with England in this matter." The crisis, Dayton warned, would "require the most delicate handling or it will be followed by consequences which every patriot must deplore."[29]

From London, Adams wrote that the current of anti-American feeling was

> still running with resistless force throughout this Kingdom. [There was] . . . an almost universal demand for satisfaction for the insult and injury thought to be endured by the action of Captain Wilkes. The members of the Government as a whole are believed not to be desirous of pressing matters to a violent issue, but they are powerless in the face of the opinion they have invited from the law-officers of the Crown. . . . There can be not a shadow of doubt that the passions of the country are up and that a collision is inevitable if the Government of the United States should . . . have assumed the position of Captain Wilkes in a manner to preclude the possibility of explanation. . . . My present expectation is that by the middle of January at farthest, diplomatic relations will have been sundered between the two countries. . . .[30]

The same mail delivery that brought Adams's pessimistic prognostication also carried disconcerting messages from two American consuls in England. From Manchester came the news that England was arming "with the greatest energy," with the people in a warlike rage. And from London, Freeman Morse had written of "the greatest possible activity here in every military department." A "strong fleet" was being assembled and loaded in the Thames, "with double gangs working the whole 24 hours, including Sundays." Although one week had passed since news of the *Trent* seizure had reached London, there had been "no abatement" of the popular bellicosity. "Nearly the whole nation" appeared to sympathize with the South and to be preparing to fight the North. "Such prompt and gigantic preparations were never known," wrote Thurlow Weed from the British capital. He begged Seward not to choose a time "for War with England, when all her people are with the Government, and when everything here is upon a war footing."[31]

When Seward went to the White House on Christmas morning to

attend the cabinet meeting called to consider a response to the British *Trent* ultimatum, it seems likely that he had made up his mind what course he wished to take. But, as he wrote his wife, his cabinet "associates" had differed with him in the past "about what I ought to do and say," even though they might have been themselves unable to offer satisfactory alternatives. Hence he would have "to feel my way."[32]

Nor was the president as yet persuaded that it would be inappropriate to temporize while asking for arbitration of the *Trent* matter. Sumner had spent many hours with him attempting to win him over to this approach. Soon after the cabinet meeting opened with a reading of the British demand for the relinquishment of Mason and Slidell, Sumner was admitted to the room in order to read letters from John Bright and Richard Cobden which tended to show, as the attorney general observed, "that in England there is . . . one feeling—all against us—about the capture. The passions of Mr. Bull are thoroughly aroused about his dignity and the honor of his flag." This impression was reinforced by a letter from Thurlow Weed, read by Seward, which warned of almost inevitable war should the United States government uphold the *Trent* seizure. It seemed clear that the British ultimatum had the almost undivided support of Her Majesty's subjects.[33]

Many Americans had hoped that England's ancient enemy, France, would automatically approve of the *Trent* abduction. But Thouvenel's dispatch of December 3, aligning the emperor's government staunchly on the side of England against the legality of Wilkes's act, reached Mercier in time for him to rush it over to the State Department, whence Assistant Secretary of State Frederick Seward was persuaded to carry it without delay to his father at the White House. There it was read aloud to the other members of the cabinet, after which there could no longer exist any doubt that, as the attorney general concluded, "the French government fully agrees with England" regarding the illegality of the capture of Mason and Slidell.[34] Even more convincing to Bates was a statement attributed to the French foreign minister, quoted in a dispatch from Dayton, "that all the foreign maritime powers with which he had conferred agreed that the act [of Wilkes] was a violation of public law." Although France would not join England in declaring war against the United States over the *Trent* question, Thouvenel had written Dayton, they would not be "indifferent spectators; the moral force of their opinions would be against us."[35]

Weed, too, had warned that the Americans could "hope for nothing friendly from France." And Richard Cobden had convincingly explained

> the ardour with which the French Press takes up the cry against you. Some of the papers most eager to push us to extremities are those which are conducted by parties who are supposed to be in the confidence of the Emperor. Spending as I did eighteen months in France, and always in close communication with the Emperor's ablest advisers, and frequently having very free audiences with himself, I came to the conclusion that *the corner-stone of his policy was friendship with England.* . . . To preserve this friendship, I believe he would submit to anything short of such a humiliation for France as would emperil his dynasty. It is to preserve this friendship that he has sought our alliance in the Crimea, in China, and in Mexico. . . . *I leave you to make an application of these facts to your present situation.*[36]

Two members of Lincoln's cabinet, both of whom had entered the discussion convinced of the desirability of refusing to release the imprisoned Southern emissaries, were greatly shaken by these revelations of the true feelings of Europeans on the *Trent* question. Attorney General Edward Bates concluded that the English were perhaps anxious "to pick a quarrel with us, on the pretense of this seisure [*sic*]," after which France would join England in smashing the blockade of the Southern cotton ports, "and consequently acknowledgeing [*sic*] the C. S. of A and that is war, and we cannot afford such a war." The secretary of the treasury, too, believed that although the United States government ought to be allowed by the English to keep "her Rebels," it would be extremely dangerous not to surrender them without delay.[37]

"In such a crisis," Bates reluctantly concluded, "with such a civil war upon our hands, we cannot hope for success in a . . . war with England, backed by the assent and countenance of France. We must evade it—with as little damage to our own honor and pride as possible." But how was this goal of "peace with honor" to be reached? No member of the cabinet save Seward had a solution to offer. The president clung to his feeling in favor of seeking arbitration, but apparently not a single cabinet member endorsed this suggestion. Only the secretary of state had a concrete plan, embodied in a draft diplomatic note in which he proposed to answer the British ultimatum by "cheerfully" yielding the four captives on the ground that Wilkes had inadvertently violated international law in seizing the men without also taking into custody their papers and the ship itself. Seward had labored long on this paper. He had studied Wilkes's own reports of the incident; he had perused a multitude of commentaries in New York and Washington newspapers; he had read the arguments, pro and con, of famous jurists; and he had examined the material his own staff had dredged up from the archives of the State Department. In the end his note had incorporated ideas drawn from all these varied sources.[38]

Because it was such a patchwork of convenience, Seward's draft note lacked the essential elements of a good legal brief—logic, consistency, and the force of authority. It was not intended, however, as a learned discussion of the legal principles involved in the *Trent* case. Rather was it meant to be a *political* paper, designed to convince first the president and the other members of the cabinet, and then, ultimately, the American people, of the expediency of yielding to the British ultimatum. Beyond this, it was also designed as a *diplomatic* document—intended to prevent an Anglo-American war. It was carefully constructed to counter what Seward called "the great difficulty in all human enterprises," which consisted "in pursuing just and worthy objects persistently when the interests and passions of men avail themselves of accidents to embarrass our movements and divert us from our course."[39]

It was no time, Seward told his cabinet colleagues, "to be diverted from the cares of the Union into controversies with other powers, even if just causes for them could be found." In response to the ultimatum calling for the return of the Southern envoys to British protection, and for "a suitable apology," the secretary of state contended in his draft note to Lyons that (1) Wilkes acted on his own, without direction from or even the knowledge of his superiors. (2) Certain allegations in the British foreign minister's description of the *Trent* incident created the impression of unwarranted discourtesy and undue violence on the part of the officers and men of the *San Jacinto* against the people on board the *Trent*, but these charges were not substantiated by the official American reports. (3) Wilkes had merely undertaken "a simple legal and customary belligerent proceeding . . . to arrest and capture a neutral vessel engaged in carrying contraband of war for the use and benefit of the insurgents." (4) Partly through charitable intentions, however, he had committed a crucial error: he had "after capturing contraband persons and making prize of the Trent in . . . a perfectly lawful manner, instead of sending her into port released her from the capture and permitted her to proceed with her whole cargo upon her voyage. He thus effectively prevented the judicial examination which might otherwise have occurred." (5) The Americans, therefore, were required by basic considerations of decency and justice "to do to the British nation just what we have always insisted all nations ought to do to us."[40]

Charles Adams had furnished the secretary of state with the crucial ingredient in his argument. Writing from London on December 3, the American minister had referred to the traditional American position "of maintenance of the privileges of neutrals to be free from search." Adams had "been particularly struck," he wrote,

> with the language used by Mr. Madison on this subject in his instructions given to Mr. Monroe to treat with the Government of Great Britain on the subjects then in dispute between the countries, dated 5 January 1804. It is scarcely possible for words to be stronger in deprecation of such acts as the one that has just been committed. It would appear that we went so far as to propose a degree of immunity to neutral vessels which was objected to on the part of the British Government on the ground of "the facility it would give to the escape of traitors and the desertion of others whose services in time of war may be particularly important to an enemy." Under these circumstances it would not seem advisable for us to insist upon assuming their position unless we are ready also to assume their old arrogant claim of the domination of the seas. Our neutral rights are as valuable to us as ever they were, whilst time has reflected nothing but credit on our steady defence of them against superior power.
>
> It has occurred to me then that at this moment it might be well to consider the expediency of renewing in some form at Washington the proposal made at the time alluded to by Mr. Madison. . . . Whatever may be the answer that will be given to the message sent out through Lord Lyons, the nature of which I do not undertake to prejudge, the offer of such a proposition may be of use as a basis of reconciliation whether

before or after the commencement of hostilities. And it will serve to break the force of the public opinion of Europe, which will certainly be against us, and if I may be permitted to say so, not without justice, should we choose to place ourselves in the position which has always heretofore earned for England the ill-will of all the other maritime nations of the globe, not excluding ourselves.[41]

Facing the "embarrassment" of appearing to support "the British side" of the *Trent* question "against my own country," Seward had received Adams's suggestion in the nick of time. Happily, he had

discovered that I was really defending and maintaining not an exclusively British interest but an old, honored and cherished American cause, not upon British authorities but upon principles that constitute a large portion of the distinctive policy by which the United States . . . have won the respect and confidence of many nations. These principles were laid down for us in 1804 by James Madison when Secretary of State . . . in instructions given to James Monroe, our minister to England. . . . The ground he assumed then was the same I now occupy, and the arguments by which he sustained himself upon it have been an inspiration to me in preparing this reply.

[Madison had written that] "whenever property found in a neutral vessel is supposed to be liable on any ground to capture and condemnation the rule in all cases is that the question shall not be decided by the captor but be carried before a legal tribunal where a regular trial may be had, and where the captor himself is liable for damages for an abuse of his power. . . ."[42]

The attorney general afterward recorded in his diary that there had been "great reluctance on the part of some of the members of the cabinet —and even the President himself"—to release the captured insurgent envoys, largely because of a fear of "the displeasure of our own people— lest they should accuse us of timidly truckling to the power of England." But, "happily for us," Bates and the others had learned, the truth was that in "yielding to the necessity of the case we do but reaffirm our old principles and carry out into practice the traditional policy of the country, as is clearly shown by Mr. Seward in quotations from Mr. Sect. of State Madison's instructions to our minister to England, Monroe, in 1804."[43]

Chase, too, was consoled, in choking down the "gall and wormwood"

of Seward's draft note, "by the reflection that . . . the surrender . . . is
but simply doing right; simply proving faithful to our own ideas and
traditions under strong temptations to violate them; simply giving to
England and to the world the most signal proof that the American Nation will not . . . commit even a technical wrong against neutrals." Nevertheless, probably because of the president's reluctance to reach a final
decision without additional time in which personally to ponder Seward's
solution, the cabinet council of December 25 was adjourned in mid-
afternoon, with the participants agreeing to resume their discussion of
the *Trent* question on the following morning. That evening at a White
House dinner the president told a senator that the cabinet had met to
consider the British ultimatum, "and had agreed not to divulge what
had occurred, but that there would be no war with England."[44]

Senator Sumner had left the cabinet meeting feeling that "the immediate pending question will be settled." And Seward told Mercier, whose
curiosity brought him into the secretary of state's path that afternoon, "that nothing had yet been decided, but that as soon as a decision
had been reached he would give me an answer [to Thouvenel's dispatch]
that could not be more friendly." The newspapers the next morning
were, with one exception, barren of definitive indications about what
had happened at the cabinet council. That exception, however, was
an important one, for the Washington correspondent of the *New York
Times*, as previously indicated, seems to have had access to highly placed
sources in the Lincoln administration—probably in the State Department. It was "understood" in the capital, he wrote, "that our Government is ready to disavow the act of Capt. WILKES, and to deliver up
MASON and SLIDELL, if that be the only means of purchasing peace with
England," on the condition that the English recognize the incident as
a binding precedent. An accompanying editorial asserted that the leaders
of the Federal government might "count, with confidence, on the public
support for whatever course [they] may deem necessary to pursue."[45]

Apparently touched off by this indication that the members of the
president's cabinet were at that very moment considering the surrender
of Mason and Slidell to England, John P. Hale of New Hampshire, an
abolitionist legislative ally of Sumner's, proclaimed in an almost empty
Senate on December 26 his bitter opposition to "an act that would sur-

render at once to the arbitarary demand of Great Britain all that was won in the Revolution, reduce us to the position of a second-rate Power, and make us the vassal of Great Britain." He would be willing, Hale declared, to consider foreign arbitration, but he "would not submit to the arbitrary, the absolute demand of Great Britain, to surrender these men, and humble our flag even to escape from a war with Great Britain." Having discussed the *Trent* affair with many citizens, the New Hampshire senator said, he had found "not a man . . . who is in favor of this surrender." Rather than relinquish the rebel envoys, he asserted, it would be better to

> let war come; let your cities be battered down, your armies be scattered, your fields barren, to preserve untarnished the national honor. . . .
>
> If this Administration will not listen to the voice of the people, they will find themselves engulfed in a fire that will consume them like stubble; they will be helpless before a power that will hurl them from their places.

Having thus emotionally expressed himself for the record, and seeing that few of his Senate colleagues appeared to approve of his outburst, Hale relinquished the floor to Sumner, who commented merely that his fellow New Englander had "spoken too swiftly," for the *Trent* question, he was confident, would be both "peaceably and honorably adjusted."[46]

Akin to Hale's chauvinism were comments like that of a Northern general who threatened if the rebel envoys were released to "snap his sword, and throw the pieces into the White House." Such histrionics, however, had no perceptible effect on events, for the decision to release the four imprisoned Southern envoys was finally made at the cabinet meeting of December 26. As Bates stated, everyone present "yielded to the necessity, and unanimously concur[r]ed in Mr. Sewards [*sic*] letter to Ld. Lyons, after some verbal and formal amendments." Then after clerks had worked overnight in the State Department to produce copies of his lengthy revised note, Seward called Lyons to his office early on December 27. According to the British minister, he "said with some emotion that he thought it was due to the great kindness and consideration which I had manifested throughout in dealing with the affair of the Trent that he should tell me with his own lips that he had been able to effect a satisfactory settlement of it." It was not without a sense of relief that he announced this, Seward added, for "he 'had been through the fires of Topet' in order to get the prisoners surrendered."[47]

After ascertaining during a hurried perusal of Seward's note that the four prisoners were "given up, immediately and unconditionally," Lyons had the document copied and sent by messenger to catch the mail packet due to leave New York at once for England. The British minister felt unable "to give an opinion upon the argumentation in Mr. Seward's voluminous note." He hoped, however, that the response to the British ultimatum would "be deemed sufficient." Until he learned otherwise from London he decided to remain at his post." For "a rupture of diplomatic relations, not followed by war, would be worse than war itself," he believed. "After that, nothing would ever convince the Americans that there was any limit to our forbearance." The secretary of state had promised to see Lyons again on the twenty-eighth in order to arrange the details of restoring the prisoners to British protection. In the meantime he requested that the British minister "keep the answer a secret." For Seward had other diplomatic notes and instructions dealing with the *Trent* question yet to write, and he desired to have those missives delivered and to have copies of the most important documents pertaining to the case sent to the newspapers before the American public should learn of the outcome from unofficial sources.[48]

After an arduous day's labor, Seward returned home early on the evening of December 27 to host a dinner for English novelist Anthony Trollope and several prominent United States senators. Afterward the secretary of state invited Senators Orville H. Browning, John J. Crittenden, Ira Harris, Preston King, and Charles Sumner to his library, where he read them the documents pertaining to the *Trent* affair which he was about to release to the newspapers. Included among those documents were the British ultimatum, his own reply thereto, Thouvenel's dispatch on the subject, Seward's reply to that, and, finally, the secretary's conciliatory instruction regarding the seizure of Mason and Slidell which he had sent on November 30 to Adams at London. When Seward finished reading all these papers, the assembled senators apparently "all agreed with him" that the captured Southern diplomats "should be given up."[49]

On Saturday morning, December 28, a large portion of the news space in the Washington *Daily National Intelligencer* was devoted to the verbatim publication of Seward's note promising to release Mason and Slidell, with the supporting documents which Seward had read to his senatorial guests. The accompanying editorial commentary was overwhelmingly favorable. It praised the "firmness and sincerity with which the Administration, resisting . . . the conceived drift of public opinion in our own country, has resolved to do what it believes to be right." The British had even been maneuvered by Seward into approving an important feature of "the law of nations, as traditionally interpreted by our Government, . . . though at the cost, it may be, of some national sensibilities waked into disproportionate activity by the temporary exacerbations of our civil feuds." These, however, were "but for a day. The law of nations is for all time."[50]

Then on Sunday morning, December 29, the great New York newspapers published the *Trent* documents. A writer for the *New York Times* suggested that Seward's note of December 26 to Lyons deserved "unqualified admiration," and he praised the Lincoln administration, "which yields not its judgment to popular desires, and which has . . . honesty of purpose enough to carry out its best judgments, even against the current of the people's wishes." A war which "would have given a certain triumph to the Southern rebellion" had been averted. The secretary of state's "masterly" note to Lyons demonstrated "very clearly that . . . the great principles of maritime law to which the United States have always adhered . . . are worth to us a thousand-fold more than the persons of MASON and SLIDELL."[51]

Telegraphic intelligence from Washington to the effect that the Southern envoys were to be released had arrived at the New York stock exchange the previous day. At once prices had risen and the news was received, one reporter testified, "with almost universal approval." Horace Greeley "heartily" endorsed the step, while James Bennett effusively praised Seward's display of "eminent ability, sagacity, dignity and decorum" in settling the *Trent* question without war. In his "masterly" note to Lyons the secretary of state had presented a "clear, sagacious and statesmanlike defence" of American principles and had thus both "sustained the honor of the United States" and gained for his country "the advantages of an honest neutrality on the part of England." History would "show him to be both a great patriot and a great statesman."[52]

Foreign diplomats stationed in Washington hastened to express their approval of the cabinet's decision, both to officials in the Lincoln administration and to their superiors at home. Mercier, for example, wrote that Seward had behaved during the crisis with "very good grace," while exposing himself to "some very spirited attacks" from those who considered that he had seriously damaged the national honor of the United States. The real motivation of such Americans, the French minister believed, had been not "a feeling of honor" at all; rather had it been to sustain a prodigious arrogance. It was therefore just and right that the Americans had been abruptly forced to realize that they were *not*, after all, "the greatest people in the world, governed by the best institutions which God has ever given man, and the bravest against their enemies." Seward, the personification of much of the innate Yankee insolence, was "becoming the most tractable of men." It should be satisfying to Frenchmen to know that not only had the emperor's government, by supporting the British demands, been able to help curb American pretentions, but Thouvenel and Mercier had also "been able to contribute to preventing the war" that had seemed about to break out over the *Trent* question.[53]

The Belgian minister, meanwhile, gave all the credit for the peaceful settlement of the *Trent* affair "to the Secretary of State, who has displayed great ability and very great courage." Seward had appeared to take "upon himself alone the entire responsibility"; his colleagues, Cuelebrouck had learned, "were only informed at the last moment" in a cabinet meeting called to consider the secretary of state's draft of a diplomatic note on the subject. Only afterward, on the evening of December 27, had Seward brought together the members of the Senate Foreign Relations Committee and told them what "*he had done.*" Cuelebrouck considered "this brave manner of proceeding . . . a happy inspiration." For the American "nation, according to all signs, will accept the *fait accompli.*"[54]

Among the dissenters from the cabinet's decision on the *Trent* affair was Captain Wilkes, who gave a New Year's day reception at his Washington home, the former James and Dolly Madison House. There he was observed complaining bitterly of the surrender of Mason and Slidell, describing the act "as a craven yielding and an abandonment of all the good ... done by [their] capture." Seward had apparently been thoughtful enough to read Wilkes his note to Lyons relinquishing the captives before he handed it to the British minister. On that occasion, and later as well, Wilkes indicated that "were I placed under similar circumstances, I should not hesitate to act again as I did in that affair." After initially favoring the seizure, Lincoln had become "weakkneed," Wilkes thought, and had by allowing Seward to have his way missed a great opportunity to serve his country. For the *Trent* question had provided the means for reuniting North and South in a common effort against a foreign enemy.[55]

Probably the best indication of how distorted were Wilkes's perceptions was the universal reaction of Southerners. "When the British Lion growled and showed his teeth," one Confederate journalist said sneeringly, "we expected that the Yankee jackal would put his tail between his legs, lower his crest, and lick the dust in abject humility, and this is exactly what he has done." Another Confederate editorial writer, noticing in Northern newspapers "very little room for doubt that the Yankee nation is about to swallow its own bluster and to surrender the Southern Commissioners ... upon the humiliating terms proposed by the English government," wondered "how the South could ever have consented so long to associate with such a craven race." In a single year the Yankees had "become the scorn and the laughing stock of mankind." But the fact was, as a Confederate agent in Europe wrote, that the release of the Southern envoys had done the insurgent cause "incalculable injury." The moment that Seward had "cowered beneath the roar of the British Lion, and surrendered Mason and Slidell," a clerk in the War Department at Richmond lamented, he had brought an end to all hope of an Anglo-Confederate alliance. "Now," he wrote, "we must depend upon our own strong arms."[56]

XIV.

The Diplomatic Settlement

*As to our [British] government wishing a war, it is out
of the question. . . . Neither glory nor gain could result
to us. . . .*

*Personally I no more believe that your government
wishes a war than ours, but I can hardly find a man to
agree with me. Some busy power is making each believe
that the other is a secret enemy. If reasonable proof can
be given to influential men that Seward does not desire
to make capital out of hostility to England, it would
do great good.*

REV. ARTHUR TO REV. M'CLINTOCK,
December 2, 1861.[1]

As a result of careful planning by Seward and Lyons, the two Southern
commissioners and their secretaries were taken from Fort Warren by a
special agent of the State Department aboard a chartered tugboat on
which they sailed surreptitiously to Provincetown, Massachusetts. There
they were quietly transferred to *H. M. S. Rinaldo*, which fought through
a howling storm to St. Thomas, where, on January 14, the four Confederates boarded the royal mail steamer *La Plata*, bound for Southampton,
England. Meanwhile, the news of their release and impending arrival
reached London on January 8. On frosty street corners throughout the
smoky city, Englishmen congratulated each other on the preservation of
peace with the United States. When the news was announced between
acts at several theaters that evening, entire audiences surged spontaneously to their feet to cheer. That night church bells rang in country
towns; dispatches flashed over telegraph wires to all the courts of Europe;
and when the news was brought to Mrs. Slidell by the British undersecretary for foreign affairs, he was disconcerted when "the poor thing

fainted—& so the daughters." Lady Russell wrote a friend: "I rejoice with all my heart and soul. John was delighted. He was very anxious up to the last moment."[2]

"I thank God," Gladstone wrote, "for the American news." During a speech delivered in Scotland he suggested that "old controversies with the Americans" should now be set aside and new ones should be dealt with "handsomely and liberally . . . in a spirit of brotherly concord." His niece, too, was ecstatic to learn that "the precious Yankees give up the commissioners and it is Peace." She was surprised to learn that "the American Government seem to have been for peace all along"; apparently, the impression of "mob brag and insolence" in America had been inaccurately conveyed by a "contemptible" Northern press. Even the old prime minister was pleased that the affair was "satisfactorily settled and that the Prisoners are given up." But he hoped that the "golden" concession by the Americans would not suddenly turn to "iron." He remained "wary of Yankees."[3]

The London press welcomed the news that the *Trent* affair had been terminated peacefully. Asserting that "to all intents and purposes, except the actual shedding of blood we have been for the last month at war with the Northern States of America," an editorial writer for the London *Times* added: "We draw a long breath, and are thankful [that] . . . we have come out of this trial with our honour safe and no blood spilt." It had been "a great victory" for British diplomacy—far better than "being obliged to conquer." For the moment the threat of chastisement had curbed "the insolence of a neighbour who took pleasure in continually provoking us, and had permitted himself at last to go beyond the possibility of suffrance." Now

the four American gentlemen who have gotten us into our late trouble, and cost us probably a million a-piece,[4] will soon be in one of our ports. . . . How, then, are we to receive these illustrious visitors? . . . They have long been known as the blind and habitual haters and revilers of this country. They have done more than any other men to get up the insane prejudice against England which disgraces the morality and disorders the policy of the Union. . . . Had they perished in the cell or on the scaffold, amid the triumphant yells of the multitude, memory would have suggested that their own bitter tirades had raised the storm, and that their death was only the natural and logical conclusion of their own calumnies and sophistries.

So we do sincerely hope that our countrymen will not give these fellows anything in the shape of an ovation. The civility that is due to a foe in distress is all that they can claim. . . . They are personally nothing to us. They must not suppose, because we have gone to the very verge of a great war to rescue them, that therefore they are precious in our eyes. We should have done just as much to rescue two of their own Negroes.[5]

The author of this editorial may have received some inspiration from official sources, for by this time a sense of relief at escaping war and a determination to avoid future Anglo-American crises, if possible, had permeated the British bureaucracy. Palmerston wrote the queen that the members of the cabinet had resolved that, although Seward's note to Lyons releasing the captured Southerners contained "many doctrines of international law . . . , which your Majesty's Government could not agree to," the American reply should nevertheless be accepted "as a full satisfaction of the demands of the British government." In a separate note to Queen Victoria, the prime minister observed that the "peaceful settlement" of the *Trent* affair was

indeed a happy event, for although there can be no doubt that your Majesty's arms would have been most successful in a war with the Northern States, yet even success in war must be purchased by a large expenditure of money, by much embarrassment to commerce, and by painful sacrifices of the lives and blood of brave men.[6]

There remained for the queen's ministers the necessity of considering the contents of Seward's *Trent* note. Having done this on January 9, they resolved, according to Granville, that the British foreign secretary should write Lyons that he "was satisfied with the surrender, but announcing an answer to be concocted by the law officers, on certain doctrines of international law laid down in Mr. Seward's despatch."[7]

As the duke of Argyll put it, Seward had been wrong in asserting that the mere fact that the British packet "was proceeding from a neutral port to another neutral port" did not negate "the right of the belligerent captor" to seize the Southern passengers as contraband of war. Such a principle, the duke wrote Palmerston, would "certainly not be admitted by us, and if acted upon, will be in danger of bringing on similar collisions every week." Rather did he agree with Thouvenel's declaration, contained in the latter's dispatch to Mercier dated December 3, that (as Argyll recapitulated it) "a vessel plying between neutral ports cannot contain contraband of war at all—and that packets such as the Trent *must* be held free from seizure by any Belligerent Power." Moreover, the duke wrote Charles Summer, "communications of any kind from one belligerent to a neutral power are not contraband, and are not liable to seizure or detention as such." Should Seward persist in maintaining otherwise, he warned the Massachusetts senator with whom he felt "on pretty intimate terms," he apprehended that "the two nations would be at the point of war every week." Neither British judicial decisions, "nor any act of our Government," he asserted in a private note to the American minister in London, "can be cited as inconsistent with this doctrine." Hence it was foolish for Americans to assume, merely because mistaken ideas had appeared in British newspapers, "that we objected to the act of Capt. Wilkes only on the narrow and technical ground that the ship was not taken into port."[8]

On January 14 an able British barrister, writing under the pseudonym of "Historicus," reiterated Argyll's theme in a letter to the editor of the London *Times*. Although he refrained from discussing Seward's "numerous legal mistakes" in detail, William Vernon Harcourt nevertheless felt obliged to point out the American secretary of state's fundamental error in ignoring the fact that "In a question of contraband, the destination of the ship is everything." No neutral ship bound for a neutral port could possibly carry contraband. Two days later, when an analysis of Seward's *Trent* note was finally forwarded to cabinet members by the crown law officers, it, too, denied that the Southern commissioners were subject to seizure as contraband of war.[9]

At its "*Council of Trent,*" the British cabinet adopted the reasoning of the law officers. They "utterly disallowed" many of the doctrines contained in what Gladstone called Seward's "long-winded & flimsy dispatch." Russell thought the law officers' report "very good in substance, tho' much involved in style." Having condensed it into a draft dispatch to Lyons, he submitted it to the lord chancellor for criticism. Then he circulated it among other members of the cabinet. Argyll, who had been aroused by the *Trent* crisis into intense lobbying in favor of peaceful relations with the Americans, was particularly vocal in desiring the softest possible language. After a last-minute scrutiny at the Foreign Office, the dispatch was finally forwarded to Lyons on January 23.[10]

In the form in which it arrived in Washington, Russell's dispatch commenced with a sly thrust based on Seward's discussion of the *Trent* case as a question of belligerent rights under international law. Since the American secretary of state had himself adopted this position, Russell wrote, "we must therefore discard entirely from our minds the allegation that the captured persons were rebels and we must consider them only as enemies of the United States at war with its Government." Citing Vattel, Scott, Wheaton, and other legal authorities, Russell argued at great length that neither the Southern envoys nor their dispatches could be considered contraband of war under the law of nations. Furthermore, the neutral destination of the *Trent* in itself exempted its passengers and their dispatches from capture.

> In view therefore of the erroneous principles asserted by Mr. Seward and the consequences they involve, Her Majesty's Government think it necessary to declare that they would not acquiesce in the capture of any British merchant ship in the circumstances similar to those of the Trent and that the fact of its being brought before a prize court . . . would not diminish the gravity of the offense against the law of nations which would thereby be committed.

As for Seward's remark that "If the safety of this Union required the detention of the captured persons it would be the right and duty of this Government to detain them," Russell replied that the bearing of such a "wrong" on the fortunes of war in the United States would not affect British objections to it. "Happily," however, "all danger of hostile collision on this subject" had been avoided "by peaceful negotiations," and Russell hoped that future differences would be likewise resolved.[11]

Disposed in the future "to be vigilant, but cautious" regarding differences with the Americans, Russell was also determined to "take care" to observe international law in all his dealings with them—especially since he feared that war on the Continent involving France and Germany was "very probable" in the near future. It would be hard to prevent such a conflict in any case, but if the British were trying to subdue the Americans and simultaneously protect Canada, Russell wrote Palmerston, "we shall be much crippled in Europe." It was "difficult to hit the exact line of neutrality" in coping with a multitude of incidents growing out of the American Civil War, especially "when the circumstances of the two belligerents are so different." Yet Russell was "heart and soul a neutral." Ruefully, he wrote Lyons: "What a fuss we have had about these two men."[12]

As soon as he received Russell's rejoinder to Seward's *Trent* note, Lyons promptly delivered it to the secretary of state. After reading it, Seward observed merely that the different interpretations of international maritime law contained in the correspondence on the *Trent* question had not prevented a peaceful settlement of that matter and that they were "not practically presented in any case of conflict now existing between the United States and Great Britain." He asked Lyons to assure the British foreign minister

> that while the United States will justly claim as their own the belligerent rights which the customary practice allows to nations engaged in war according to our present convictions, there is no melioration of the maritime law or of the actual practice of maritime war that the leading maritime States including Great Britain shall think desirable which will not be cheerfully assented to by the United States, even to the most liberal asylum for persons and the extreme point of exemption of private property from confiscation in maritime war.[13]

Happy though he was with the outcome of the *Trent* crisis, Lyons claimed, nevertheless, that "the real cause" of the surrender of Mason and Slidell "was nothing more nor less than the military preparations made in England."[14] Supported by the French dispatch, and reinforced by the courteous and moderate British ultimatum, the widely publicized military movements of the Palmerston ministry had "in all probability ... prevented war." People who were not already well acquainted with the Americans, Lyons wrote Russell,

> will probably be much more surprised than I am at the surrender of the prisoners. I was sure from the first that they would give in, if it were possible to convince them that *war* was really the only alternative. My

difficulty has been to make them aware that it was surrender or war, without making such threats as would render the humiliation too great to be borne, even by them.[15]

From the British foreign minister, Lyons received hearty congratulations on the "favourable result." Russell attributed it at least partly to Lyons's "silence, forebearance, & friendly discretion." Terming the episode "a trial of our patience," Russell did not "regret its occurrence. The unanimity shown here, the vigourous despatch of troops & ships, the loyal determination of Canada," he believed, "may save us a contest for a long while to come, & in fact the cost incurred may be true economy." But feeling "a great weight not only off my mind but off the mind and heart of the nation," he admitted that in one respect, at least, the *Trent* crisis had opened his eyes. He no longer believed "that Seward has any animosity to this country. It is all buncom[be]."[16]

In the London *Observer*, which Thurlow Weed called "one of Earl Russell's journals," an editorial asserted that

the manner of the concession by the Secretary of State, at Washington, goes far to obliterate the bad feeling engendered on this side. No man has done more to brush aside all the sophistries that have been accumulated upon so simple a case, than Mr. Seward himself, and the authors of the silly chatter that has been uttered on both sides of the Atlantic must hide their heads in the presence of the very straightforward and candid admission of the American Secretary of State.[17]

In Washington, plaudits poured into the State Department from relieved American diplomats in Europe. "The course of our Government, in reference to Mason and Slidell," wrote Dayton, "is approved by everybody. We have made character, not lost, by it." From London, Adams wrote that the *Trent* settlement would "meet with very general approbation" in Europe. Throughout the British capital city, he wrote, expressions of satisfaction were heard everywhere, "in remarkable contrast with the feeling which animated almost everybody only six weeks ago." It appeared almost as if British public opinion, "for the moment," had shifted in favor of the Northern cause against that of the rebels. And Seward's management of "the various difficulties and complications attending this unfortunate business" had won the renewed "admiration" of Adams himself.[18]

From Berlin, Norman Judd wrote that "the disposition of the Trent affair was eminently wise and judicious—a statesman's conduct of the question." Many German political leaders, as well as foreign diplomats, had offered Judd their congratulations, not only because war had been averted, but also because Seward's manner of dealing with the crisis had left the United States in a strong moral position, "reflecting the highest credit" both upon the secretary of state and upon his country. Similar sentiments were forwarded by the American ministers at Madrid, at Vienna, and at St. Petersburg. Motley wrote, for example, that Count Rechberg, the Austrian foreign minister, had extended his "congratulations for the able, temperate, courageous and statesmanlike manner in which the [United States] government had borne itself throughout these trying circumstances," and especially had he commended Seward's concluding note to Lyons. As for Cassius Clay, his reaction on hearing that the Southern Commissioners had been relinquished had been to "rejoice at the good sense of our people. . . . Let 'one war at a time' be our motto. . . . And may God save the Republic."[19]

"Everybody I see," Sanford wrote from Brussels, "is delighted & is chuckling over the discomfiture of England." The effect of the *Trent* settlement, he thought, was "highly favorable to us in continental Europe." As James S. Pike wrote from The Hague, the peaceful resolution of the crisis had helped to dispel the conviction, widely held in Europe, that the American government was "under the control of an unthinking mob, instead of being in the hands of persons of moderation and wisdom." All over Europe it had been "believed and avowed by the ruling classes that at such a crisis a headlong democracy was sure to drive the Government into the broad road to national ruin." Having acted discreetly and courteously in dealing with the *Trent* emergency, the leaders of the American government were sure at last to win from Europeans "their involuntary respect and admiration."[20]

From Turin, Seward received a similar appraisal. The cause of the Union, George Marsh wrote, would "be essentially advanced by [the] . . . wisdom and skill" with which "an apparently unlucky accident" had been converted "into an instrument of good." The *Trent* settlement would aid immeasurably in "dispelling an error almost universal among European statesmen, . . . the assumption namely that the American Union is less a republic than an unbridled democracy, of which the federal government is but a blind instrument." As Bishop McIlvaine, too, wrote home from Europe, the outcome ought to have shown conclusively that the government of the United States *could* contend with the mythical mob and do justice in its foreign relations.[21]

The American secretary of state had demonstrated, during the *Trent* affair, that his reputation among his critics—like Senator Sumner—for carelessness and precipitancy was unjustified. Rather had he appeared to vacillate so long regarding the great topic of the day that his London representative had complained bitterly to Thurlow Weed and others of being "left in utter ignorance of the views of the Department of State . . . on this Trent affair." Not a word of guidance had Adams received "during six weeks of the most trying anxiety and suspense." "To be indebted to British ministers for what he knows about negotiations at Washington," Weed added, was not for Adams a mode of existence "either profitable or pleasant."[22]

These reproaches soon brought Weed several letters from Seward in which the American secretary of state protested that he could not have prevented "the delay and suspense in the Trent affair" without using the telegraph, which was hardly a suitable method of sending dispatches devoted to a sensitive subject. He was unable, moreover, to comprehend how Weed and Adams had convinced themselves

> that from the . . . inception of the recent difficulty I knew and could have intimated from day to day . . . what would be the solution of the affair.
> Pray understand now that I neither can advise Mr. Adams beforehand nor even know myself what will be the action of the Government two days in advance of the actual decision it may make. . . . The consideration of the Trent case was crowded out by pressing domestic affairs until Christmas day. It was considered on my presentation of it on the 25 & 26 December. The Government when it took up the request had no idea of the grounds upon which it would explain its action, nor did it believe then that it would concede the case. Yet it was heartily

unanimous on the actual result after two days' examination—and in every word of the defense.

Remember that in a Council like ours, there are some strong wills to be reconciled, and some voluble elements. . . .

Lord Lyons submitted the case to me only on Friday & on the Friday following the matter was disposed of. It would have been disposed of in exactly the same way had the British Government and British Press and American Press and American Correspondents held their temper and their patience—that is to say, it would have been so decided if it had been left with me. But I could not know that it would be so left, and I could not assume it so against the overruling authority I am to consult in all cases.

Adams, concluded Seward, had been told all that was positively known in Washington, "as fast as I knew it. I have had to feel my way."[23]

This criticism by two of his closest friends seems to have cut Seward deeply. He wrote Weed that he thought himself to be as industrious as anyone in Washington, and reasonably versatile; yet Weed seemed to have forgotten "how little time official consultations and audiences leave me to work at all." It was unreasonable to have expected him to write Adams private notes "when the Trent affair was pending," especially when he had not known what the official decision would be on that matter until it was actually rendered. Nor had he considered it prudent to entrust mere speculation on the subject to letters that might be opened and published, after which Seward might well, as he had before, "be reproved for false prophecies," or at least have his words misinterpreted in ways that might injure his country.[24]

As soon as peace returned to North America, Seward wrote, he yearned to "leave public life forever." He desired "to rest during what remains of life free from the suspicions and jealousies of enemies and the reproofs of friends." The Newcastle falsehood, the echoes from Europe of Sumner's and Lyons's lies about his alleged warmongering, and the malicious gossip to the effect that he was a drunkard, an opportunist, and a liar, all combined with overwork and the unusually onerous anxieties springing out of the *Trent* crisis to depress Seward's usually ebullient spirits. Adams thought it evident, after reading Seward's unhappy letters to Weed, "that the difficulties of his position wear upon him. My wonder is that he has stood under them at all. In all my experience of public abuse and private slander of a statesman I have never known a parallel instance."[25]

In a private letter to the secretary of state, Adams denied having "given the smallest credit to any of the numerous charges which I have found circulating [in England] to the injury of your public and private character." He had "uniformly replied" to all who related such stories by asserting "that they were pure calumnies, and only a part of a system which I saw had been originated immediately on your accession to office, and persevered in with a ferocity beyond belief." Seward should not permit himself "to suspect for a moment that those who are acting under you suffer their confidence in you to be weakened" by slanders spread by enemies of all varieties. Adams believed that already a reaction in the secretary's favor was beginning to show itself both in America and in Europe. Had Seward's "bloodymindedness towards all Englishmen" been more than a ridiculous myth, the *Trent* affair could not have been peaceably settled. And people in London were beginning to show themselves "a little ashamed" of quoting the duke of Newcastle's strange story.[26]

These reassurances brought forth a reply in kind from a secretary of state seemingly restored to better spirits by rest and prospects of Union military victories. Expressing regret once more at the "ignoble" position in which he had been placed by calumnies and misunderstandings, Seward affirmed his belief that "all those lies" were gradually dying a natural death. Although he had prepared himself months before "for bonds or beheading," Seward wrote, he still "had no taste for martyrdom in the form of slander and defamation." He had, however, suppressed all "sensibilities except when Mr. Weed has 'tended' my wounds with the brave purpose of healing them." Adams himself had expressed a troubled attitude regarding reports circulated in Europe that some aspects of his chief's diplomacy were unappreciated even in Washington. "Nothing could be more erroneous" than such tales, Seward wrote. "Still it was not unnatural," he added, for both Adams and himself to suffer unjust criticism and even vicious slanders. For wars always created a "tempest of passion," in which, as during the *Trent* crisis, "everybody and every thing have of course been misunderstood." Such misunderstanding was "the penalty we must pay for the conscientious discharge of public duties."[27]

"I am inclined to believe," Charles F. Adams had written, "that the happening of the affair of the *Trent* just when it did, with just the issue that it had, was rather opportune than otherwise." Seward agreed. He, too, considered it "fortunate that the Trent affair occurred, even with all its exasperations." For festering animosities between the English and their Yankee cousins, which had been intensifying since the outbreak of the slaveholders' rebellion in America, had been alleviated by the favorable resolution of the crisis that had revealed them. Now, with serenity restored to the foreign relations of the United States, it was time to get on with the task of quelling the Southern insurrection and restoring tranquility to the American Union.[28]

Notes

CHAPTER I: THE DEPARTURE OF MASON AND SLIDELL

1. Chesnut, *Diary from Dixie*, 92, 124.

2. *ORN*, Ser. 2, III, 110; *Life of Mason*, 198. This memoir is useful for quotations from documents, but a new, more objective and thorough study is needed.

3. *ORN*, Ser. 2, III, 110–12. Mason may have been considered "intelligent, esteemed, and worthy" by Jefferson Davis, and Robert B. Rhett, Jr., may have really believed that "Mr. Mason and Mr. Slidell possess character, ability, and, what is no less important, eminent social fitness for their respective posts," but Mary Chesnut, daughter of a former governor, congressman, and U. S. senator from South Carolina, wrote in her diary, on hearing of Mason's appointment: "My wildest imagination will not picture Mr. Mason as a diplomat. He will say 'chaw' for 'chew,' and he will call himself 'Jeems,' and he will wear a dress coat to breakfast. . . . He will . . . chew tobacco. In England a man must expectorate like a gentleman. . . ." (*Charleston Mercury*, 29 Oct 61, p. 5; Chesnut, *Diary from Dixie*, 123–24.)

4. *ORN*, Ser. 2, III, 257–61.

5. *Ibid.*

6. *Ibid.*, 263–64.

7. *DAB* XVII, 209–11; *ORN*, Ser. 2, III, 112–14, 265–73; *Life of Mason*, 200. Two studies of Slidell's diplomacy are of little help to the serious historian. Willson, *Slidell*, is a fictionalized account, without documentation, devoted almost exclusively to Confederate diplomatic activity in Paris during the years from 1862 to 1865; while the same activity is barely summarized in Sears, *Slidell*, a book apparently based on very meager research.

8. *DAB* III, 191–92; *ORN*, Ser. 2, III, 112, 115; *Life of Mason*, 200.

9. Bulloch, *Secret Service* I, 117.

10. Trescot (1822–98), a Charleston lawyer, later became a Confederate army officer.

11. *ORN*, Ser. 2. III, 276–77.

12. *Ibid.*, 257, 265, 275–77.

13. *Ibid.,* 276–77.

14. *Ibid.,* 276–78.

15. *ORN,* Ser. 2, III, 281–82; *Life of Mason,* 200; Mason to Jefferson Davis, 11 Oct 61, Special Collections, Emory Univ.; *Charleston Mercury,* 31 Oct 61, p. 2.

16. *ORN,* Ser. 2, III, 282; *Life of Mason,* 200–201; *ORN,* Ser. 1, VI, 407. It took the U.S. consul at Nassau almost two weeks to get a dispatch off to Seward saying he had "learned from good authority that the so-called steamer *Theodora* is the Charleston packet *Gordon . . . ,*" and to report "that the steamer was en route to Havana with a large number of passengers on their way to England." (Whiting nos. 32, 33 to Seward, 25–26 Oct 61, NA.) I have found no indication that anyone in the State or Navy departments discerned from Whiting's dispatches that the *Theodora's* passengers included Mason and Slidell.

17. *Life of Mason,* 201–203; *ORN,* Ser. 2, III, 282–83.

18. *ORN,* Ser. 1, I, 113; DuPont, *Civil War Letters* I, 165.

19. *ORN,* Ser. 1, I, 114–17.

20. *ORN,* Ser. 2, III, 104–105, 225–26, 274–75, 284–86.

21. *Ibid.,* 284–85, 291–92.

22. *Life of Mason,* 202–203.

23. *Ibid.,* 202–204.

Chapter II: The British Anticipate a Crisis

1. Motley to Seward, 20 Sept 61, NA.

2. *ORN,* Ser. 1, I, 120–29, and Ser. 1, VI, 443–44, 454–55; Moran, *Journal,* 902, 911–12; Adams, Diary, 5–8 Nov 61, R76, and Adams to Marchand, 5 Nov 61, R166, both AP; Adams no. 69 to Seward, 8 Nov 61, NA; Morse to Sanford, 11 Nov 61, Box 139, SaP; Palmerston to Hammond, 9 Nov 61, FO391/7.

3. Palmerston to Hammond, 9 Nov 61, FO391/7.

4. Hammond to Palmerston, 9 Nov 61, GC/HA/248, PP.

5. Sir John Harding, queen's advocate; Sir Roundall Palmer, solicitor general; and Sir William Atherton, attorney general.

6. Hammond to Palmerston, 11 Nov 61, FO391/7; Palmerston to Delane, 11 Nov 61, AT.

7. Hammond to Palmerston, and Palmerston to Hammond, both 11 Nov 61, FO391/7; Palmerston to Delane, 11 Nov 61, AT.

8. Adams, Diary, 12 Nov 61, R76, AP; Adams "Confidential" to Seward, 15 Nov 61, NA; Palmerston to Delane, 11 Nov 61, AT.

9. Adams "Confidential" to Seward, 15 Nov 61, NA. The U.S. consul at Southampton believed that Palmerston had done Cdr. Marchand an injustice by suggesting that he was intemperate. (Weed to Seward, 11 Jan 62, SeP.)

10. Adams "Confidential" to Seward, 15 Nov 61, NA.

11. "We have had an alarm about the American ship, which we thought might be sent here to intercept the British packet with Mason & Slidell on board. Adams says it was all a false alarm & wonders at our susceptibility & exaggerated notions. Still, we are not quite out of the wood." (Russell to Lyons, 16 Nov 61, PRO30/22/96.)

12. Adams "Confidential" to Seward, 15 Nov 61, NA; C. F. Adams, Jr., "Trent Affair," 55.

13. Palmerston to Delane, 12 Nov 61, AT; *Letters of Queen Victoria, 1st Ser.* III, 467; Palmerston to Hammond, 12 Nov 61, and Palmerston to Russell, 13 Nov 61, both PRO30/22/21.

14. Italics added.

15. Encl. 1 to Russell no. 440 to Lyons, 30 Nov 61, FO115/249/III. See also Baxter, "Papers Relating to Belligerent and Neutral Rights," 84–86, and "The British Government and Neutral Rights," 15–16. Baxter does not attempt to treat the law officers' report in the context of contemporary events. He says "either the law officers changed their minds on what proved to be the crucial point [that of whether the envoys might be removed from the packet without also making it a prize], between their oral statement of November 11 and their written opinion dated the following day, or else, as seems more probable, Palmerston misunderstood their oral opinion. . . ." A third explanation, however, appears to me to be the correct one. Hammond's two memoranda to the prime minister, dated Nov 9 (GC/HA/248, PP) and Nov 11 (FO391/7), both indicate doubt whether the Southerners might not be taken out of the packet, but the latter memorandum declares that this question will be "decided hereafter." It seems obvious, therefore, that the point was left unresolved at the meeting of November 11, and was then ruled on for the first time by the law officers in their written opinion issued the next day.

16. Palmerston to Newcastle, 7 Nov 61, Add. MS 48,582, BM.

CHAPTER III: TWISTING THE LION'S TAIL

1. WP.

2. Warren, "The *Trent* Affair," 7, refers to "the forty-year-old Wilkes."

3. The sources from which this chapter has been drawn are as follows: (1) Capt. Charles Wilkes's official reports to the secretary of the navy, 15 and 16

Nov 61; Wilkes's instructions to Lt. Fairfax, 8 and 11 Nov 61; reports dated 12 or 13 Nov 61 to Wilkes from various officers or petty officers of the *San Jacinto* who participated in the seizure of Mason and Slidell on board the *Trent*; a statement about the seizure dated 9 Nov 61, addressed to Wilkes by the Southern emissaries, along with Wilkes's rejoinder to them, dated 13 Nov 61; subsequent official correspondence relating to the voyage of the *San Jacinto* from the coast of Cuba to Boston Harbor; and two official memoranda relating to the seizure of the Southern commissioners by Commander Richard Williams, R.N. (ret.), dated 9 and 27 Nov 61. All of these documents have been printed in *ORA*, Ser. 2, II, 1076–1115, *passim*. (2) D. MacNeill Fairfax, "Captain Wilkes's Seizure of Mason and Slidell," *Battles and Leaders of the Civil War* II, 135–42. (3) Virginia Mason, *The Public Life and Diplomatic Correspondence of James M. Mason*. (4) Charles D. Wilkes, manuscript "Diary, 1861," and his "Autobiography," both in Charles D. Wilkes Papers, LC. (5) Official log of U.S.S. *San Jacinto*, 4 Aug through 30 Nov 61. RG24, NA. (6) "The *Trent* Affair, November 8, 1861," *ORN*, Ser. 1, I, 64–65, 119–20, 129, *et seq*. (7) "Prisoners of War," Civil War Papers, Box 9, folders 61 and 81, RG59, NA. I have also cautiously drawn information from many newspapers and magazines. Among the most valuable secondary accounts are: (1) Daniel Henderson, *The Hidden Coasts*, a biography of Wilkes which unfortunately lacks citations of authorities; (2) R. M. Hunter, "The Capture of Mason and Slidell," a short eyewitness account; (3) William Jeffries, "The Civil War Career of Charles Wilkes," a Ph.D. dissertation; (4) John Long, "Glory-Hunting Off Havana: Wilkes and the Trent Affair," a short article; and (5) Gordon Warren, "The *Trent* Affair, 1861–1862," a Ph.D. dissertation. Two older works, often cited by others, I have elsewhere (*Civil War Books: A Critical Bibliography* I, 256, 270) dismissed as follows: (1) T. L. Harris, *The Trent Affair*, "Unscholarly, unreliable, and badly written," and (2) Evan John [Simpson], *Atlantic Impact, 1861*, "A short, dramatic, shallow account, lacking documentation and containing serious inaccuracies." See the bibliography at the end of this book for additional works of all classes and varying value which discuss the earliest stages of the *Trent* affair.

4. Sometimes referred to by her officers and crew as the "Saucy Jack." (*New York Daily Tribune*, 25 Nov 61, p. 5.)

5. The British Consul General, Joseph T. Crawford, later wrote Lyons "that I neither presented nor accompanied these gentlemen [Mason and Slidell] to the Captain-general, in uniform or otherwise." This protest notwithstanding, it is plain from Mason's account of his sojourn in Havana that

Crawford performed "many acts of courtesy and hospitality" for the Southerners, including a personal visit to the Spanish captain general to procure for them an interview on the following day. (*ORA*, Ser. 2, II, 1125.)

6. Shufeldt objected to seizing the Southern envoys from the *Trent*, declaring that such an act "would seem to be a violation of the rights of neutrals upon the ocean." (Shufeldt no. 79 to Seward, 9 Nov 61, NA.)

7. An international commission of arbitration later declared Wilkes at fault and awarded the sum of $9,500 to the French plaintiff. (Warren, "Trent Affair," 9.) The text of the official complaint of the French master appears in the *New York Times*, 20 Dec. 61, p. 2.

8. These were sailors. A second boat contained about ten Marines carrying muskets with bayonets attached.

9. He did. According to the Paris correspondent of the London *Daily News*, Slidell's dispatches were placed in his wife's hands before he left his cabin to go aboard the *San Jacinto*, and the Southern envoy allegedly told her to "sit at the port-hole, and that if an attempt was made to take the box from her, to drop it into the sea. Mrs. Slidell obeyed his orders, was not molested, and took the dispatches safely to England." (*New York Times*, 19 Dec 61, p. 1.)

10. According to one eyewitness of this episode, Moir supposedly exclaimed when Fairfax asked for his passenger list: " 'For a damned impertinent, outrageous puppy, give me, or don't give me, a Yankee. You go back to your ship, young man, and tell her skipper that you couldn't accomplish your mission, because we wouldn't let ye. I deny your right of search. D'ye understand that?' . . . As Captain Moir made his assertion regarding the right of search the passengers applauded." (Hunter, "The Capture of Mason and Slidell," 797–98.)

11. In a report made out almost three weeks later, Cdr. Richard Williams stated that he had told Fairfax: "In this ship I am the representative of Her Britannic Majesty's Government and in the name of that Government I protest against this illegal act—this violation of international law—this act of piracy which you would not dare to attempt on a ship capable of resisting such aggression."

12. Perhaps the most dramatic account of this portion of the episode was presented, early in December, at the Royal Western Yacht Club of England, by Cdr. Williams. Referring to published reports that Fairfax had denied "that the marines made a rush towards Miss Slidell at the charge with fixed bayonets," Williams proclaimed, nevertheless, clapping his hand over his heart, that, "as I hope for mercy on the day of Judgment, it is true that they

did so." When the Marines charged the helpless girl, the heroic English officer had "*just time to put my body between their bayonets and Miss Slidell* ... and I said to them ... 'Back you——cowardly poltroons.'" "Bravo!" and "Capital!" rang round the room as the commander terminated his narrative. In a mocking commentary on Williams's speech, a New York journalist wrote that all parties to the *Trent* affair now had authentic heroes—for the Americans had Wilkes; the rebels had Miss Slidell; and the English had Williams, "letter carrier to Her Majesty the Queen, exponent of international law, and general remonstrator and protector of indignant females in distress." The English people should be "very proud" of Williams, but "should never permit him to make speeches." (*New York Herald*, 30 Dec 61, p. 8, and 31 Dec 61, pp. 6, 7.)

13. A somewhat different version of this phase of the incident recounts that no less than thirty armed sailors and Marines followed Fairfax as he pursued Slidell to his stateroom, at which point "Miss Slidell" blocked the doorway and cried out: "'I swear to heaven you shall not go into this cabin to my father.' ... Just then Mr. Slidell began a most ungraceful movement out of the window of his cabin. ...'" (Hunter, "The Capture of Mason and Slidell," 798–99.)

14. Hunter, "The Capture of Mason and Slidell," says Matilda Slidell was "in the enjoyment of an aggravated attack of hysterics [with] other lady passengers similarly occupied."

15. Hunter, "The Capture of Mason and Slidell," declares that "Mr. Eustis ... was more violent than either of the principals, and made a demonstration in the direction of striking Lieutenant Greer with his fist. He passed into the boat *sans ceremonie.*"

16. As Slidell descended the *Trent*'s gangway, he allegedly called up to his wife: "Good-bye, my dear, we shall meet in Paris in 60 days." His prediction was exactly three weeks off the mark.

17. A story which was widely quoted from the Brooklyn *Times* alleged that when Slidell was residing in New York he stole away Wilkes's fiancée and married her, but Wilkes had never actually met his rival until the Southern envoy was brought aboard the *Trent*. "Such is the romance of war," a journalist commented. "We congratulate the bold Charles upon having at last 'got more than even.'" (*Boston Daily Evening Transcript*, 22 Nov 61, p. 4.) It was ironic that Wilkes and Fairfax, a New Yorker and an aristocratic Virginian, should have thus taken into custody another New Yorker and another aristocratic Virginian.

18. The second stateroom had been occupied by a passenger, Capt. Alfred

Taylor, U.S.N., who was carrying dispatches to Washington from the African coast.

19. Before leaving Havana, Wilkes later recalled, he had added to his ship's supplies "every provision for entertainment, particularly in the stores of eatables and drinkables, well knowing the propensities of these commissioners to indulge in the alcoholic beverage."

20. Although there were many British complaints that the capture had been rudely and violently accomplished, the pro-Confederate Liverpool *Mercury* later contradicted such statements "on the authority of a lady member of the family of one of the Commissioners," declaring that, on the contrary, Fairfax "behaved with the utmost courtesy, and personally conducted himself like an officer and a gentleman." (Quoted in *Daily National Intelligencer*, 24 Dec 61, p. 3.) Malakoff, meanwhile, wrote from Paris that a Spaniard, who was a passenger on the *Trent*, had told "everybody" in Paris "that the English accounts of the manner of arrest" of Mason, Slidell, and their secretaries were "grossly exaggerated." Fairfax and his men had been "very polite and proper." (*New York Times*, 24 Dec 61, p. 1.)

21. Writing a report of this incident the next day, Williams related that Fairfax also demanded that Capt. Moir "should proceed on board the San Jacinto, but as he expressed his determination not to go unless forcibly compelled likewise this latter demand was not carried into execution." I doubt whether such a "demand" was made. Possibly some kind of invitation was extended as a matter of courtesy. According to Lt. Greer, Cdr. Williams, "a pompous and shaggy little individual, . . . burst into a loud stream of talk about what he called this outrage on a British ship," and he "tried several times to get me into a discussion of the matter. I told him that I was not there for that purpose. He was very bitter." He threatened: " 'You take off these men if you dare! I will report the act at the Admiralty, and in twenty days England, England, sir, will open the blockade!' " Therefore, Williams added, "the Northerners might as well give up now. . . . Most all the officers of the vessel showed an undisguised hatred for the Northern people and a sympathy for the Confederates." (Greer's official report, printed in *ORA*, Ser. 2, II, 1084–85, was later supplemented by a more colorful recollection, found in the *New York Times*, 29 Nov 61, p. 6.)

22. Marshal Murray reported that the "traps" of the rebel commissioners brought ashore to Fort Warren included "six or eight trunks, six valises, several cases of brandies, wines and liquors, a dozen or more boxes of cigars, two casks (pints and quarts) of bottled Scotch ale." (*New York Daily Tribune*, 26 Nov 61, p. 8.)

23. One account, however, describes Fort Warren as a "pentagonal granite-hewn fortress, surrounded by a thirty-foot wide ditch," with scanty armaments and a relatively small garrison to guard approximately eight hundred confederate captives and prisoners of state. (Warren, "Trent Affair," 24.)

CHAPTER IV: UNION OPINION-MAKERS
CONFRONT THE *Trent* CRISIS

1. *Boston Daily Evening Transcript*, 22 Nov 61, p. 2.
2. In this chapter, I suggest the inaccuracy of the supposition, long accepted in British and American historical literature, that at the outset of the *Trent* affair Northerners were virtually unanimous in belligerence against England. Actually, press opinion in the North generally was at first elated but not bellicose, and later, as soon as uncertainty developed about the legality of the *Trent* seizure, the editors of most of the North's leading newspapers, without waiting to hear from London, called for conciliation and peaceful adjustment of any Anglo-American dispute that might arise out of the incident, even including, if necessary, the relinquishment of the rebel envoys. This trend among Northern journalists paralleled a similar development of points of view among influential private citizens. I regret that requisite cuts in the length of this book prior to publication forced me to omit a large number of quotations and much other evidence through which I had hoped vividly to demonstrate how "public opinion" developed as the *Trent* affair progressed.
3. *Boston Daily Evening Transcript*, 18 Nov 61, p. 2.
4. *Ibid.*, 18 Nov 61, p. 2, and 30 Nov 61, p. 2; *New York Times*, 17 Nov 61, pp. 1 and 4; *Albany Evening Journal*, 20 Nov 61, p. 2; *New York Daily Tribune*, 27 Nov 61, p. 5.
5. *New York Daily Tribune*, 18 Nov 61, pp. 4 and 5; *Boston Daily Evening Transcript*, 16 and 18 Nov 61, both p. 2, and 27 Nov 61, p. 1; *Albany Evening Journal*, 16 Nov 61, p. 3; *New York Times*, 17 Nov 61, pp. 1 and 4; *New York Herald*, 17 Nov 61, p. 1; *Daily National Intelligencer*, 18 Nov 61, p. 3; Monck to Newcastle, 24 Nov 61, NeC.
6. Lousada to Lyons, 17 Nov 61, LP; Trollope, *North America*, 138; *New York Times*, 17 Nov 61, p. 1, and 13 Dec 61, p. 4; *New York Herald*, 17 Nov 61, p. 1.
7. *Daily National Intelligencer*, 18 Nov 61, p. 3; *New York Times*, 17, 18, 19, 21, 22, and 24 Nov 61, all p. 4, and 23 Nov 61, p. 3; *ORA*, Ser. 2, II, 1098–99; *New York Daily Tribune*, 18, 21, and 23 Nov 61, all p. 4; *Albany Evening*

Journal, 18 Nov through 13 Dec 61, *passim*, especially 18 and 19 Nov 61, both p. 2.

8. *New York Times*, 18 Nov and 3 Dec 61, both p. 4, and 25 Nov 61, p. 5, and 26 Nov 61, pp. 4 and 8, and 27 Nov 61, pp. 2–4.

9. *New York Times*, 20 and 26 Nov 61, and 7 and 8 Dec 61, all p. 4, and 5 Dec 61, p. 2, and 8 Dec 61, pp. 1 and 4; *Washington Evening Star*, 12 Dec 61, pp. 1–2; *New York Herald*, 21 Nov 61, p. 2.

10. The most significant exception to this trend was the violently anti-British *New York Herald*, whose editor, James Gordon Bennett, consistently maintained that turning Mason and Slidell over to the British was "altogether out of the question," and who was possibly the only editor of an influential American newspaper to advocate fighting England rather than relinquishing the captured commissioners. This was a position consistent with Bennett's advocacy earlier in the year of a war against England in order to annex Canada. (*New York Herald*, 15 Nov 61, p. 4, and 16 Nov 61, p. 6, and 17 Nov 61, pp. 1 and 4, and 18 Nov 61, pp. 1 and 4, and 22 Nov 61, p. 4, and 6 Dec 61, p. 4.)

11. *Boston Daily Evening Transcript*, 19 Nov 61, p. 2, and 21 Nov 61, p. 1, and 29 Nov 61, p. 2, and 7 Dec. 61, p. 2; *New York Daily Tribune*, 22 Nov 61, p. 6, and 24 Dec 61, p. 6; Everett to Seward, 18 Nov 61, cited in Warren, "Trent Affair," 41–42; *New York Times*, 22 Nov 61, p. 6, and 4 Dec 61, p. 4; *Daily National Intelligencer*, 22 Nov 61, p. 2; Frothingham, *Everett*, 437; McLaughlin, *Cass*, 353–55; *ORA*, Ser. 2, II, 1127–39.

CHAPTER V: ON THE VERGE OF WAR

1. Newton, *Lyons* I, 15.

2. Britton to Adams, 21 Nov 61, R555, and Adams, Diary, 21 Nov 61, R76, both AP; Moran, *Journal*, 909.

3. *Insurgent Privateers*, 8–9. The *Nashville* had been sent to England to show Confederate naval power at close range and to display the Confederate flag in European waters. (Huse, *Supplies for the Confederate Army*, 32–33.)

4. Adams, Diary, 21 Nov 61, R76, AP; Morse no. 38 to Seward, 23 Nov 61, *London Consular Despatches*, vol. 29, NA.

5. Adams, Diary, 22–23 Nov 61, R76, AP; Morse no. 38 to Seward, 23 Nov 61, *London Consular Despatches*, vol. 29, NA; Moran, *Journal*, 909–10; *Insurgent Privateers*, 6–8.

6. Layard nos. 430 and 436 to Lyons, 23 and 28 Nov 61, w/numerous encls., FO115/248/VI and FO115/249/I.

7. *Insurgent Privateers*, 10; Hammond to Admiralty, 22 Nov 61, encl. to Layard no. 430 to Lyons, 23 Nov 61, FO115/248/VI; Adams, Diary, 23 Nov 61, R76, AP; Moran, *Journal*, 911; Russell to Layard, 23 Nov 61, Add. MS 38,987, BM. Palmerston was kept closely informed of developments in the *Nashville* case. (See, for example, Hammond to Palmerston, 21 Nov 61, GC/HA/249, PP, and Russell to Layard, Add. MS 38,987, BM.)

8. Adams, Diary, 22 Nov 61, R76, and Morse to Adams, 22 Nov 61, R555, both AP; *Insurgent Privateers*, 5–6, 10; Moran, *Journal*, 910; Morse no. 39 to Seward, 30 Nov 61, *London Consular Despatches*, vol. 29, NA.

9. Schuyler to Adams, 23 Nov 61, R555, and Adams to Schuyler, 25 Nov 61, R166, both AP.

10. Moran, *Journal*, 911–12; Moran to Adams, 25 Nov 61, R555, AP; Adams no. 79 to Seward, 29 Nov 61, NA. James Pike, U.S. minister at The Hague, wrote his colleague at Brussels: "That Nashville can be cut out & burned for 10,000 £, surely. There must be pluck enough & American sailors enough in London & Liverpool to do it. Damn neutrality." (Pike to Sanford, 23 Nov 61, Box 139, SaP.)

11. Layard to Russell, 24 Nov 61, and Russell to Layard, 25 Nov 61, both Add. MS 38,987, BM; Layard no. 436 to Lyons, 28 Nov 61, w/encl., FO115/249/I; *Insurgent Privateers*, 12–13.

12. Layard no. 436 to Lyons, 28 Nov 61, w/encl., FO115/249/I; Morse no. 39 to Seward, 30 Nov 61, *London Consular Despatches*, vol. 29, NA; Moran, *Journal*, 912, 918; C. Wilson to Seward, 27 Nov 61, reel 29, no. 13148, ALP; Morse to Adams, 6 Dec 61, R556, AP; London *Times*, 26 Nov 61, p. 9.

13. Milnes's backing of the Union cause did not prevent him from making jocular references to Adams as "the minister for the Dis-United States." (Pope-Hennessy, *Milnes* II, 167.)

14. Moran, *Journal*, 911 and 913; Henry Adams, *Education*, 119. Typically, the first secretary of the London legation did not even know where the minister was. He thought Adams was "spending a day in the country with Mr. Milner Gibson." (C. Wilson to Seward, 27 Nov 61, reel 29, no. 13148, ALP.)

15. Adams, Diary, 25–27 Nov 61, R76, AP.

16. *Ibid.*; Adams to Everett, 27 Nov 61, R166, AP.

17. Adams, Diary, 27 Nov 61, R76, and Adams, "Reminiscences," R296, and Moran (telegram) to Adams, 27 Nov 61, R555, all AP.

18. Adams, Diary, 27 Nov 61, R76, and Adams, "Reminiscences," R296, both AP; Toy, *Castles of Great Britain*, 123–25; D'Auvergne, *English Castles*, 192–98.

19. Adams, Diary, 27 Nov 61, R76, AP; Reid, *Forster* I, 343. In 1861,

Forster was Adams's best friend in England, "I might say," the American wrote in his diary on July 25, "the only real one." It is strange, however, that only four weeks before he joined Adams at Fryston Hall, Forster addressed a letter to "His Excellency J. Q. Adams," the U.S. minister in London. (Forster to Adams, 1 Nov 61, R555, AP.) Reid, *Milnes* I, 463–64, contains an inaccurate account of the Adams visit to Fryston Hall and the American envoy's receipt of the disquieting news of the *Trent* seizure.

20. Adams, Diary, 28 Nov 61, R76, AP; Moran, *Journal*, 914–15; Layard to Russell, 28 Nov 61, Add. MS 38, 987, BM; "Letters of John Bright, 1861–1862," MHSP XLV, 149.

21. Layard (3) to Russell, and Russell (3) to Layard, and Layard to Palmerston, and Palmerston to Layard, all 27 Nov 61, and Layard to Russell, 28 Nov 61, all Add. MS 38,987, BM; Russell, *Recollections*, 275.

22. Palmerston to Lewis, 27 Nov 61, GC/LE/236, PP. Unlike his colleague at the Foreign Office, Palmerston seemed not to consider the abduction of the Southerners from the *Trent* as an emergency requiring hasty cabinet action; rather did he appear to regard it as an unpleasant addition to a long series of irritations, which should be dealt with methodically in due course.

23. Lewis to Palmerston, 27 Nov 61, GC/LE/147, PP.

24. Palmerston to Gladstone, 29 Nov 61, Add. MS 44,272, BM; Palmerston to Layard, 29 Nov 61, Add. MS 38,987, BM; Palmerston to Russell, 29 Nov 61, PRO30/22/21; London *Times*, 29 Nov 61, p. 6. Some strange stories about the prime minister's actions at this time have crept into histories of the *Trent* affair. For example, a former diplomat recalled, *over forty years later*, that the premier's private secretary had told him (on the day the first cabinet meeting was held to consider the abduction of Mason and Slidell) "that Lord Palmerston, on entering the room where the Ministers met in Downing Street, threw his hat on the table, and at once commenced business by addressing his colleagues in the following words: 'I don't know whether you are going to stand this, but I'll be d———d if I do!'" (Rumbold, *Recollections* II, 83.) This may actually have happened, but I doubt it. Palmerston was habitually cool and careful in such exigencies, and there is nothing in contemporary correspondence to indicate that he was otherwise in this particular instance. Philip Guedalla, in his impressionistic biography of *Palmerston* (p. 465), repeats a story told *over half a century after the event* by George Putnam, who related that "some twenty years after the close of the war," he had been told, by a son of Confederate commissioner A. D. Mann, that "during the later months of 1861, Palmerston made a practice of coming from evening to evening to [Mann's] . . . office in Suffolk Street, Pall Mall,

East." On the evening of November 27, Mann's son allegedly related, "I remember very vividly the tall figures of Palmerston and my father standing before a map of the States ... which hung on the wall and deciding together at what points the first action of the British fleet or of the combined fleets could be taken to best advantage. New York and Philadelphia were to be assailed," and a combined French and British force was to sail up the Potomac River and capture Washington, after which, Palmerston was supposed to have exclaimed, "France and England will be in a position to demand the immediate cessation of the war and to exercise a rightful influence in regard to the terms of peace." (Putnam, *Memories*, 209–11; Putnam, "The London 'Times' and the American Civil War," p. 184.) Although often repeated, this story is unworthy of credit.

25. *Stanleys of Alderley*, 319; Argyll to Gladstone, 29 Nov 61, Add. MS 44,099, BM.

26. It is possible that Westbury was also absent from this meeting. (Cowley, *Secrets of the Second Empire*, 224.) London *Times*, 28 Nov 61, p. 9.

27. London *Times*, 28 Nov 61, p. 9.

28. *Ibid.*

29. *Ibid.*

30. Manchester *Guardian*, 28 Nov 61, p. 2; Birmingham *Daily Post*, 28 Nov 61, quoted in London *Times*, 29 Nov 61, p. 10; London *Chronicle* and London *News*, both 28 Nov 61, and both quoted in *New York Herald*, 13 Dec 61, p. 2.

31. London *Morning Post*, 28 Nov 61, quoted in the *New York Times*, 14 Dec 61, p. 4.

32. London *Times*, 29 Nov 61, p. 6. The full opinion of the crown law officers, dated 28 Nov, may be found as an enclosure in Russell no. 440 to Lyons, 30 Nov 61, FO115/249/III.

33. Adams to Everett, 27 Nov 61, R166, and Adams, Diary, 29 Nov 61, R76, both AP; Moran, *Journal*, 912 and 915; Adams nos. 78–80 to Seward, 29 Nov 61, NA.

34. Adams, Diary, 29 Nov 61, R76, AP; Adams no. 80 to Seward, 29 Nov 61, NA.

35. Russell no. 445 to Lyons, 30 Nov 61, FO115/249/V; Adams, Diary, 29 Nov 61, R76, AP; Adams no. 80 to Seward, 29 Nov 61, NA.

36. Baxter, "Papers Relating to Belligerent and Neutral Rights," 86–87; Guedalla, *Queen and Mr. Gladstone*, 123; *Letters of Queen Victoria, 1st Ser.* III, 595–97. The author of *Atlantic Impact*, Simpson, misinforms his readers

by claiming (p. 155) that Palmerston asked the crown law officers to alter their first opinion, made in relation to the *James Adger*, because: "Nothing else would satisfy Lord Palmerston, for nothing else would satisfy the English public, on whose support his career was dependent. That public was beginning to shout aloud. . . ." I do not think the prime minister, nearing the end of a long life, worried much about "his career" in dealing with the *Trent* affair.

37. *Letters of Queen Victoria, 1st Ser*. III, 595–96. Wilkes had no such orders.

38. *Stanleys of Alderley,* 319–20; *Letters of the Right Hon. Sir George Cornewall Lewis,* 405–406.

39. Palmerston to Russell, 1 Dec 61, PRO30/22/21; Tenterden to Gladstone, 17 Dec 70, Add. MS 44,428, BM; Morley, *Gladstone* II, 73–74; Argyll, *Memoirs* II, 179; Gibson to Cobden, 2 Dec 61, Add. MS 43,662, BM; "Letters of John Bright, 1861–1862," *MHSP* XLV, 149–50. It appears that within an hour or two after the British cabinet had determined upon its course of action in regard to the seizure of Mason and Slidell, the Confederate commissioners in London were furnished with full particulars. "What a noble statesman Lord Palmerston! His heart is as young as it was 40 years ago." So wrote one of the Southerners to the Confederate secretary of state in Richmond. (*ORN*, Ser. 2., III, 307.) I doubt whether Palmerston or any other member of the cabinet bothered to send the news directly to the Southern envoys. Rather should the above statement be attributed to the efforts of a pro-Southern subordinate in the British government, or, more likely yet, to supposition based on gossip and newspaper commentary.

40. Queen Victoria to Russell, 1 Dec 61, PRO30/22/21; Bell, *Palmerston* II, 294–95; Martin, *Prince Consort* V, 421–23; *Letters of Queen Victoria, 1st Ser*. III, 597. For a discussion of the role of the prince consort in the *Trent* affair, see Ferris, "The Prince Consort, 'The Times,' and the 'Trent' Affair."

41. Palmerston to Russell, 1 Dec 61, PRO30/22/21; Russell no. 444 to Lyons, 30 Nov 61, FO115/249/V.

42. Russell nos. 446–48 to Lyons, all 30 Nov 61, FO115/249/V.

43. Russell to Lyons, 1 Dec 61, PRO30/22/96.

CHAPTER VI: ENGLAND MOBILIZES FOR WAR

1. Add. MS 43,659, BM.

2. Lyons no. 678 to Russell, 19 Nov 61, FO115/258.

3. *Ibid.*

4. *Ibid.* I have found little evidence to support Lyons's estimate that the popular exultation in the North was owing principally to a conviction that England had been insulted, rather than simply to a belief that two diabolical traitors had been caught and were to be jailed. Lyons seemed to think that most Americans were obsessed by hatred for Great Britain.

5. *Ibid.*

6. Lyons nos. 674 of 18 Nov 61, and 677 and 682 both of 19 Nov 61, all to Russell, FO115/258.

7. Lyons nos. 677 and 678, both 19 Nov 61, FO115/258.

8. Hammond to Palmerston, 3 Dec 61, GC/HA/750/1–2, PP; Palmerston to Russell, 6 Dec 61, PRO30/22/21.

9. Lewis, *Letters of Sir George Cornewall Lewis*, 406; Cardwell to de Grey, 3 Dec 61, Add. MS 43,551, BM; *Stanleys of Alderley*, 320–21.

10. Gladstone to Argyll, 3 Dec 61, Add. MS 44,099, and Gladstone to Sir Robertson Gladstone, 7 Dec 61, Add. MS 44,532, both BM; Argyll, *Memoirs* II, 179–82.

11. Gibson to Cobden, 2 Dec 61, Add. MS 43,662, and Villiers to Bright, 3 Dec 61, Add. MS 43,386, both BM; Weed to Seward, 4 Jan 62, SeP; Cowley, *Secrets of the Second Empire*, 224.

12. Russell no. 447 to Lyons, 30 Nov 61, FO115/249/IV.

13. Coleridge, *Life and Correspondence of Coleridge* II, 11; Grote to Layard, 1 Dec 61, Add. MS 38,987, BM.

14. London *Morning Post*, 28 Nov 61, as quoted in *New York Times*, 14 Dec 61, p. 4; Manchester *Guardian*, 28 Nov 61, p. 2.

15. *New York Daily Tribune*, 19 Dec 61, p. 6.

16. *Ibid.*, 25 Dec 61, p. 8.

17. Lyons to Russell, 22 Nov 61, PRO30/22/35.

18. *Ibid.*

19. J. Russell, *Later Correspondence* II, 321–22; Russell to Clarendon, 6 Dec 61, CP.

20. Russell to Lyons, 7 Dec 61, PRO30/22/96. Randall (*Lincoln the President* II, 47–48) argues that the "diplomatic maneuver" of the British "can hardly be regarded as an ultimatum in the accepted sense of that word." Even if one adopts Randall's own criteria, which hold that "an ultimatum involves a situation in which all the elements—demand, time limit, and threat as to what would happen on non-compliance—are communicated to the threatened government," it is evident that the British demand was clearly

and concretely presented; that the time limit was known; and that the frantic military preparations in England and in Canada, the sudden shipment of thousands of fighting men to Canada, and the posting of a large number of warships to the North American station, all together comprised a threat the nature of which was obvious to American political leaders, as well as to the American press and public. Lyons's official dispatches and private letters, not to mention the reports of Lyons's diplomatic colleagues in Washington, none of which Randall apparently read, clearly show that an ultimatum was delivered.

21. Russell to Layard, 27 Nov 61, and Layard to Russell, 28 Nov 61, both Add. MS 38,987, BM; Palmerston (2) to Russell, both 29 Nov 61, PRO30/ 22/21.

22. Palmerston (2) to Russell, both 29 Nov 61, PRO30/22/21; Palmerston to Granville, 29 Nov 61, PRO30/29/18.

23. Somerset to Lewis, 1 Dec 61, GCLP.

24. The two leaders of the Conservative Party, Benjamin Disraeli and the earl of Derby.

25. Palmerston to Lewis, 2 Dec 61, GCLP.

26. Lewis to Palmerston, 2 and 3 Dec 61, both GC/LE/148–49, PP.

27. Russell to Palmerston, 7 [?] Dec 61, GC/RU/683, PP.

28. Palmerston to Russell, 6 [?] Dec 61, PRO30/22/21. This letter is obviously an answer to Russell's note, previously cited, which was dated 7 Dec.

29. Palmerston allegedly wrote the queen on 5 Dec that "A War Committee will meet tomorrow at 2 o'clock at the War Department to consider generally the precautionary measures the best to be adopted." (Connell, *Regina Vs. Palmerston*, 347.) My guess is that Palmerston's note bore the date of December 8.

30. Mackay to Layard, 4 and 6 Dec 61, Add. MS 39,102, BM; Monck to Newcastle, 22 Nov 61, NeC; Milne to Somerset, 24 Jan 62, 107/1, Milne Papers; Bourne, *Britain and the Balance of Power*, 212–28, 238–45. (See also Winks, *Canada and the United States*, 81–88; Rhodes, *History of the United States* II, 526; Martin, *Prince Consort* V, 419n; Stacey, *Canada and the British Army*, 119–21; Hitsman, "Winter Troop Movement to Canada, 1862," 127– 35; British *Sessional Papers* LXXII, 663; *Hansard's*, 3d Ser., CLXV, 396; and contemporary newspapers.) As far as I can tell, Bourne's figures appear correct and his narrative accurate, which cannot be said of most other accounts, but Bourne is the only scholar, I believe, who has examined most of the pertinent archival sources. Among the papers mentioned by Bourne, relative to

the question of British military reinforcements to Canada during December, I should say that two memoranda by de Grey, dated 8 and 13/17 Dec 61, both in GCLP, are most important.

31. Maxwell, *Clarendon* II, 250; Bourne, *Britain and the Balance of Power*, 245.

32. Wilding to F. W. Seward, 29 Nov 61, corroborated by Dudley to Seward, 11 Dec 61, both *Liverpool Consular Despatches*, vol. 20, and Morse nos. 40–41 to Seward, 29 Nov 61, and Morse no. 43 to Seward, 6 Dec 61, all *London Consular Despatches*, vol. 29, all NA.

33. *New York Daily Tribune*, 23 Dec 61, p. 7; Weed to Seward, 2, 5 and 6 Dec 61, SeP.

34. Cobden to Paulton, 1 Dec 61, Add. MS 43,662, BM; *New York Times*, 25 Dec 61, p. 1; Adams no. 84 to Seward, 6 Dec 61, NA.

35. Adams, Diary, 29 Nov 61, R76, AP; Henry Adams, *Education*, 125–26, 183–84, 187–92. Bright wrote a friend: "I spent a long evening with Adams. I found him quiet and serious. He believed the seizure of the Commissioners to be without authority from the government and he thought the act unfortunate and impolitic." Adams seemed far from sanguine and, to Bright, overly passive in the emergency. The Englishman wondered if "a man of more force would be better for his government in any transactions with ours in the present state of affairs." (Bright to Cobden, 9 Dec 61, RCP.) Weed, too, had written even before he arrived in England that he was "not sure that Mr. Adams is the man we so much need" in Europe; the United States, he believed, would fare better with "the services of a live, live man (like the Rev. Dr. M'Clintock) abroad." (Weed to Sanford, 20 Oct 61, Box 132, SaP.) Louis Mallet received the impression from Weed in London that the United States was "wretchedly represented" there; that "Adams has done nothing here—neglected the Press and wasted his time." (Mallet to Cobden, 8 Dec 61, RCP.) M'Clintock, however, wrote: "I think Adams suits them very well [in London]. He is a cold, cautious man—very much of an Englishman himself—and really will do more good there than a man of more impulsive nature could do." (Crooks, *M'Clintock*, 303.)

36. Adams, Diary, 30 Nov 61, R76, AP. The minister's quaint parable notwithstanding, the British position was sound. As the secretary at the Methodist Mission house in London commented: "We give every policeman the right to arrest a person accused and carry him before a tribunal; but let the highest police officer in the land assume to deal out justice and he will soon be dismissed." George T. Curtis, in a letter to the Boston *Journal*, put

the same argument into judicial terminology. (Crooks, *M'Clintock*, 311; *ORA*, Ser. 2, II, 1137–39.)

CHAPTER VII: A DESPERATE STRUGGLE FOR PEACE BEGINS

1. Henry Adams, *Education*, 119; Adams no. 81 to Seward, 29 Nov 61, NA. Adams, Diary, 30 Nov 61, R76, AP.

2. W. C. Ford, *Cycle* I, 75–76; H. Adams to C. F. Adams, Jr., 30 Nov 61, R555, AP.

3. Moran, *Journal*, 917. Some writers have allowed themselves poetic license in describing the clamor in Great Britain. Carl Sandburg, wrote for example, that the "London *Morning Chronicle* tore its hair." (Sandburg, *War Years* I, 362.)

4. Bigelow, *Retrospections* I, 412; Reid, *Milnes* II, 75; Coleridge, *Life and Correspondence of Coleridge* II, 11; Adams, Diary, 4 Dec 61, R76, AP; Reid, *Forster* I, 343–44.

5. Morley, *Cobden*, 571, 574; Hobson, *Cobden*, 292–94; Adams, Diary, 3 and 6 Jan 62; R77, AP; Cobden to Layard, 29 Nov 61, Add. MS 39,101, BM.

6. *New York Daily Tribune*, 19 Dec 61, p. 7.

7. Villiers to Bright, 3 Dec 61, Add. MS 43,386, BM.

8. Cobden to Bright, 3 Dec 61, RCP.

9. Bright, *Speeches on Questions of Public Policy* I, 167–95, *passim*.

10. *Ibid*. Regarding "the tone of the Times and other Newspapers," Edward Twisleton wrote, there was "no doubt" that they had contributed to the "very bitter feeling in the North against England. . . ." (Twisleton to Lewis, 28 Nov 61, GCLP.) Argyll, too, observed sadly that a great part of the passionate hatred which has made this outrage so popular in America has flowed directly from the insulting & taunting articles of the 'Times,' & the other Papers." (Argyll to Gladstone, 7 Dec 61, Add. MS 44,099, BM.)

11. Bright, *Speeches on Questions of Public Policy* I, 167–95, *passim*. According to Thomas Dudley, who sat beside Bright while he delivered his Rochdale address, Bright was at the time "exceedingly depressed" because Cobden, reluctant to make the political sacrifice, had refused to join Bright in speaking at the meeting. (Dudley, "Three Critical Periods," 40–42.) Dudley must have misunderstood Bright, who knew perfectly well that Cobden had a serious bronchial condition and had determined not to aggravate it by speaking at *any* public meeting that winter. (Cobden to Sumner,

27 Nov 61, Add. MS 43,676, BM.) It was Cobden, however, who, besides writing Senator Sumner in Washington several long letters urging a pacific approach to the *Trent* question, also encouraged the secretary of the English Peace Society, the Rev. Henry Richard, to demand arbitration of the incident. (Cobden to Richard, 3 Dec 61, Add. MS 43,659, BM; London *Times*, 11 Dec 61, p. 5.)

12. Trevelyan, *Bright*, 313; Clay to Bright, 13 Dec 61, Add. MS 43,391, BM.

13. Trevelyan, *Bright*, 313; Bigelow to Bright, 8 Dec 61, Add. MS 43,390, and Clay to Bright, 13 Dec 61, and Dudley to Bright, 6 Dec 61, both Add. MS 43,391, all BM. The latter file contains dozens of letters from Americans thanking Bright for his Rochdale speech.

14. Mallet to Bright, 6 Dec 61, Add. MS 43,389, BM; Cobden to Bright, 6 Dec 61, RCP; Morley, *Cobden*, 571–72. William Gladstone, however, lamented that "John Bright and John Bull seem to agree worse and worse, and I see no prospect of reconciliation." It was, Gladstone thought, naïve of Bright to think that a Northern victory in the American Civil War would ensure the triumph of democracy in the New World. For the fact was that the conflict was "doing immense mischief, not merely to democratic but to all popular and liberal principles whatever." (Gladstone to Denison, 16 Aug 61, Add. MS 44,532, BM.)

15. Bright to Gibson, 7 Dec 61, Add. MS 43,388, BM.

16. *Ibid.* Bright wrote Bigelow that he was doing all he could to persuade British leaders to adopt "a prudent and friendly course" toward the United States. But he had "no influence" with Palmerston or the Foreign Office; all he could do was "to urge certain members" of the cabinet "to avoid the bottomless pit into which they may be tempted to be drawn." (Bigelow, *Retrospections* I, 459.)

17. Bright to Cobden, 9 Dec 61, RCP.

18. London *Times*, 6 Dec 61, p. 6 and 7 Dec 61, p. 8; *Punch* XLI (21 Dec 61), 246. Preceding the *Times*'s second blast at Bright was an editorial calling Jefferson Davis "one of the most vigorous and astute politicians that America has produced," and praising the Confederate president's message to the Southern Congress as "a bold and confident manifesto."

19. Gasparin, *A Word of Peace*, 6; *Correspondence of Motley* II, 218–19, 223.

20. Adams to Motley, 4 Dec 61, R166, AP.

21. Clarendon to Granville, 14 Sept 61, PRO30/29/29.

22. Weed to Seward, 4 Dec 61, & Hughes to Seward, 5 and 11 Dec 61, all

SeP; Fogg to Adams, 2 Dec 61, R556, AP; Judd no. 14 to Seward, 14 Dec 61, and Adams no. 84 to Seward, 6 Dec 61, both NA. On the same subject, see Adams to Fogg, 9 Dec 61, R166, AP; Schurz no. 44 to Seward, 7 Dec 61, and Marsh no. 34 to Seward, 23 Dec 61, both NA.

23. Sanford no. 2 to Seward, 12 May 61, NA; Sanford to Seward, 2 (2) and 9 Dec 61, Box 99, and Sanford to Seward, 3 Dec 61, and Sanford to Beckwith, 7 Dec 61, both Box 100, all SaP; Sanford "private" to Seward, 5, 13, 17 and 31 Dec 61, NA.

24. The terms of the British ultimatum were read by Russell to the French ambassador in London on November 29. At once they were forwarded to Paris. (Flahault to Thouvenel, 30 Nov 61, vol. 8, Papiers de Thouvenel, FMAE, MD.)

25. See, for example, Marsh nos. 32 and 36 to Seward, 9 Dec 61 and 6 Jan 62, and Schurz no. 43 to Seward, 30 Nov 61, and Perry no. 17 to Seward, 28 Dec 61, and Clay no. 13 to Seward, 10 Dec 61, and Sanford "private and confidential" to Seward, 2 Dec 61, all NA.

26. Marsh no. 32 to Seward, 9 Dec 61, NA; Adams to Motley, 26 Dec 61, R166, AP.

27. Cowley to Crampton, 3 Dec 61, FO519/229; Case and Spencer, *US & France: CW Diplomacy*, 196–97.

28. Flahault to Thouvenel, 30 Nov 61, vol. 8, Papiers de Thouvenel, FMAE, MD; Cowley nos. 1397 and 1409 to Russell, 3 and 5 Dec 61, FO27/1399. Thouvenel showed Cowley a note from Napoleon saying that he thoroughly approved of the British ultimatum and that they were to be assured of his "full sympathy to the end." (Cowley to Russell, 5 Dec 61, PRO30/22/56.)

29. Thouvenel no. 32 to Mercier, 3 Dec 61, vol. 125, FMAE, AD, EU. A translation of Thouvenel's dispatch is found in Case and Spencer, *US & France: CW Diplomacy*, 202–204, in the course of an able discussion of its formulation and its impact, both in London and in Washington.

30. Russell to Palmerston, 6 Dec 61, GC/RU/682, PP; Russell no. 457 to Lyons, 6 Dec 61, FO115/249/V; Palmerston to Russell, 6 Dec 61, PRO30/22/21. Russell wrote Cowley that Thouvenel's dispatch "will, I think, have its effect, and may give Lincoln a loophole—unless the Devil looks over him as he does over his namesake." This last was probably a reference to the Duke of Newcastle. (Russell, *Later Correspondence* II, 321–22.)

31. Lewis, *Letters of Sir George Cornewall Lewis*, 406–407; Cowley to Bulwer, 5 Dec 61, FO519/229; Cowley to Layard, 5 Dec 61, Add. MS 39,102, BM; Cowley to Hammond, 6 Dec 61, FO391/5.

32. Cowley, *Secrets of the Second Empire*, 223–25.

33. Cowley no. 1404 to Russell, 3 Dec 61, FO27/1399.

34. McIlvaine to Chase, 26 Oct and 6 Nov 61, and Hughes to Seward, 29 Oct and 13 and 20 Nov 61, and Weed to Seward, 6 Nov 61, all SeP; Hughes to Weed, 29 Oct 61, and Seward to Weed, 7 Nov 61, both WP; *Seward at Washington* II, 20. Randall, among others, has suggested that "In Paris . . . Weed was an informal emissary of Seward." (Randall, *Lincoln the President* II, 46.) This is untrue. Shortly after Hughes and Weed arrived in England, Russell received word from Lyons that it was "generally supposed" in the United States that the two men had been commissioned by the Lincoln administration "to counteract the endeavours" of Mason and Slidell in Europe. Lyons admitted, however, that he had "no ground but the general public belief, for supposing that either Dr. Hughes or Mr. Weed has any mission from this government, or indeed that either has any political object in visiting Europe." (Lyons no. 633 to Russell, 8 Nov 61, FO115/257.)

35. Hughes to Seward, 20 Nov 61, SeP; London *Times*, 28 Nov 61, p. 6; *Albany Evening Journal*, 20 Dec 61, p. 2.

36. *New York Times*, 24 Dec 61, p. 1; Cowley to Russell, 2 Dec 61, PRO30/22/56.

37. Cowley to Russell, 29 Nov and 2 Dec 61, both PRO30/22/56; Cowley to Layard, 2 Dec 61, Add. MS 39,102, BM. The rumor about Scott's alleged assertion that the Washington cabinet initiated the *Trent* seizure probably came to France via a British newspaper. (*Letters of Queen Victoria*, 1st Ser. III, 595–96.) But it might also have originated with Archbishop Hughes, who proudly wrote Seward that he had told Americans and "distinguished French gentlemen" alike, who anxiously called on him at his Paris hotel on November 28, that the *Trent* capture (about which he actually knew almost nothing) had been "a measure of wisdom and necessity." Lincoln's cabinet, Hughes said he had added, would not "shrink in the least from the ordeal" of war with England, should hostilities be initiated because of the abduction of Mason and Slidell. (Hughes to Seward, 28 Nov 61, SeP.) There was also support in U.S. newspapers for Cowley's supposition. The Washington correspondent of the New York *Evening Post*, for example, had written (early enough for Cowley to have read his words) that, shortly before the Southern commissioners were taken from the *Trent*, "persons in the State Department were engaged in looking up this subject, which would indicate that Mr. Seward is prepared for it." That the seizure was legal, the *Post*'s correspondent affirmed, "is given as the opinion of an important *attaché* of the State Department, and as a slight indication of the course the Secretary of State will pursue in the matter. Mr. Seward will not only take the ground that the

act was perfectly justifiable, but he might, if he pleased, make a demand upon Lord Lyons for the surrender of the vessel." (Reprinted in *Albany Evening Journal*, 20 Nov 61, p. 2.) This erroneous information probably came from Adam Gurowski.

38. Cowley to Layard, 2 Dec 61, Add. MS 39,102, BM; Doyle to Cowley, 3 Dec 61, encl. to Cowley no. 1404 to Russell, 3 Dec 61, FO27/1399.

39. Bigelow, *Retrospections* I, 387–90; Weed to Seward, 2 Dec 61, SeP; London *Times*, 6 Dec 61, p. 7; E. D. Adams, *GB & Amer. CW* I, 218.

40. Bigelow, *Retrospections* I, 396–97; Cobden to Slagg, 6 Dec 61, Add. MS 43,676, and Cobden to Richard, 6 Dec 61, Add. MS 43,659, both BM; M'Clintock to Arthur, 4 Dec 61, Special Collections, Emory Univ.

41. Weed to Seward, 2, 4, and 5 Dec 61, SeP.

42. Weed to Seward, 6 Dec 61, SeP; Cobden to Bright, 7 Dec 61, RCP; Bright, *Diaries*, 257–58. Palmerston was aware of Weed's presence in London and mentioned him to the queen as having allegedly advised Seward "to yield to the British demands absolutely and immediately." (Connell, *Regina Vs. Palmerston*, 347.) The standard biography of Weed is by Glyndon Van Deusen. An *Autobiography* and a *Memoir* of Weed by Barnes are both unreliable.

CHAPTER VIII: THE "BÊTE NOIRE"

1. *Cycle* I, 88–89.

2. London *Times*, 29 Nov 61, p. 5; Arthur to M'Clintock, 29 Nov 61, and M'Clintock to Arthur, 30 Nov 61, both Special Collections, Emory Univ.

3. Arthur to M'Clintock, 30 Nov 61, Special Collections, Emory Univ. Three days later, specifically in response to M'Clintock's inquiry, Arthur wrote that it was indeed "seriously believed on all hands that Seward wishes a war." Among the few British leaders who, according to the English pastor, "know better & look deeper," the opinion prevailed that Seward desired rather "to make capital out of a show of menacing us, & this is to *men* the more offensive supposition of the two." (Arthur to M'Clintock, 2 Dec 61, Special Collections, Emory Univ.)

4. M'Clintock to Arthur, 2 Dec 61, Special Collections, Emory Univ.

5. Weed to Seward, 2 and 4 Dec 61, SeP; M'Clintock to Arthur, 4 Dec 61, Special Collections, Emory Univ.

6. *Albany Evening Journal*, 30 Dec 61, p. 2; Weed to Seward, 6 Dec 61, SeP; Weed to Hughes, 7 Dec 61, copy in WP.

7. Sideman and Friedman, *Europe Looks at the Civil War*, 101; London

Daily News, quoted in *New York Daily Tribune,* 16 Dec 61, p. 5; London *Times,* 2 Dec 61, p. 6.

8. London *Morning Post,* quoted in both *Boston Daily Evening Transcript,* 16 Dec 61, p. 1, and *New York Daily Tribune,* 16 Dec 61, p. 5; Edinburgh *Scotsman,* quoted in *New York Times,* 20 Dec 61, p. 6; Fergusson's report found in GC/DE/70/2–7, PP.

9. Cowley, *Secrets of the Second Empire,* 223.

10. Lyons to Russell, 19 Nov 61, PRO30/22/35; Weed to Seward, 5 and 7 Dec 61, both SeP; Adams to C. F. Adams, Jr., 3 Jan 62, R557, AP; "Letters of John Bright, 1861–1862," 152; Arthur to M'Clintock, 4 Dec 61, Special Collections, Emory Univ.

11. Argyll, *Memoirs* II, 182; Newcastle to Monck, 5 Dec 61, NeC; Villiers to Bright, 14 Dec 61, Add. MS 43,386, BM.

12. Odo Russell to Layard, 8 Dec 61, Add. MS 39,102, BM; Marsh no. 36 to Seward, 6 Jan 62, and Motley no. 3 to Seward, 20 Jan 62, both NA; Kean, *Inside the Confederate Government,* 17; Malakoff in *New York Times,* 24 Dec 61, p. 1.

13. *New York Times,* 22 Nov 61, p. 8.

14. *Cycle* I, 75–76.

15. London *Times,* 14 Dec 61, p. 7.

16. Adams, Diary, 13 Dec 61, R76, AP; *Albany Evening Journal,* 13 Dec 61, p. 2; London *Times,* 14 Dec 61, p. 6; Weed to Seward, 16 Dec 61, SeP. This episode is recounted in Weed, *Memoir,* 354–61.

17. London *Times,* 14 Dec 61, p. 6.

18. *Seward at Washington* I, 471; London *Chronicle* editorial, widely reprinted or referred to in American newspapers, such as the *New York Times,* 26 and 27 Dec 61, both p. 4; the *New York Daily Tribune,* 27 Dec 61, p. 6; and the *Albany Evening Journal,* 27 Dec 61, p. 2.

19. London *Times,* 14 Dec 61, p. 7; *Albany Evening Journal,* 30 Dec 61, p. 2; Weed to Seward, 6, 7, and 10 Dec 61, and 22 Jan 62, SeP; Mallet to Cobden, 8 Dec 61, RCP.

20. Weed to Seward, 7, 18, and 25 Dec 61, SeP; Weed to Hughes, 7 and 22 Dec 61, copies in WP.

21. Clipping from London *Daily Telegraph* annexed to Weed to Seward, 8 Jan 62, SeP. Seward's own comment on this letter was that the *Telegraph* story "was utterly groundless. My speech in Canada was so flattering to the *British* that the *French* took offense." (Seward to Weed, 30 Jan 62, WP.) Joseph G. Whelan (in "William Henry Seward, Expansionist") says that

throughout his public career Seward adhered to the belief that "the American Republic . . . could expand . . . not by war and conquest, but by peace."

22. London *Times*, 2 and 9 Dec 61, both p. 6.

23. London *Times*, 2 Dec 61, p. 6.

24. London *Times*, 14 Dec 61, p. 6; article from *Saturday Review*, 30 Nov 61, quoted in *ibid.*, 2 Dec 61, p. 8.

25. Adams no. 93 to Seward, 20 Dec 61, NA; London *Times*, 2, 9, and 14 Dec 61, all p. 6; Weed to Seward, 2 Dec 61, SeP.

26. Adams no. 93 to Seward, 20 Nov 61, NA.

27. *Ibid.*

28. Seward, *Works* IV, 394–95, 405–406.

29. *Ibid.*, 646; *New York Times*, 24 Dec 60, p. 8.

30. *New York Times*, 24 Dec 61, p. 8; Head to Lewis, 17 Feb 61, GCLP.

31. *New York Herald*, 15 Nov 61, p. 4, and 16 Nov 61, p. 6, and 17 Dec 61, p. 6, and 21 Dec 61, p. 4, and 31 Dec 61, p. 6.

32. *New York Daily Tribune*, 31 Dec 61, p. 4.

33. Ever since Bancroft published his biography of Seward over seventy years ago, in which he spoke approvingly of "the balance of good judgment that characterized Lord Lyons," while often criticizing Seward for lacking this quality, the legend of the latter's intemperate brusquerie has won almost universal acceptance among historians. (Bancroft, *Seward* II, 298–99, 370–72.)

34. Thornton, *Nine Lives of Citizen Train*, 115–20; *New York Herald*, 30 Dec 61, p. 8; Walden no. 198 to Russell, 9 Dec 61, encl. to Hammond no. 478 to Lyons, 14 Dec 61, FO115/250/III.

35. Trollope, *North America*, 139.

36. *New York Daily Tribune*, 21 Nov 61, p. 4; Lyons to Russell, 22 Nov 61, with encl. clipping from Sunday *Evening Transcript*, 17 Nov 61, PRO30/22/35. Lyons, in suggesting that the editor of the *Transcript* gave an accurate portrayal of American public opinion on the *Trent* question, once again showed his considerable powers of imagination.

37. Pierce, *Sumner* IV, 48–49; Bright to Cobden, 4 Nov 61, RCP; Weed to Seward, 31 Dec 61, SeP; Adams, Diary, 6 Dec 61, R76, AP.

38. Adams to Seward, 31 Jan 62, SeP.

39. Twisleton to Lewis, 28 Nov and 4 Dec 61, both GCLP.

40. Lyons nos. 740 and 742 to Russell, both 6 Dec 61, FO115/258 and 259.

41. *New York Times*, 22 Nov 61, p. 8; Sanford "private" to Seward, 5 Nov 61, NA. The only important American I have discovered offering ad-

verse criticism of Seward's October imprisonment note to Lyons was Senator Sumner, who called it "unfortunate." (Lieber to Sumner, 28 Dec [?] 61, LI3501, HL.)

42. *The Saturday Review* XII, no. 321 (21 Dec 61), pp. 624–27.

43. *New York Daily Tribune*, 17 Dec 61, p. 5. Of course there were no such offensive "earlier despatches." With few exceptions, Seward had published those containing his strongest expressions.

44. Lieber to Sumner, 19 Dec 61, LI3498, HL; *New York Daily Tribune*, 18 Dec 61, p. 4.

45. Weed to Seward, 4 Jan 62, SeP; Weed to Blatchford, 12 Jan 62, WP; Russell to Lyons, 28 Nov [probably Dec] 61, PRO30/22/96. It should be added, however, that Weed himself recalled, in a letter to Seward, that he had asked him earlier in the year, "when you read me an important Despatch to Mr. Adams, whether it could not be softened." (Weed to Seward, 7 Jan 62, SeP.)

46. London *Times*, 3 Dec 61, p. 8, and 10 Dec 61, p. 9.

47. *Ibid.*, 2 and 9 Dec 61, both p. 6, and 10 Dec 61, p. 8.

48. *Illustrated London News* XXXIX, no. 1120 (7 Dec 61), p. 573; Cyrus Redding, "England and America," *The New Monthly Magazine* CXXIV (Jan. 1862), p. 65; *Punch* XLI (14 Dec 61), p. 236.

49. Cowley, *Secrets of the Second Empire*, 225; Argyll to Gladstone, 29 Nov 61, Add. MS 44,099, BM.

50. *Stanleys of Alderley*, 321; Twisleton to Lewis, 4 Dec 61, GCLP.

51. Palmerston to Russell, n.d. (*ca.* Jan 62), PRO30/22/21; Connell, *Regina Vs. Palmerston*, 347.

CHAPTER IX: CHALLENGED BY AN ANGRY LION

1. *New York Daily Tribune*, 21 Nov 61, p. 4.

2. *New York Herald*, 9 Dec 61, pp. 1 and 4; *New York Times*, 9 Dec 61, pp. 2 and 4; *New York Daily Tribune*, 9 Dec 61, pp. 4 and 6, and 13 Dec 61, p. 6; *Boston Daily Evening Transcript*, 10 Dec 61, p. 2; *Daily National Intelligencer*, 10 Dec 61, p. 3; *Albany Evening Journal*, 9 Dec 61, p. 2.

3. *New York Times*, 9 Dec 61, p. 2; *Albany Evening Journal*, 10 Dec 61, p. 2.

4. *New York Times*, 13 Dec 61, pp. 1 and 4; *Daily National Intelligencer*, 13 Dec 61, p. 3, and 14 Dec 61, p. 2.

5. *New York Times*, 16 Dec 61, pp. 1 and 4; *Boston Daily Evening Tran-*

script, 16 Dec 61, p. 1; *Albany Evening Journal*, 16 Dec 61, p. 2. Similar headlines appeared in the *Daily National Intelligencer*, 16 Dec 61, p. 3, and the *New York Daily Tribune*, 16 Dec 61, pp. 1 and 4, and the *New York Herald*, 16 Dec 61, p. 1, and in many more Northern newspapers.

6. *Albany Evening Journal*, 16 Dec 61, p. 2; *New York Times*, 16 Dec 61, pp. 4 and 5; *New York Daily Tribune*, 17 Dec 61, pp. 4, 5 and 6.

7. *New York Herald*, 16 Dec 61, p. 4, and 17 Dec 61, p. 6.

8. *Albany Evening Journal*, 16 Dec 61, p. 2; *New York Daily Tribune*, 17 Dec 61, p. 4.

9. *Boston Daily Evening Transcript*, 16 Dec 61, p. 2.

10. *New York Times*, 15, 16, and 17 Dec 61, all p. 4.

11. *Ibid.*, 16 Dec 61, p. 4. The *New York Herald*, 17 Dec 61, p. 7, printed a collection of comments on the British ultimatum from leading newspapers in Philadelphia, Baltimore, Pittsburgh, Louisville, Cincinnati, Cleveland, Detroit, Chicago, and Buffalo, which exhibited a wide variety of opinion about how the United States government should respond. Recommendations ranged all the way from declaring war against England, to seeking arbitration, to apologizing and releasing the captured Southern envoys.

12. *New York Herald*, 19 Dec 61, p. 2; *Albany Evening Journal*, 21 Dec 61, p. 3; *New York Daily Tribune*, 19 Dec 61, p. 7; *Albany Evening Journal*, 21 Dec 61, p. 3, and 26 Dec 61, p. 2; *New York Times*, 19 Dec 61, pp. 1 and 4, and 20 Dec 61, p. 2, and 25 Dec 61, p. 2.

13. *New York Herald*, 20 Nov 61, p. 5, and 17 Dec 61, p. 7; *New York Daily Tribune*, 18 and 20 Nov 61, p. 5, and 18 Dec 61, p. 3; *New York Times*, 20 Dec 61, p. 2.

14. *Life of Mason*, 234.

15. *Ibid.*, 232; *ORA*, Ser. 2, II, 1094, 1110, 1114, and 1119; Seward to Dimick, 5 Dec 61, "Letters Sent Regarding Prisoners of War and Intercepted Messages, Aug. 1861–Feb. 1863," RG59, NA; *Boston Daily Evening Transcript*, 14 Dec 61, p. 1.

16. *Boston Daily Evening Transcript*, 23 Nov 61, p. 2, and 14 Dec 61, p. 2; *New York Daily Tribune*, 14 Dec 61, p. 4.

17. *Life of Mason*, 205–208, 234–35.

18. *Ibid.*, 234–35; Seward to Dimick, 5 Dec 61, "Letters Sent Regarding Prisoners of War and Intercepted Messages, Aug. 1861–Feb. 1863," RG59, NA; *New York Daily Tribune*, 26 Dec 61, p. 8. Faulkner, too, lived well during his brief sojourn at Fort Warren. While stopping overnight on his way to Richmond he was overheard boasting "of the wines and turkeys,

thirty in one day, and other courtesies he received from Boston flunkies."
(*Ibid.*, 16 Dec 61, p. 4.)

19. *New York Daily Tribune*, 21 Nov 61, p. 8, and 25 Nov 61, p. 6; *New Orleans Bee*, 5 Dec 61, p. 1; Jones, *Rebel War Clerk's Diary*, 55–56; *Charleston Mercury*, 20 Nov 61, p. 1, and p. 4 also for editorials quoted from *Richmond Enquirer* and *Richmond Examiner*.

20. Chesnut, *Diary from Dixie*, 160–61; Richmond *Whig*, Petersburg *Express*, Savannah *Republican*, and New Orleans *Crescent* and *Delta*, all quoted in *Charleston Mercury*, 20 Nov 61, p. 4, and 23 Nov 61, p. 1.

21. Petersburg *Express*, Savannah *Republican*, and New Orleans *Crescent* and *Delta*, all quoted in *Charleston Mercury*, 20 Nov 61, p. 4, and 23 Nov 61, p. 1.

22. *Daily Nashville Patriot*, 19 and 26 Nov 61, both p. 2; *New Orleans Bee*, 5 Dec 61, p. 1.

23. *Charleston Mercury*, 18 and 21 Dec 61, both p. 1; *Charleston Daily Courier*, 24 Dec 61, p. 2, and 30 Dec 61, p. 1; *New Orleans Bee*, 20 Nov and 19 and 23 Dec 61, all p. 1.

24. *Richmond Examiner* and *Richmond Enquirer*, both of 19 Dec 61, and both quoted in *Albany Evening Journal*, 26 Dec 61, p. 2; Jones, *Rebel War Clerk's Diary*, 61.

25. Cuelebrouck no. 230 to de Vrière, 17 Nov 61, BPCUS, G&B, roll 6; Stoeckl no. 68 to Gortchakov, 18 Nov 61, ESD, LC; Mercier no. 69 to Thouvenel, 19 Nov 61, vol. 125, FMAE, AD, EU. The false rumor that Seward had ordered Wilkes to seize Mason and Slidell probably originated at the State Department with the eccentric Count Gurowski. (Bates, *Diary*, 206.)

26. Mercier nos. 69 and 70 to Thouvenel, 19 and 25 Nov 61, both vol. 125, FMAE, AD, EU; Stoeckl no. 68 to Gortchakov, 18 Nov 61, ESD, LC.

27. Cuelebrouck no. 230 to de Vrière, 17 Nov 61, BPCUS, G&B, roll 6; Bates, *Diary*, 205; Mercier no. 70 to Thouvenel, 25 Nov 61, vol. 125, FMAE, AD, EU.

28. Cuelebrouck no. 236 to Rogier, 8 Dec 61, BPCUS, G&B, roll 6; Mercier no. 72 to Thouvenel, 3 Dec 61, vol. 125, FMAE, AD, EU.

29. Cuelebrouck no. 230 to de Vrière, 17 Nov 61, BPCUS, G&B, roll 6; Stoeckl no. 68 to Gortchakov, 18 Nov 61, ESD, LC; Mercier nos. 69 and 72 to Thouvenel, 19 Nov and 3 Dec 61, both vol. 125, FMAE, AD, EU.

30. Lyons nos. 674, 677, 678, and 682 to Russell, 18 and 19 Nov 61, all FO115/258; Lyons to Earl of Mulgrave, 25 Nov 61, and Lyons to Milne, 25 Nov and 1 Dec 61, and Lyons to Monck, 28 Nov 61, and Lyons to Hammond, 2 Dec 61, all LP.

31. *New York Herald* and *New York Daily Tribune*, both 20 Nov 61, p. 5.

32. Lyons nos. 690 and 705 to Russell, 22 and 25 Nov 61, both FO115/258; *New York Herald*, 23 Nov 61, p. 1; Lyons to Russell, 25 Nov 61, PRO30/22/35.

33. Lyons no. 716 to Russell, 29 Nov 61, FO115/258; Lyons to Milne, 25 Nov and 1 Dec 61, both LP; Lyons to Russell, 29 Nov and 3 Dec 61, both PRO30/22/35.

34. Lyons nos. 668, 669, and 674 to Russell, all 18 Nov 61, and Lyons no. 738 to Russell, 6 Dec 61, all FO115/258.

35. Lyons nos. 728, 735, and 740 to Russell, 3 and 6 Dec 61, all FO115/258; Lyons no. 742 to Russell, 6 Dec 61, FO115/259; Lyons to Russell, 29 Nov 61, PRO30/22/35; Lyons to his sister, 3 Dec 61, LP.

36. Lyons no. 742 to Russell, 6 Dec 61, FO115/259; Lyons to Russell, 3 and 6 Dec 61, both PRO30/22/35.

37. Lyons no. 742 to Russell, 6 Dec 61, FO115/259; Lyons to Russell, 3 and 6 Dec 61, PRO30/22/35.

38. Lyons to Milne, 1 and 9 Dec 61, MLN/107, Milne Papers; Lyons to Monck, 9 Dec 61, LP. The British minister may have been apprehensive just at this time that Seward might discover that Lyons had received communications directed to Mason and Eustis from some of their female relations, who took it for granted that Her Majesty's minister in Washington would gladly intercede in favor of the captured Southern envoys, "at least," wrote Mason's daughter, "until England's voice can be heard." (Anna Mason Ambler to Lyons, 21 Nov 61, and Louise M. Eustis to Lyons, 30 Nov 61, both LP.)

39. Lutz, "Rudolf Schleiden and the Visit to Richmond," 214; Cuelebrouck no. 239 to Rogier, 16 Dec 61, BPCUS, G&B, roll 6; L. M. Sears, "The London *Times'* American Correspondent in 1861: . . . ," 256.

CHAPTER X: WHAT WILL THEY DO?

1. Most of Lincoln's biographers have exhibited little critical discrimination in treating the president's attitude towards the *Trent* affair. When one discards from their accounts unverified rumors and unsubstantiated reminiscences of old men, little remains to indicate that Lincoln had reached any conclusion whatever about the *Trent* topic prior to the arrival of the British ultimatum.

2. *New York Herald*, 19 Nov 61, p. 3, and 20 Nov 61, p. 5. This con-

temporary statement alleging that Lincoln was initially adamant about cling-
ing to Mason and Slidell is probably more reliable than assertions to the
contrary that appeared many years later. (Cf., Rice, *Reminiscences*, 245;
Welles, *Lincoln and Seward*, 185–89; and Lossing, *Pictorial History* II, 156–
57.) Less easy to discount, however, is a near-contemporary assertion that
Lincoln "from the start . . . was for giving the traitors up." (Gurowski,
Diary, 135.) I would nevertheless hesitate to accept as conclusive *anything*
which came unverified from the eccentric Gurowski. I think he probably
based his statement on the testimony of a Washington journalist, which may
be found in the *New York Tribune*, 31 Dec 61, p. 5. Since what is asserted
there is contradicted, at least in part, by Edward Bates's diary, the allegations
about Lincoln's position are open to question.

3. *Daily National Intelligencer*, 18 Nov 61, p. 3; F. W. Seward to Shufeldt, 22 Nov 61, and Shufeldt no. 79 to Seward, 9 Nov 61, both NA;
Gurowski, *Diary*, 109. Several Northern newspapers referred to continuing
"investigations in the State Department" regarding legal precedents for the
Trent seizure. (See, for example, *New York Daily Tribune*, 25 Nov 61, p.
5.) Gurowski, wrong as usual, told a reporter that he was "certain that Great
Britain will not take exception to the act," since British legal precedents
justified it. (*New York Times*, 19 Nov 61, p. 1.)

4. London *Times*, 3 Dec 61, p. 8; *New York Times*, 19 Nov 61, p. 1; *ORA*,
Ser. 2, II, 1109; West, *Welles*, 137; Bates, *Diary*, 202; Seward *"Confidential"*
and 136 to Adams, 27 and 30 Nov 61, both NA. Bates thoroughly agreed
with the *Daily National Intelligencer* editorial of 18 Nov upholding the
legality of the *Trent* seizure. Chase, according to Lt. Fairfax, commended
him for disobeying his orders and not taking possession of the *Trent* as a
prize, after Fairfax had asserted he did it in order to avoid giving the English a pretext for declaring war against the U.S. (Fairfax, "Captain Wilkes's
Seizure of Mason and Slidell," 141.) Although the evidence supporting it is
meager (see Welles, *Lincoln and Seward*, 186), I am not prepared to contest
the assertion of W.C. Smith that the postmaster general at once denounced
Wilkes's seizure of Mason and Slidell and suggested that the *San Jacinto*'s
captain be ordered personally to deliver them to a British recipient. (Smith,
Francis Preston Blair Family II, 194.) Some historians have taken seriously
the testimony of Gideon Welles, published in 1874, that "no man was more
elated or jubilant over the capture of the emissaries than Mr. Seward, who
for a time made no attempt to conceal his gratification and approval of the
act of Wilkes." (Welles, *Lincoln and Seward*, 185.) Since Welles misrepre-

sented his own role in the affair, and since there is no reliable contemporary corroboration of his statement about Seward, I judge it worthless. Nor do I consider definitive a statement by Jeremiah Black, who had been Seward's inept predecessor as secretary of state, that Montgomery "Blair denounced the conduct of Wilkes as an indefensible outrage which would be sure to make trouble, while Mr. Seward was as much delighted as if one of his deputy kidnappers had broken the head of an honest judge or dragged an independent editor to prison." Published in 1874 in *Galaxy* magazine as part of the same series of anti-Seward memoirs as those of Welles, this diatribe contains numerous distortions. (Black, "Mr. Black to Mr. Adams," 116–17.)

5. *Seward at Washington* II, 22; *New York Times*, 4 Dec 61, p. 4; *New York Herald*, 6 Dec 61, p. 4; Browning, *Diary*, 513–14; Wilkes, "Autobiography," X, 2308; Skelton, *Life of Galt*, 316.

6. Lyons no. 777 to Russell, 19 Dec 61, FO115/259; W.H. Russell to Delane, 20 Dec 61, AT; *New York Herald*, 19 Dec 61, p. 7.

7. Mercier no. 75 to Thouvenel, 19 Dec 61, vol. 125, FMAE, AD, EU.

8. Lyons no. 777 to Russell, 19 Dec 61, FO115/259.

9. *Ibid.*; Lyons to Russell, 19 Dec 61, PRO30/22/35.

10. Lyons to Russell, 19 Dec 61, PRO30/22/35.

11. *Ibid.*; Lyons to Russell, 20 Dec 61, PRO30/22/35; Lyons to S. Cunard, 16 Dec 61, FO115/283; *New York Daily Tribune*, 18 Dec 61, p. 4; Lyons to Milne, 19 Dec 61, MLN/107, Milne Papers. The remark to Milne was virtually identical with what Lyons wrote Russell on 19 Dec 61, PRO30/22/35.

12. "In the State Department a large amount of manuscript advice from all parts of the country, touching the English question, are awaiting a reader." (*New York Daily Tribune*, 20 Dec 61, p. 5.)

13. Lyons nos. 790 and 791 to Russell, both 23 Dec 61, FO115/259.

14. Mercier no. 76 to Thouvenel, 23 Dec 61, vol. 125, FMAE, AD, EU; Lyons to Russell, 23 Dec 61, PRO30/22/35; Lyons no. 799 to Russell, 27 Dec 61, FO115/259.

15. Lyons to Russell, 23 Dec 61, PRO30/22/35. Lyons thought it was "not *quite* certain" that Seward's answer to the British ultimatum "will be a refusal." (Lyons to Milne, 23 Dec 61, MLN/107, Milne Papers.)

16. Cuelebrouck no. 240 to Rogier, 23 Dec 61, BPCUS, G&B, roll 6; W.H. Russell to Delane, 20 Dec 61, AT.

17. *Daily National Intelligencer*, 19 Dec 61, p. 3; *New York Times*, 19 Dec 61, p. 1, and 21 Dec 61, p. 4, and 22 Dec 61, pp. 1 and 4; *New York Daily Tribune*, 20 Dec 61, pp. 3, 4, and 5; *New York Herald*, 21 Dec 61, p. 1.

18. *New York Herald*, 19 Dec 61, pp. 6–7, and 21 Dec 61, p. 4.

19. Everett to Adams, 21 Dec 61, R556, AP; W.H. Russell to Delane, 20 and 22 Dec 61, AT; London *Times*, 10 Dec 61, p. 9.

CHAPTER XI: POISED UPON THE BRINK

1. Maxwell, *Clarendon* II, 251.

2. M. Adams to C. F. Adams, Jr., 6 Dec 61, R556, AP; *New York Times*, 30 Dec 61, p. 1.

3. Adams to R. H. Dana, Jr., 13 Dec 61, R166, AP.

4. *New York Times*, 26 Dec 61, p. 4; M'Clintock to Arthur, 4 Dec 61, Special Collections, Emory Univ.; London *Times*, 2 Dec 61, p. 5.

5. Brougham to Gladstone, 10 Dec 61, Add. MS 44,114, BM; Delane to W.H. Russell, 11 Dec 61, AT. Edward Everett, the orator, and George Bancroft, the historian, had both based successful political careers upon frequent references to American military victories over England.

6. Cowley to Russell, 9 Dec 61 (2), PRO30/22/56; *Letters and Recollections of John Murray Forbes* II, 243n; Holland to Cobden, 16 Dec 61, Add. MS 43,670, and Gladstone to Paxton, 18 Dec 61, Add. MS 44,532, both BM.

7. Gladstone to Paxton, 18 Dec 61, Add. MS 44,532, BM; Russell to Palmerston, 16 Dec 61, GC/RU/685, PP. Ellice was soon in touch with Weed, who wondered "what he wants or expects to make of me." Apparently what was desired was merely personal contact, so that Seward and Palmerston had an alternative channel of informal communication. After breakfasting together the two men continued to exchange ideas. (Weed to Hughes, 22 Dec 61, copy in WP; Weed to Seward, 18 and 31 Dec 61 and 11 Jan 62, all SeP.)

8. *Illustrated London News* XXXIX, no. 1121 (14 Dec 61), p. 596; Cobden to Richard, 3 Sept 61, Add. MS 43,659 and Cobden to Sumner, 12 Dec 61, Add. MS 43,676, both BM; Weed to Sanford, 7 Dec 61, Box 132, SaP.

9. Gaines to Cobden, 18 Dec 61, Add. MS 43,659, and Cobden [to Slagg], *ca.* 20 Dec 61, Add. MS 43,676, both BM; Cobden to Bright, 11 Dec 61, RCP.

10. Cobden to Bright, 3 Sept and 1 Nov and 11 Dec 61, and Bright to Cobden, 6 Sept 61, all RCP; Cobden to Sumner, 19 Dec 61, Add. MS 43,676, BM. Bright growled about the waste and provocation involved in the hectic British war preparations. He thought that if the captive Southern commissioners were released promptly upon receipt in Washington of the British demand, "our friends in the Cabinet ought to go to Newgate [prison] on bread and water for the rest of their natural lives." (Bright to Cobden, 18 Dec 61, RCP.)

11. Cobden to Slagg, *ca.* 20 Dec 61, and Cobden to Sumner, 19 Dec 61, both Add. MS 43,676, BM; Cobden to Bright, 14 Dec 61, and Bright to Cobden, 6 Sept and 13 Dec 61, all RCP.

12. Cobden to Bright, 11 Dec 61, RCP; Argyll, *Memoirs* II, 180; Gibson to Gladstone, 18 Dec 61, Add. MS 44,397, and Gladstone to Phillimore, 10 Dec 61, Add. MS 44,532, and Gladstone to Somerset, 13 Dec 61, Add. MS 44,304, all BM. Perhaps even more worried than Gibson was his friend Villiers, who discovered that the *Trent* dispute was "not favourable to my habit of insomnia." He had "not the least idea" of what might happen, but he apprehended that war was "inevitable." (Villiers to Bright, 14 Dec 61, Add. MS 43,386, BM.)

13. R. H. Dana, III, "Trent Affair," MHSP XLV, 528; E. D. Adams, *GB & Amer. CW* I, 224; *Lady John Russell: A Memoir*, 194.

14. London *Times*, 9 Dec 61, p. 6; Mackay to Layard, 9 Dec 61, Add. MS 39,102, BM.

15. Adams, Diary, 8 and 9 Dec 61, R76, and Adams to Fogg, 9 Dec 61, R166, both AP.

16. Morse no. 45 to Seward, 18 Dec 61, *London Consular Despatches*, vol. 29, NA; Jordan and Pratt, *Europe and the American Civil War*, 136; Adams to Fogg, 9 Dec 61, R166, AP.

17. Adams to Palfrey, 13 Dec 61, R556, AP; W. C. Ford, *Cycle* I, 81–84.

18. *Memoir of Weed*, 352–53; Weed, *Autobiography*, 643–44; Weed to Seward, 18 Dec 61, SeP; Adams, Diary, 9 and 13 Dec 61, R76, AP.

19. Adams, Diary, 16–18 Dec 61, R76, AP; *ORA*, Ser. 2, II, 1102; Moran, *Journal*, 927; *ORN*, Ser. 1, I, 168–69; Adams no. 93 to Seward, 20 Dec 61, NA; Weed to Seward, 18 Dec 61, SeP. In the newspaper stories received in the same mail delivery that brought Seward's conciliatory instruction, the British secretary for war discerned "ominous" and "decidedly threatening" signs, and former Foreign Secretary Clarendon heard, despite the lord chancellor's conviction that Lincoln's administration was "preparing for concessions to our demands," that, nevertheless, "the news from America is thought by the government, and indeed by everybody, to confirm the notion that war is inevitable." (Lewis to Gladstone, 17 Dec 61, Add. MS 44,236, BM; Maxwell, *Clarendon* II, 254–55.)

20. Russell no. 483 to Lyons, 19 Dec 61, FO115/250/III; Adams no. 93 to Seward, 20 Dec 61, NA. Russell said that he had avoided discussing the Bunch affair at this interview because the correspondence on it had already been terminated. Otherwise his arguments, according to Adams, "carried with them much force."

21. Adams no. 93 to Seward, 20 Dec 61, NA.

22. *Ibid.*; Russell no. 483 to Lyons, 19 Dec 61, FO115/250/III.

23. C.F. Adams, Jr., "Trent Affair," 140; Adams, Diary, 19 Dec 61, R76, AP; Adams nos. 93 and 102 to Seward, 20 Dec 61 and 17 Jan 62, both NA; Moran, *Journal*, 928; *Seward at Washington* II, 31; *Lady John Russell: A Memoir*, 194.

24. Adams no. 102 to Seward, 17 Jan 62, NA; Weed to Sanford, 20 Dec 61, Box 132, SaP; Moran, *Journal*, 928; Adams, Diary, 20 and 21 Dec 61, R76, AP; Weed to Seward, 20 and 25 Dec 61, SeP; Dudley to Seward, 20 Dec 61, *Liverpool Consular Despatches*, vol. 20, NA.

25. W. C. Ford, *Cycle* I, 88–89.

26. Sanford to Cox, Foster, and Goodrich, all 20 Dec 61, and Sanford to Bigelow, 21 Dec 61, and Sanford to Anthony, 24 Dec 61, all Box 100, SaP.

27. Lewis to Gladstone, 20 Dec 61, Add. MS 44,236, and Argyll to Gladstone, 30 Dec 61, Add. MS 44,099, and Gladstone to Brougham, 27 Dec 61, Add. MS 44,532, and Mallet to Bright, 19 Dec 61, Add. MS 43,389, all BM; Weed to Hughes, 22 Dec 61, copy in WP.

28. Russell to Palmerston, 20 Dec 61, GC/RU/686/1–2, PP; Argyll to Gladstone, 30 Dec 61, Add. MS 44,099, BM. Twenty Dec was a bad day for the testy Russell, who sent Lyons on that date three dispatches: (1) protesting that Lincoln's "cruel plan" of blocking up Southern harbors with sunken hulks was "a project worthy only of times of barbarism" and should be abandoned; (2) threatening that if the U.S. government tried in case of war with England to take possession of the Panama railroad, "force will be met by force"; and (3) suggesting that if the U.S. and Great Britain "should ever unhappily be at war against each other, Her Majesty would be ready to . . . abolish privateering," provided that President Lincoln would make the same engagement. These ridiculous dispatches furnish revealing evidence of Russell's tendency to bustle and bluster unrealistically during periods of crisis, which at times made him a dangerous foreign minister. (Russell nos. 487, 488 and 489 to Lyons, all 20 Dec 61, FO115/250/IV.)

29. Russell to Palmerston, 21 Dec 61, GC/RU/687, PP; Palmerston to Russell, 20 and 22 Dec 61, both PRO30/22/21.

30. Somerset to Newcastle, 19 Dec 61, NeC; Somerset to Granville, 21 Dec 61, PRO30/29/24; Lewis to Palmerston, 24 Dec 61, GC/LE/150/1–2, and Russell to Palmerston, 11 Dec 61, GC/RU/684/1–3, both PP; Twisleton to Lewis 24 Dec 61, and de Grey to Lewis, 26 Dec 61, both GCLP.

31. Lindsay to Layard, 10 Dec 61, Add. MS 39,102, and Layard to Russell, 17 Dec 61, Add. MS 38,987, both BM.

32. Palmerston to Granville, 26 Dec 61, PRO30/29/18. Palmerston had the Speaker of the House of Commons scrambling to determine "the length of notice necessary before P[arliament] could be summoned for despatch of business." Mid-January, Denison discovered, would probably be the earliest possible time. ("Speaker's Diary" for 1860–62, OsC.)

33. Fitzmaurice, *Granville* I, 405; Maxwell, *Clarendon* II, 254–55; Cowley, *Secrets of the Second Empire*, 228–30; Brougham to Delane, 15 Dec 61, AT; Lewis to Gladstone, 17 Dec 61, Add. MS 44,236, BM. Correspondence on file in PRO30/29/31 covering the month of December, 1861, supported by documents printed in such sources as *Letters of Queen Victoria, 1st Ser.* III, and Russell, *Later Correspondence* II, 322–23, indicates that the queen, her household, and many members of the cabinet were almost entirely occupied during most of that month with the prince's illness and death and had little inclination to reconsider the action taken initially in regard to the *Trent* question.

34. Maxwell, *Clarendon* II, 251; Cobden to Gladstone, 11 Dec 61, Add. MS 44,136, BM.

35. Gladstone to Cobden, 13 Dec 61, Add. MS 44,136, BM. Gladstone also thought, in his usual positive way, that "the nearly unanimous opinion of the civilized world" opposed the Northern effort to restore the American Union, which he called "one of the blindest enterprises on record in human history, for if (and what an if!) they could conquer the South they would only find themselves confronted by political and civil problems which are, especially under the conditions afforded by their institutions, wholly insoluble." Cobden, too, believed that the Northerners might, "if they choose to make the ruinous sacrifice themselves, persist until they make a ruin & desolation of the South I don't doubt." But such would be in truth a pyrrhic victory. (Gladstone to Sinclair, 19 Dec 61, Add. MS 44,532, and Cobden to Paulton, 27 Dec 61, Add. MS 43,662, both BM.)

36. Gibson to Bright, 18 Dec 61, Add. MS 43,388, and Villiers to Bright, 25 Jan 62, Add. MS 43,386, both BM.

37. "Letters of John Bright, 1861–1862," MHSP XLV, 155; Bright to Cobden, 16 and 21 Dec 61, RCP.

38. Bigelow, *Retrospections* I, 441–42.

39. Cobden to Slagg, 18, 19 and 21 Dec 61, Add. MS 43,676, and Cobden to Richard, 11 Dec 61, Add. MS 43,659, all BM.

40. Bigelow, *Retrospections* I, 417–18.

41. Adams, Diary, 22 Dec 61, R76, and Adams to Motley, 27 Dec 61, R166, both AP; Moran, *Journal*, 930.

42. Adams, Diary, 24–26 Dec 61, R76, AP.

Chapter XII: Awaiting the American Response

1. W.C. Ford, *Cycle* I, 90.

2. *Diaries of Lady Frederick Cavendish* I, 120–21; Gladstone to Eversley, 28 Dec 61, Add. MS 44,532, and Brougham to Gladstone, 31 Dec 61, Add. MS 44,114, both BM; Newcastle to Young, 26 Dec 61, NeC.

3. Davis, *Rise and Fall of the Confederate Government* I, 482; Yancey to Davis, 30 Dec 61, Special Collections, Emory Univ.; Sanford to Weed, 31 Dec 61, and 3 Jan 62, both WP.

4. Bright to Cobden, 16 Dec 61, and Cobden to Bright, 17 and 18 Dec 61, all RCP; Villiers to Bright, 14 Dec 61, Add. MS 43,386, and Cobden to Slagg, 17 and 21 Dec 61, Add. MS 43,676, and Cobden to Richard, 18 Dec 61, Add. MS 43,659, all BM; "Letters of John Bright, 1861–1862," MHSP XLV, 154; Catt to Cobden, 14 and 18 Dec 61, Add. MS 43,670, and Cobden to Catt, 16 and 18 Dec 61, Add. MS 43,677, both BM.

5. Dudley to Seward, 20 Dec 61, *Liverpool Consular Despatches*, vol. 20; Gaines to Cobden, 18 Dec 61, Add. MS 43,659, BM; *Illustrated London News* XL (4 Jan 62), 10.

6. Bigelow, *Retrospections* I, 440–41.

7. Weed to Seward, 31 Dec 61, SeP; McIlvaine to Bedell, 23 Dec 61, copy in WP.

8. Jordan and Pratt, *Europe and the American Civil War*, 38–39; London *Times*, 20 Dec 61, pp. 6 and 10, and 25 Dec 61, p. 6, and 26 Dec 61, pp. 5 and 6.

9. Palmerston to Russell, 3 Apr 61, GC/RU/1137, PP; Palmerston to Russell, 9 Sept 61, Add. MS 48,582, BM; Gladstone to Sinclair, 10 Dec 61, and Gladstone to Russell, 12 Dec 61, both Add. MS 44,532, and Gladstone to Talmadge, 10 Dec 61, Add. MS 44,397, all BM; London *Times*, 9 Dec 61, p. 6; Lewis to Clarendon, 9 Dec 61, CP.

10. Russell to Gladstone, 13 Dec 61, Add. MS 44,292, BM.

11. Cowley to Russell, 5 Dec 61, PRO30/22/56; Palmerston to Russell, 27 Dec 61, PRO30/22/21; Russell to Palmerston, 27 Dec 61, GC/RU/688, PP.

12. Westbury to Palmerston, 30 Dec 61, GC/WE/132, PP; Palmerston to Westbury, 31 Dec 61, Add. MS 48,582, BM.

13. Westbury to Palmerston, 3 Jan 62, GC/WE/134, PP; London *Times*, 9 Dec 61, p. 6.

14. Watson to Gladstone, 27 Dec 61, Add. MS 44,397, BM.

15. Bright to Cobden, 1 Jan 62, RCP; Argyll to Gladstone, 1 Jan 62, Add. MS 44,099, BM.

16. Palmerston to Russell, 1 Jan 62, PRO30/22/22; Russell to Palmerston, 1 Jan 62, GC/RU/691, PP.

17. *Lady John Russell: A Memoir*, 10; Newton, *Lyons*, 67–70; E. D. Adams, *GB & Amer. CW* I, 230.

18. Russell to Granville, 1 Jan 62, PRO30/29/18; Palmerston to Granville, 2 Jan 62, PRO30/29/24; Layard to de Grey, 2 Jan 62, Add. MS 43,550, and Palmerston to de Grey, 2 Jan 62, Add. MS 43,512, both BM; Clarendon to Lewis, 2 Jan 62, and Lewis to Clarendon, 3 Jan 62, both CP; Fitzmaurice, *Granville* I, 406.

19. Forster to de Grey, 2 Jan 62, Add. MS 43,536, and Eversley to Gladstone, 3 Jan 62, Add. MS 44,398, both BM; Derby to Granville, 3 Jan 62, PRO30/29/18.

20. Gladstone to Russell, 2 and 6 Jan 62, and Gladstone to Somerset, 5 Jan 62, and Gladstone to Sumner, 8 Jan 62, all Add. MS 44,532, and Russell to Gladstone, 4 Jan 62, Add. MS 44,292, all BM.

21. Adams no. 95 to Seward, 27 Dec 61, NA; Adams, Diary, 29 Dec 61, R76, and 1 Jan 62, R77, both AP.

22. Adams no. 97 to Seward, 2 Jan 62, NA; W. C. Ford, *Cycle* I, 86; C. F. Adams, Jr., to H. Adams, 25 Dec 61, R556, AP.

23. *Congressional Globe*, 37 Cong., 2 sess. (26 Dec 61), 176–77; Frothingham to Adams, 24 Dec 61, R556, AP.

24. Adams to C. F. Adams, Jr., 3 Jan 62, R557, AP.

25. *Ibid.*; Adams, Diary, 10 Dec 61, R76, AP.

26. Argyll to Gladstone, 10 Dec 61, Add. MS 44,099, BM.

27. Gibson to Cobden, 2 Dec 61, Add. MS 43,662, BM; Atkins, *Russell* II, 89.

28. Russell nos. 459 and 499 to Lyons, 7 and 28 Dec 61, FO115/250/I and V; Hammond to crown law officers, 16 Dec 61, and law officers to Russell, 21 Dec 61, and Harding to Russell, 21 Dec 61, all FO83/2212; M'Clintock to Arthur, 2 Dec 61, Special Collections, Emory Univ.; Pierce, *Sumner* IV, 59. One British legal authority discovered several cases dating back to the Napoleonic era which justified the *Trent* seizure. "It would seem to have been our principle in 1806," wrote Edward Twisleton, "that a belligerent might seize any of his enemies on a neutral vessel, without taking them before a prize court." Hence it appeared that Wilkes had "not gone beyond" principles upheld by British Admiralty judges during the last great war against France. Although such decisions, in Twisleton's opinion, were not sound, the fact that they had been rendered meant that it would be "a strong measure" to

make war *"at once"* against the United States, should Lincoln express "an opinion that the Commodore's act was legal." (Twisleton to Lewis, 10 Dec 61, GCLP.)

29. Seward to Adams, 20 Dec 61, R556, and Adams, Diary, 2 and 6 Jan 62, R77, and Adams to Frothingham, 8 Jan 62, R166, all AP; Moran, *Journal*, 937, 939. Everett had written that he knew Seward favored a peaceful settlement. But it was not Seward who worried Adams. In the privacy of his diary he lamented that the American government was "in a perilous condition with a chief so little fitted to direct it." (Everett to Adams, 21 Dec 61, R556, and Adams, Diary, 10 Dec 61, R76, both AP.)

30. Layard to de Grey, 6 Jan 62, Add. MS 43,550, BM.

31. Layard to de Grey, 7 Jan 62, Add. MS 43,550, and Ryan to Gladstone, 8 Jan 62, Add. MS 44,398, both BM; Argyll to Denison, 7 Jan 62, OsC; Russell to Palmerston, 7 Jan 62, GC/RU/692, PP; Stanley to Granville, 8 Jan 62, PRO30/29/24; Newcastle to Derby, 8 Jan 62, NeC; Maxwell, *Clarendon* II, 257. Gladstone was elated to see a newspaper report that Sumner had declared in the U.S. Senate "that there would be peace. If you said so," he wrote the Bostonian, "it can have but one meaning & God be thanked." (Gladstone to Sumner, 8 Jan 62, Add. MS 44,532, BM.)

CHAPTER XIII: A DECISION AT LAST

1. *Boston Daily Evening Transcript*, 18 Nov 61, p. 2, and 26 Nov 61, p. 2; *New York Times*, 17 Nov 61, p. 4, and 6 Dec 61, p. 5. I believe that no silver service was ever actually given to Wilkes. The mayor of Boston, however, presented Wilkes with the promised ceremonial sword six months later. (C. F. Adams, Jr., "The Wilkes Sword," MHSP XLV [1912], 590–91.) Ultimately, the sword found its way to the Smithsonian Institution in Washington, D.C. (Long, "Glory-Hunting Off Havana," 143n.)

2. *New York Times*, 2 Dec 61, p. 1, and 5 Dec 61, p. 5. The idea that the primary task of the historian is "commemoration" was well represented by the main speaker of the evening, Benson J. Lossing, in his own books.

3. *New York Daily Tribune*, 6 Dec 61, p. 6, and 9 Dec 61, p. 5.

4. *ORA*, Ser. 2, II, 1109. Welles expressed essentially the same ideas in his annual departmental report to the president three days later. (*Ibid.*, 1113–14.) Many of Wilkes's fellow naval officers opposed his abduction of the Southern envoys from the *Trent*. Commodore Samuel F. DuPont, politically a Northern Democrat, wrote his wife that *"not one word* of commendation went up from this squadron for [Wilkes's] act, except possibly from myself." It had

been "the inward thought of every man that one war at one time was about as much as we could stand." All recognized that Mason and Slidell "could do no harm" in Europe; and that, in any case, "they can be replaced immediately." Hence there had been "no exultation" in DuPont's fleet "at the capture of those commissioners—it was considered so impotent in any results. . . . Mrs. Slidell, permitted to go on, [was] worth two of her husband." (DuPont, *Civil War Letters* I, 290 and 294.) Meanwhile, Commodore L. M. Goldsborough agreed that "A war with England at this time . . . would be simply a national suicide. Better . . . to give up ten thousand such concerns as Slidell and Mason than to bring England down on us at such a crisis." (Fox, *Confidential Correspondence of Gustavus Vasa Fox* I, 224 and 227.)

5. *Ibid.*, 1113 and 1115; *New York Times*, 3 Dec 61, pp. 1 and 4; *Congressional Globe*, 37 Cong., 2 sess. (2 Dec 61), 10 and 13.

6. *New York Daily Tribune*, 16 Dec. 61, p. 4; *New York Herald*, 16 Dec 61, p. 8.

7. Wilkes, "Autobiography," 580; *New York Daily Tribune*, 19 Dec 61, p. 4; *New York Herald*, 22 Dec 61, p. 4.

8. *Boston Daily Evening Transcript*, 16 Dec 61, p. 2; *Congressional Globe*, 37 Cong., 2 sess. (17 Dec 61), 101. Greeley asserted that "The fiercest advocates of war with England at all hazards, the noisiest blusterers about the American eagle and the British lion, are men who have long been suspected of being rebels at heart. Vallandigham is the loudest-mouthed patriot of all, and Cox is not far behind him. Those who wish the rebellion put down are not so anxious to precipitate hostilities." (*New York Daily Tribune*, 18 Dec 61, p. 4.)

9. Lutz, "Rudolf Schleiden and the Visit to Richmond," 214; Sumner to S. G. Howe, 22 Dec 61, HM23336, HL; Sumner to Bright, 15 Oct 61, Add. MS 43,390, BM; *New York Daily Tribune*, 25 Dec 61, p. 5.

10. Sumner to Bright, 23 Dec 61, Add. MS 43,390, BM; Pierce, *Sumner* IV, 60–61; H. Woodman to Sumner, 20 Dec 61, Sumner Papers, Houghton Library. Lincoln told Senator Browning on December 10 that he had been informed by Mercier "that the law officers of England had decided that we were justifiable by the law of Nations in the arrest of Mason and Slidell, and there would probly [*sic*] be no trouble about it." (Browning, *Diary* I, 513–14.) This rumor, based on a misunderstanding of the crown law officers' memorandum of 12 Nov, had been published in Northern newspapers. (W. H. Russell, *Diary*, 577.) By 19 Dec, Lincoln had learned from Seward that Mercier had misled him. Later, I imagine, Charles Sumner either showed Lincoln or told him about a letter forwarded from Boston, in which Edward

Twisleton had accurately summarized both memoranda of the crown law officers—that of 12 Nov and that of 28 Nov—and had quoted the crucial passages. It appears at least possible that Lincoln knew the truth about the British legal position before the ultimatum of that government was delivered by Lyons. (Extract from Twisleton to Dwight, 7 Dec 61, MHSP XLVII, 107–109.)

11. Cobden to Sumner, 27 and 29 Nov 61, both Add. MS 43,676, BM.

12. Cobden to Sumner, 27 and 29 Nov and 5 Dec 61, all Add. MS 43,676, BM.

13. Cobden to Sumner, 5 and 6 Dec 61, both Add. MS 43,676, BM.

14. Cobden to Sumner, 6 Dec 61, Add. MS 43,676, BM. This suggestion was outlined in detail in Cobden to Slagg, 6 Dec 61, Add. MS 43,676, BM, and mentioned in Cobden to Richard, 6 Dec 61, Add. MS 43,659, BM. Somewhat the same proposition was expressed in Sanford to Seward, 2 and 9 Dec 61, both Box 99, SaP.

15. Cobden to Sumner, 6 Dec 61, Add. MS 43,676, BM.

16. *Ibid.*

17. Bright's letter to Cobden comparing their respective suggestions to Sumner about how to deal with the *Trent* crisis is a masterpiece of tact. "I return the letters . . . to Mr. Sumner," Bright wrote. "*Your scheme is too great and too wise* to have a chance of being listened to by any other government than that of the United States, and I think *is above its mark.* I wrote to Sumner on Saturday, confining myself to this pressing question of the 'Trent.' I advised that they should . . . offer . . . to refer the whole matter to the decision of any one or two of the governments of Europe. . . . I think this a course, *probably not wiser than yours*, but more likely to be adopted by the Washington government." (Bright to Cobden, 9 Dec 61, RCP; italics mine.)

18. "Letters of John Bright, 1861–1862," MHSP XLV, 150–51.

19. There is in the Lincoln papers a letter from James R. Doolittle of the Senate foreign relations committee, who suggested on 19 Dec that when the British ultimatum arrived, the president should reply that he felt the arrest justified but would refer the matter to arbitration by the French emperor and the Russian czar. (Doolittle to Lincoln, 19 Dec 61, Ser. I, no. 13478, ALP, LC.) This missive may have influenced the president somewhat, but in my opinion Lincoln was guided more by Bright's advice, for he adopted the Englishman's position almost unaltered, even to using Bright's very language. It is possible that Doolittle had been persuaded by Sumner to write Lincoln—essentially to *support* Bright's arguments.

20. Lincoln's *Works* V, 62–64. The date of 10 Dec assigned to this docu-

ment by Nicolay and Hay in their earlier edition of Lincoln's *Works*, and adopted here by Basler, is obviously wrong. The evidence indicates 20 Dec is the most probable date of authorship, although it is possible that the president reworked the paper after a talk with Sumner on 22 Dec. In any case the existence of this conciliatory draft note tends to undermine the credibility of W.H. Russell's assertion that, at approximately the same time, Lincoln "put down his foot" against surrendering Mason and Slidell to England, telling "an old Treasury official the other day, 'I would sooner die than give them up.'" (W.H. Russell, *My Diary*, 588.)

21. Browning, *Diary* I, 516–17; Sumner to Bright, 23 Dec 61, Add. MS 43,390, BM.

22. Sumner to Bright, 30 Dec 61, Add. MS 43,390, BM; "Letters of John Bright, 1861–1862," MHSP XLV, 152–53; *New York Daily Tribune*, 24 Dec 61, p. 4.

23. *New York Herald*, 21 Dec 61, p. 4. Later Sumner acknowledged that arbitration was an unrealistic remedy for the *Trent* problem, writing Bright that "it was necessary that the case should be decided at once. Its pendency caused a paralysis upon all our naval and military movements against the rebellion, which gave us a foretaste of the certain effect of a British war." (Sumner to Bright, 30 Dec 61, Add. MS 43,390, BM.) Another reason why arbitration was impossible was that any European arbitrator almost surely would have assumed the existence of Confederate belligerent rights, which were unlikely to be conceded by the Lincoln administration.

24. *New York Times*, 19 Dec 61, p. 4, and 22 Dec 61, p. 1; *New York Daily Tribune*, 24 Dec 61, p. 4.

25. *New York Herald*, 24 Dec 61, p. 3, and 25 Dec 61, p. 1; *New York Daily Tribune*, 25 Dec 61, pp. 5 and 6; Pierce, *Sumner* IV, 58. Some writers (see, for example, Warren, "Trent Affair," 195–96) have, I think, misinterpreted the significance of an entry in the diary of the London *Times*'s special American correspondent, wherein W.H. Russell related that he had encountered the secretary of state at a diplomatic dance, on which occasion Seward allegedly exclaimed that if Great Britain forced a war upon the United States, the latter power would "wrap the whole world in flames!" This, however, seems to have been a favorite phrase less of Seward's than of Russell's; moreover, Russell himself testified that Seward seemed to speak "in a very good humor"—and on the following day when Russell had dinner at Seward's house the secretary, by this time well aware of the excitement in England over the *Trent* seizure, puzzled the English journalist by continuing to behave "in the best of spirits." Very much in contrast "with the irritation

he displayed in May and June" toward England, Seward's "good humor" was "not intelligible," unless it was interpreted as indicative of a conciliatory attitude. (W.H. Russell, *My Diary*, 587.) As for George Bancroft's recollection of Seward's "vulgar" and "loud" behavior at the same diplomatic party, one must recall that Bancroft was an old political opponent of Seward's. (Bancroft, *Life and Letters* II, 148.)

26. Weed to Seward, 2 Dec 61, SeP; Dayton no. 87 to Seward, 30 Nov 61, and Adams no. 82 to Seward, 3 Dec 61, both NA.

27. *ORA*, Ser. 2, II, 1106–1108. In February, 1862, Mackay went to New York to become the London *Times*'s special correspondent there. Reflecting the views of his editors, his writing was permeated with anti-American bias.

28. The *America* arrived at New York on 24 Dec with letters and dispatches from England through 7 Dec and information slightly older from the continent. (*New York Daily Tribune*, 25 Dec 61, pp. 5 and 8.)

29. Dayton no. 88 to Seward, 3 Dec 61, NA. The grim tidings from Paris were reinforced by word from Madrid, from The Hague, and from Brussels. (Schurz no. 43 to Seward, 30 Nov 61, and Pike no. 29 to Seward, 4 Dec 61, and Sanford "Private and Confidential" to Seward, 2 Dec 61, all NA; Sanford to Seward, 2 Dec 61, Box 99, SaP.) I refrain from speculating about the effect on Seward of a ridiculous letter from Paris in which his friend Archbishop John Hughes recommended that "while John Bull is getting on his sea-legs and military boots," Mason and Slidell and their secretaries should be tried for treason, which would doubtless end in their being condemned to death; but the president might then commute their sentences and send them via any neutral vessel into enforced exile. (Hughes to Seward, 5 Dec 61, SeP.)

30. Adams no. 84 to Seward, 6 Dec 61, NA.

31. Lord to Seward, 5 Dec 61, *Manchester Consular Despatches*, and Morse no. 43 to Seward, 6 Dec 61, *London Consular Despatches*, vol. 29, both NA; Weed to Seward, 7 Dec 61, SeP. The New York and Washington newspapers backed up these reports with their own accounts of war preparations in both England and Canada. See, for example, the *New York Times*, 24 Dec 61, p. 1, and the *New York Daily Tribune*, 24 Dec 61, p. 4, and the *Daily National Intelligencer*, 23 Dec 61, p. 3.

32. *Seward at Washington* I, 627; Seward to Weed, 30 Dec 61, WP. The special correspondent of the London *Times* was frustrated that he found no intimation anywhere of the view taken by Seward of the British ultimatum. "If Mason and Slidell are not given up," he wrote, "war is—I fear—inevitable." (L.M. Sears, "The London *Times*' American Correspondent in 1861: . . . ," 256.)

33. Bates, *Diary*, 213–14; Weed to Seward, 2 Dec 61, SeP. It is difficult to determine which letters of Bright and Cobden were read by Sumner at the Christmas Day cabinet session. Senator Browning testified that Lincoln told him that the Massachusetts senator read one letter from Bright and two from Cobden. (Browning, *Diary* I, 519.) It is probable that Cobden's letters of Nov. 29 and Dec. 5 were read, as well as Bright's letter of Dec. 5.

34. Professor Lynn Case quotes copiously from the comments of contemporary journalists, diplomats, and governmental leaders on both sides of the Atlantic to make a strong circumstantial case in favor of "the crucial part which the French note played in giving Seward a diplomatic and legal instrument for convincing the president, the cabinet, and the Northern people of the wisdom of releasing the two Confederate envoys." In dramatic language he depicts "Mercier's, Lyons', and Seward's agonizing wait for the arrival of the one documentary piece which would turn the trick." And he brands Seward's statement that Lincoln had "decided upon the disposition" of the *Trent* question prior to the arrival of Thouvenel's note as a falsehood which one century later still caused historians "to ignore half of the 'Trent' story." (Case and Spencer, *US & France: CW Diplomacy*, 227–47, 591. See also the *New York Times*, 31 Dec 61, p. 5.) I believe that Case gives the French note undue weight. Although the document was published by Seward afterward in order to help convince Americans that the British ultimatum had the support of continental statesmen, I doubt whether the decision of the cabinet would have been different had Thouvenel's note never arrived. As for Seward's statement that Lincoln had already decided what to do before Thouvenel's note arrived, I think Seward probably meant that the president had decided to do what was required to avert a war with England, not that Lincoln had actually made up his mind about exactly *how* this would be accomplished.

35. Mercier no. 77 to Thouvenel, 27 Dec 61, vol. 125, FMAE, AD, EU; Bates, *Diary*, 215; Lyons (telegram) to Russell, 26 Dec 61, PRO30/22/35; Browning, *Diary* I, 518–19; Dayton no. 91 to Seward, 6 Dec 61, NA; Lyons no. 799 to Russell, 27 Dec 61, FO115/259.

36. Weed to Seward, 2 Dec 61, SeP; Cobden to Sumner, 5 Dec 61, Add. MS 43,676, BM. John Bigelow, the U.S. consul at Paris, had written Seward a warning, received on 25 Dec, that the French "press and people and government" were united in opposition to the *Trent* seizure, and that the emperor, in case of war, would support England without actively engaging in the conflict. (Bigelow to Seward, 5 Dec 61, SeP.)

37. Bates, *Diary*, 215; Chase, *Inside Lincoln's Cabinet*, 55.

38. Bates, *Diary*, 215–16; *Seward at Washington* II, 46.

39. Seward no. 150 "Confidential" to Adams, 27 Dec 61, NA.

40. *Ibid.*; Seward to Lyons, 26 Dec 61, NA.

41. Adams no. 82 "Confidential" to Seward, 3 Dec 61, NA. Adams was later pleased to discover in Seward's note to Lyons relinquishing Mason and Slidell "the traces of my Despatch of the 3rd of December." (Adams, Diary, 9 Jan 62, R77, AP.) The minister's son, Henry, too, recognized the role of "the Chief" of the London legation in providing the crucial element in Seward's note to Lyons. (W.C. Ford, *Cycle* I, 100.)

42. Seward to Lyons, 26 Dec 61, NA. A pamphlet published in New York, probably about this time, quoted James Madison in support of the statement "that we must in a great measure abandon forever the freedom of the seas and the external interests of neutral States, . . . if from [neutral] ships, not even brought to adjudication, may be forcibly removed any citizen or subject of his enemy" by a belligerent. (Pro Lege, *A Legal View of the Seizure of Messrs. Mason and Slidell*, 26.)

43. Bates, *Diary*, 215–16.

44. Chase, *Inside Lincoln's Cabinet*, 55; Bates, *Diary*, 213; Browning, *Diary* I, 518. In 1891, Frederick W. Seward published an oft-quoted version of what happened at the December 25 cabinet meeting. I think that the younger Seward's account was probably faithful to the *spirit* of the conversations he reports. (*Seward at Washington* II, 25–26, reiterated some 25 years later in F. W. Seward, *Reminiscences*, 188–90.) Years later, Bates recalled that Lincoln told him before the cabinet met that Mason and Slidell would have to be released; indeed, a contemporary newspaper report virtually confirms this statement. Lincoln is supposed to have doubted whether Wilkes's course could be justified by international law and to have said that, "at all events, he could not afford to have two wars upon his hands at the same time." Yet I doubt the truth of this, in view of the entirely different version recorded in Bates's contemporary diary. It is probably a less accurate version of the situation, in fact, than an unqualified declaration of another Washington writer on 26 Dec "that the President was opposed to the surrender of the rebel prisoners under any circumstances, but he is willing to do whatever he shall be convinced is necessary for the public good." (Rice, *Reminiscences*, 245; *New York Daily Tribune*, 31 Dec 61, p. 5; *New York Herald*, 27 Dec 61, p. 1; Bates, *Diary*, 216–17.)

45. Sumner to Lieber, 25 Dec 61, Sumner Papers, Houghton Library; Mercier no. 77 to Thouvenel, 27 Dec 61, vol. 125, FMAE, AD, EU; *New York Times*, 26 Dec 61, pp. 1 and 4.

46. *Congressional Globe*, 37 Cong., 2 sess. (26 Dec 61), pp. 176–77. Such jingoistic pronouncements as Hale's caused W.H. Russell to remark that evening that there could be but one answer to the British demands. "Press, people, soldiers, sailors, ministers, senators, congressmen, people in the street, the voices of the bar-room—all are agreed. 'Give them up? Never! We'll die first!'" Apparently, Senator Sumner, with whom Russell dined that day, pretended that he had no information about a release of the captive Confederate commissioners. (W.H. Russell, *My Diary*, 591–92.)

47. Bates, *Diary*, 216; W.H. Russell, *My Diary*, 593; Lyons no. 801 to Russell, 27 Dec 61, FO115/259; Lyons to Russell, 27 Dec 61, PRO30/22/35. The fact that many amendments were apparently added by others to Seward's draft note to Lyons tends in my opinion to invalidate much of the criticism directed by contemporaries and by historians later on against Seward because of the poor reasoning allegedly found in the document. Warren ("Trent Affair," p. 214), for example, calls it "a monument to illogic." I do not see how Seward can be required to assume responsibility for the entire wording of a document to which apparently many modifications were made during the cabinet discussions of the secretary of state's draft. Thus Cobden, for example, may have been unfair to Seward in observing that "There was a nasty piece of Buncumb in Seward's long dispatch in which he said he would have kept the men if necessary for the Union. There is a want of moral perceptions in the man." (Cobden to Richard, 30 Jan 62, Add. MS 43,659, BM.)

48. Lyons nos. 800 and 801 to Russell, 27 Dec 61, FO115/259; Lyons to Russell, 27 Dec 61, PRO30/22/35. Lyons also sent Russell four copies of a telegram to be carried to England by four different mail packets which announced the release of the prisoners into his custody. (Lyons no. 803 to Russell, 27 Dec 61, FO115/259.)

49. Browning, *Diary* I, 519; Trollope, *Autobiography*, 151; *Seward at Washington* II, 26.

50. *Daily National Intelligencer*, 28 Dec 61, pp. 2 and 3.

51. *New York Times*, 29, 30, and 31 Dec 61, all pp. 1 and 4.

52. *New York Daily Tribune*, 30 Dec 61, pp. 4 and 8; *New York Herald*, 29 Dec 61, p. 4, and 31 Dec 61, pp. 6 and 7. See *Albany Evening Journal*, 31 Dec 61, p. 2, for many extracts from newspapers all over the United States, all praising the decision to release Mason and Slidell. Acquiescence in the step was perhaps stimulated by the wide dissemination in Northern newspapers of war-scare missives from Europe, such as a letter from Weed dated 7 Dec, in which the Albany editor wrote that in London everyone expected war with the United States, "and all accept it, and generally with less reluctance

than I anticipated." British preparations for the conflict to come were "on a gigantic scale." Weed asked that Americans, "for the sake of peace," be magnanimous toward Great Britain in regarding the *Trent* affair. For the United States was simply unprepared for a trans-Atlantic war, which would greatly aid the Southern traitors. Such warnings as Weed's made it easier for Northerners to accept the decision to release Mason and Slidell. (*Albany Evening Journal*, 28 Dec 61, p. 2.)

53. Mercier to Thouvenel, 27 and 30 Dec 61 and 3 Jan 62, all in vol. 13, Papiers de Thouvenel, and Mercier no. 78 to Thouvenel, 31 Dec 61, vol. 125, FMAE, AD, EU; Bates, *Diary*, 216–17.

54. Cuelebrouck no. 244 to Rogier, 29 Dec 61, BPCUS, G&B, roll 6.

55. Bates, *Diary*, 214; Long, "Glory-Hunting," 142–43; Wilkes, "Autobiography," LC; C. F. Adams, Jr., "The Wilkes Sword," MHSP XLV (1912), 590.

56. *New Orleans Bee*, 3 Jan 62, p. 1; *Charleston Mercury*, 30 Dec 61, p. 1; Jones, *Rebel War Clerk's Diary*, 63; Hotze to Hunter, 11 Mar 62, Pickett Papers, LC.

CHAPTER XIV: THE DIPLOMATIC SETTLEMENT

1. Special Collections, Emory Univ.

2. Lyons to Russell, 27 and 31 Dec 61, PRO30/22/35; *Seward at Washington* II, 36; Lyons nos. 805 and 806 to Russell, 31 Dec 61, FO115/259; Lyons to Milne, 28 Dec 61, MLN/107, Milne Papers; F. W. Seward to Col. Dimick, 28 Dec 61, "Letters Sent Regarding Prisoners of War and Intercepted Messages, Aug. 1861–Feb. 1863," RG59, NA; *Life of Mason*, 208, 235–46; Moran, *Journal*, 939–40; *Memoir of Weed*, 978–79; "P. E. de S." to Gladstone, 9 Jan 62, Add. MS 44,938, BM; *Lady John Russell: A Memoir*, 195.

3. Gladstone to Cavendish, 9 Jan 62, Add. MS 44,532, BM; Diaries of Lady Frederick Cavendish, 122; Guedalla, *Gladstone and Palmerston*, 197; London *Times*, 13 Jan 62, p. 6.

4. According to the British secretary for war, the expense of sending arms and troops to Canada as a result of the *Trent* crisis somewhat exceeded one million pounds. He thought it "safe to say that it will fall short of a million and a half." Apparently, this estimate included the cost of ocean transportation. (Lewis to Palmerston, 18 Jan and 6 Feb 62, GC/LE/154–55, PP.)

5. *Life of Mason*, 238–46; London *Times*, 9 Jan 62, p. 8, and 10 and 11 Jan 62, both p. 6.

6. *Letters of Queen Victoria, 2d Ser.* I, 7–8; Connell, *Regina Vs. Palmer-*

ston, 359–60. In the first of these two notes to the queen, the premier recommended that Lyons, having "conducted the very difficult and important negotiations" of the *Trent* affair "with great ability and judgment, and [with] . . . great discretion," should be decorated a "Knight Grand Cross of the Civil Order of the Bath." The queen approved, and the award was made. (See also Palmerston to Russell, 12 Jan 62, PRO30/22/14C and Russell no. 20 to Lyons, 17 Jan 62, FO115/284/II.)

7. Granville to Newcastle, 9 Jan 62, NeC; Russell no. 11 to Lyons, 10 Jan 62, FO115/284/I.

8. *ORA*, Ser. 2, II, 1117, 1149; Pierce, *Sumner* IV, 54n; Argyll to Gladstone, 1 Jan 62, Add. MS 44,099, BM; Argyll to Palmerston, 11 Jan 62, GC/AR/24/1–2, PP; C. F. Adams, Jr., "Trent Affair," 77.

9. London *Times*, 14 Jan 62, p. 6.

10. Lewis to de Grey, 14 Jan 62, Add. MS 43,533, and Gladstone to Brougham, 16 Jan 62, Add. MS 44,532, both BM; Clarendon to Lewis, 19 Jan 62, and Lewis to Clarendon, 20 Jan 62, both CP; Russell to Palmerston, 17 and 20 Jan 62, both GC/RU/696 and 698/1–2, PP.

11. Russell no. 39 to Lyons, 23 Jan 62, FO115/284/III.

12. Russell to Palmerston, 31 Dec 61, and 12 and 15 Jan 62, all GC/RU/690, 693, and 695, PP; Russell to Hammond, 16 Jan 62, FO391/7; Russell to Lyons, 8 Feb 62, LP.

13. Lyons no. 131 to Russell, 21 Feb 62, FO115/298; Seward to Lyons, 21 Feb 62, NA.

14. Lyons to Russell, 31 Dec 61, PRO30/22/35.

15. Lyons no. 807 to Russell, 31 Dec 61, FO115/259; Lyons to Russell, 27 Dec 61, PRO30/22/35. Lyons's protestation that he was "sure from the first" that the Americans would yield to the threat of force does not coincide with Anthony Trollope's testimony that during the afternoon of December 26, 1861, "I and others had received intimation through the Embassy that we might probably have to leave Washington at an hour's notice." (Trollope, *Autobiography*, 151.)

16. Russell, *Later Correspondence* II, 324; Russell to Lyons, 8 Feb 62, LP; Lewis to de Grey, 22 Jan 62, Add. MS 43,533, BM; Russell to Gladstone, 26 Jan 62, Add. MS 44,292, BM.

17. Weed to Seward, 11 Jan 62, SeP.

18. Dayton to Seward, 14 Jan 62, and Adams nos. 99 and 103 to Seward, 10 and 17 Jan 62, all NA; Adams to Everett, 10 Jan 62, R166, and Adams to C. F. Adams, Jr., 10 Jan 62, R557, both AP.

19. Judd no. 16 to Seward, 14 Jan 62, and Perry no. 22 to Seward, 10 Jan

62, and Motley no. 3 to Seward, 29 Jan 62, and Clay no. 16 to Seward, 10 Jan 62, all NA.

20. Sanford no. 43 to Seward, 9 Jan 62, and Sanford to Seward, 14 Jan 62, and Pike nos. 30 and 33 to Seward, 11 Dec 61 and 9 Jan 62, all NA.

21. Marsh no. 37 to Seward, 13 Jan 62, NA; McIlvaine to Bedell, 13 Jan 62, copy in SeP.

22. Pierce, *Sumner* IV, 60–61; Adams no. 85 to Seward, 11 Dec 61, NA; Adams, Diary, 9 Dec 61, R76, AP; W.C. Ford, *Cycle* I, 84; Moran, *Journal* II, 916 and 937; Weed to Seward, 10 Dec 61, and 7 and 8 Jan 62, all SeP.

23. Seward to Weed, 30 Dec 61, and 22 and 30 Jan 62, all WP.

24. Seward no. 163 to Adams, 11 Jan 62, NA; Seward to Weed, 22 Jan and 7 Mar 62, both WP.

25. Seward to Weed, 7 Mar 62, WP; Adams, Diary, 31 Jan 62, R77, AP.

26. Adams to Seward, 31 Jan 62, R167, AP. One of Adams's closest friends had recently written him from Boston: "What a shame & pity it is, now, that the personal & political enemies of Mr. Seward have been so industrious in making him suspected and disliked abroad, & by the diplomatic circles here! I think his despatches . . . do him great credit, & have restored confidence in him here." (Dana to Adams, 17 Dec 61, R556, AP.)

27. Seward to Adams, 19 Feb 62, R557, AP; Adams no. 85 to Seward, 11 Dec 61, and Seward no. 152 to Adams, 30 Dec 61, both NA.

28. Adams no. 114 to Seward, 13 Feb 62, and Seward no. 13 to Motley, 4 Mar 62, and Seward no. 171 to Adams, 31 Jan 62, all NA.

Sources

The following compilation of sources consists mainly of those cited in Notes. The *Trent* affair has probably been written about more than all other topics of American Civil War diplomatic history combined, and it is therefore not feasible here to mention, much less to try to characterize, all the books and articles, or even all of the documentary materials, that bear on this subject. One who wishes to investigate possibilities for additional reading about the *Trent* affair may consult standard historical bibliographies and the section entitled "Diplomacy" in *Civil War Books, A Critical Bibliography*, ed. by A. Nevins, J. Robertson, Jr., and B. Wiley (Baton Rouge, La., 1967, I, 241–78), and compiled by the author.

Throughout my notes I have used the shortest possible citations. Certain files of documents located in public archives and various collections of manuscripts have been identified as follows:

ALP. Papers of Abraham Lincoln, Library of Congress.

AP. Papers of Adams Family, Massachusetts Historical Society, Boston, especially the following rolls from the microfilm edition: R76–77 for C.F. Adams's Diary; R165–67 for C.F. Adams's Letterbooks; R296 for C.F. Adams's Reminiscences; and R554–58 for C.F. Adams's Letters Received and Other Loose Papers.

AT. Archives of *The Times*, Printing House Square, London, England, with special thanks to archivist J. Gordon Phillips and William Rees-Mogg, ed.

BM. British Museum, London. Documents used in writing this book have been cited by manuscript number as follows: 38,987–39,102 for Papers of Sir Austen Henry Layard; 43,386–43,391 for Papers of John Bright; 43,512–43,551 for Papers of George Frederick Samuel Robinson, earl de Grey and marquis of Ripon; 43,659–43,677 for Papers of Richard Cobden; 44,099–44,938 for Papers of William Ewart Gladstone; and 48,582 for a letterbook of Henry John Temple, 3d viscount Palmerston.

BPCUS, G&B. Belgian Political Correspondence, United States, General and

Bound. Includes dispatches of Belgian minister in Washington. Microfilm copies in National Archives.

Cᴘ. Papers of George William Frederick Villiers, 4th earl of Clarendon, Bodleian Library, Oxford University.

Emory University. Special Collections. Papers of Jefferson Davis, James M. Mason, and John M'Clintock.

Esᴅ. Dispatches of Edouard Stoeckl, Russian minister in Washington. Copies at Library of Congress.

Fᴍᴀᴇ, ᴀᴅ. Archives of the French Ministry of Foreign Affairs, Paris, "Archives diplomatiques, Angleterre," vols. 719, 720, and "Archives diplomatiques, Etats-Unis," vols. 124, 125.

Fᴍᴀᴇ, ᴍᴅ. Archives of the French Ministry of Foreign Affairs, Paris, "Memoirs et Documents, Papiers de Thouvenel," vols. 8, 13.

Fᴏ. British Foreign Office records, located in ᴘʀᴏ.

Gᴄʟᴘ. Papers of Sir George Cornewall Lewis, Harpton Court Collection, National Library of Wales, Aberystwyth. Special thanks to Professor Alan Conway for assistance in seeing this collection.

Houghton Library, Harvard University, Cambridge, Mass. Papers of Charles Sumner.

Hʟ (or ʜᴍ). Manuscripts of Charles Sumner and Francis Lieber and Thomas Dudley, all at Huntington Library, San Marino.

Hssᴘ. See SaP.

Hwʟᴘ. Papers of Henry W. Longfellow, Craigie House, Cambridge, Mass.

Jʙᴘ. Papers of John Bigelow, New York Public Library.

Jᴍᴍᴘ. James Murray Mason Papers, Library of Congress.

Jsᴘᴘ. James Shepherd Pike Papers, Library of Congress.

Lᴄ. Library of Congress. Manuscript Division has the "Journal" of Benjamin Moran and Papers of Francis Lieber, Abraham Lincoln (ᴀʟᴘ), James M. Mason (ᴊᴍᴍᴘ), James S. Pike (ᴊsᴘᴘ), Rudolf Schleiden (ʀsᴅ), and Charles D. Wilkes, as well as the so-called Pickett Papers of the Southern Confederacy. Here may also be found diplomatic correspondence pertaining to the United States during 1861 and 1862 of Russia (ᴇsᴅ) and England (FO115 and FO5) in either photostat or microfilm form.

Lᴘ. Papers of Richard Bickerton Pemell, 1st earl Lyons, Arundel Castle, England, with the permission of the former duke of Norfolk.

Mʜsᴘ. Massachusetts Historical Society *Proceedings*, pub. at Boston. The society contains manuscripts of the Adams family, of Governor Andrew, and of Richard Henry Dana, Jr.

Mʟɴ. Papers of Sir Alexander Milne, National Maritime Museum, Greenwich, England, used with the permission of the trustees of the National Maritime Museum.

NA. National Archives, Washington, D.C. Among the records I have consulted there are (1) log of U.S.S. *San Jacinto* for the period from Aug. 4 to Nov. 30, 1861, RG24; (2) dispatches of U.S. ministers at London, Paris, Brussels, Turin, St. Petersburg, The Hague, Madrid, Vienna, Lisbon, and Berlin to Seward, and the secretary of state's instructions to these envoys in Europe, all for the period from Mar. 1861 to Feb. 1862; (3) diplomatic notes exchanged during 1861 by Seward and Lyons; (4) dispatches received by Seward during 1861 from U.S. consuls at Liverpool, London, and Manchester, and at Havana and Nassau; (5) "Correspondence Regarding Prisoners of War, 1861–1862, Parr-Sullivan," Box no. 9, folders nos. 61, 75, 81, "Civil War Papers," and "Instructions to Special Agents," vol. 21, and "Letters Sent Regarding Prisoners of War and Intercepted Messages, Aug. 1861–Feb. 1863," and "Miscellaneous Letters of the Department of State," all in RG59.

NeC. Papers of Henry Pelham Fiennes Pelham Clinton, 5th duke of Newcastle, University of Nottingham, used with the permission of the trustees of the Newcastle estate.

New York Public Library. Horace Greeley papers.

ORA. *War of the Rebellion: Official Records of the Union and Confederate Armies.*

ORN. *Official Records of the Union and Confederate Navies in the War of the Rebellion.*

OsC. Papers of John Evelyn Denison, viscount Ossington, University of Nottingham.

PP. Papers of Henry John Temple, 3d viscount Palmerston, consulted at the Historical Manuscripts Commission, Chancery Lane, London, by permission of the trustees of the Broadlands Archives.

PRO. Public Record Office, London, where I have consulted the following records: (1) dispatches exchanged between the Foreign Office and the British legation in Washington which, for the period covered by this book, are found in files FO115/238 through FO115/259 and FO115/283–84; (2) supplementary materials not located in the FO115 files were found in FO5/776 and FO5/906; (3) dispatches exchanged between the Foreign Office and the British Embassy in Paris which I have cited appear in FO27 and in FO519/11; (4) the Russell Papers, as designated by PRO30/22, include not only the private correspondence between Lords Russell and Cowley in PRO30/22/56 (as well as in FO519/228–29), but also private correspondence between Lords Russell and Lyons in PRO/30/22/35 and PRO30/22/96, and private correspondence between Lords Russell and Palmerston in PRO30/22/4, PRO30/22/14, PRO30/22/21 and PRO30/22/22; (5) cabinet memoranda which I have cited may be found in PRO30/22/27, while Russell's correspondence with officials like Somerset may be seen in PRO30/22/24; (6) in the Granville Papers, especially PRO30/29/18, PRO30/29/24, PRO30/29/29, and PRO30/29/31, is valuable information; (7) pertinent records were found in records of the Colonial Office designated as CO42/626-29; (8) memoranda exchanged between the Foreign Office and the crown law officers were discovered in FO83/2212; while (9) in the Hammond Papers, especially FO391/5-7, I found indispensable information.

RCP. Papers of Richard Cobden, West Sussex County and Diocesan Record Office, Chichester, with thanks to Mrs. Patricia Gill, county archivist, for much kind assistance.

RCSA. Records of the Confederate States of America, also called the "Pickett Papers," Library of Congress.

RHDP. Papers of Richard Henry Dana, Jr., Massachusetts Historical Society, Boston.

RSD. Dispatches of Rudolf Schleiden, minister of Bremen at Washington, copies of which are in the Library of Congress.

SaP. Papers of Henry Shelton Sanford, Florida National Bank, Sanford, Fla., with thanks to Mrs. Harriet Owsley for generous assistance in locating them. See especially boxes 99, 100, 132, 139, and 140.

SeP. Papers of William H. Seward, Rush Rhees Library, University of Rochester.

University of Georgia. Special Collections. T. Cobb Papers.

WP. Papers of Thurlow Weed, Rush Rhees Library, University of Rochester.

Some collections of primary source materials which I did not find useful in writing this book, but which another writer with a different perspective may need to use include: (1) the dispatches to the British Foreign Office of Joseph T. Crawford, British consul general at Havana, Cuba, during 1861 and 1862, in FO72/1013 and FO72/1041, both PRO; (2) the papers of Simon Cameron, William H. Seward, and Robert W. Shufeldt (U.S. consul general at Havana), all LC; and (3) the papers of Edward Ellice and Alexander T. Galt at the Public Archives of Canada, Ottawa.

UNSIGNED ARTICLES IN NEWSPAPERS AND MAGAZINES

In the notes to this book I have cited articles (including editorials) published in the following newspapers and magazines, exclusive of those whose authorship was clearly established, in which case they were listed below among other printed sources: *Albany Evening Journal. Boston Daily Evening Transcript. Charleston Mercury.* Charleston *Courier. Commercial Review. Daily Nashville Patriot.* Washington *Daily National Intelligencer.* Washington *Evening Star. Illustrated London News.* London *Morning Post.* Manchester *Guardian. New Monthly Magazine. New Orleans Bee. New York Daily Tribune. New York Herald. New York Times. Punch. Quarterly Review. Saturday Review.* London *Times.*

Remaining Printed Sources and Other Authorities

For convenience in locating other sources consulted in writing this book which are cited in the notes above, I have compiled them hereafter alphabetically, by author. Included, with brief evaluations given of each item, are Ph.D. dissertations, articles in scholarly journals, monographs, and standard works. Some of these sources have also been characterized in my notes. Since I finished writing the narrative section of this volume some five years prior to its actual publication, many books and articles treating the *Trent* affair in one way or another have come to my attention, and a few are so significant in Civil War diplomatic history that they deserve to be mentioned in this compilation of sources, although I was unable to read them in time for my book to benefit from the insights of their authors. Such items are marked with an asterisk.

A Cycle of Adams Letters, 1861–1865. Ed. by Worthington C. Ford. 2 vols. Boston, 1920. Contains selected wartime correspondence of the Adams family.

Adams, Brooks. "The Seizure of the Laird Rams," Massachusetts Historical Society *Proceedings* XLV (Dec. 1911), 242–333. A ground-breaking essay by a son of the U.S. minister in London.

Adams, Charles, F., Jr. "The British Proclamation of May, 1861," Massachusetts Historical Society *Proceedings* XLVIII (Jan. 1915), 190–241. Bases a defense of British recognition of Confederate belligerent rights on limited research and shaky reasoning.

————. *Charles Francis Adams.* Boston, 1900. An unscholarly study by one of the sons of the American minister in London.

————. *Charles Francis Adams, 1835–1915: An Autobiography.* Boston, 1916. Reveals the author's antagonism toward his famous father.

————. "The Negotiation of 1861 Relating to the Declaration of Paris of 1856," Massachusetts Historical Society *Proceedings* XLVI (Oct. 1912),

23–84. A distorted but (unfortunately) influential essay drawn in part from unreliable sources.

————. *Richard Henry Dana, A Biography*. 2 vols. Boston, 1890. An appreciative reminiscence by a family friend.

————. *Studies Military and Diplomatic, 1775–1865*. New York, 1911. Discusses several topics of Civil War diplomatic history argumentatively.

————. "The Trent Affair," Massachusetts Historical Society *Proceedings* XLV (Nov. 1911), 35–148. Offers an opinionated discussion, with supporting documents, which is summarized in "The Trent Affair," *American Historical Review* XVII (Oct. 1911–July 1912), 540–62. An undistinguished article.

————. "The Wilkes Sword," Massachusetts Historical Society *Proceedings* XLV (May 1912), 589–92. Adds a fillip to the story of Wilkes's role in the *Trent* affair.

Adams, Ephraim D. *Great Britain and the American Civil War*. Reprint (2 vols. in 1). New York, 1958. A valuable, pretentious, pro-British study.

Adams, Henry B. "The Declaration of Paris. 1861." In *The Great Secession Winter of 1860–61 and Other Essays*, ed. by George Hochfield, pp. 363–89. New York, 1958. Comprises a series of shaky suppositions.

————. *The Education of Henry Adams*. Boston, 1918. Offers sardonic, stimulating comments on London and its leading men during the *Trent* crisis.

————. *The Letters of Henry Adams, 1858–1891*. Ed. by Worthington C. Ford. Boston, 1930. Prints a few revealing letters from the U.S. legation in London during the Civil War.

Argyll, George Douglas, 8th duke of. *Autobiography and Memoirs*. Ed. by dowager duchess of Argyll. 2 vols. London, 1906. Shows the salubrious influence exerted on Anglo-American relations by a powerful member of the British cabinet.

Ashley, Evelyn. *The Life and Correspondence of Henry John Temple, Viscount Palmerston, 1846–1865*. 2 vols. London, 1876. Reproduces several important letters.

Atkins, John B. *The Life of Sir William Howard Russell*. 2 vols. New York, 1911. Summarizes the experiences in Civil War America of the famous war correspondent of the London *Times*.

Baker, George E. *The Life of William H. Seward, With Selections from His Speeches*. New York, 1855. A "campaign biography."

Baker, Philip. "The Confederacy and England: The Editorial Opinion of the

Richmond *Examiner,* the Charleston *Mercury,* and the Augusta *Chronicle and Sentinel,*" M.A. thesis, Emory Univ., 1955. Offers a convenient selection of Southern commentary on the *Trent* affair.

Bancroft, Frederic. *The Life of William H. Seward.* Reprint. 2 vols. Gloucester, Mass., 1967. A "standard" life which is now three quarters of a century old.

Barnes, Thurlow W. *Memoir of Thurlow Weed.* Boston, 1884. Prints valuable letters from Europe during the *Trent* affair.

Bates, Edward. *The Diary of Edward Bates, 1859–1866.* Ed. by Howard K. Beale as vol. IV of the *Annual Report* of the American Historical Association for the Year 1930. Washington, D.C., 1933. An absolutely essential document for Civil War historians that sheds light on cabinet discussions of the *Trent* affair.

Baxter, James P. III. "The British Government and Neutral Rights, 1861–1865," *American Historical Review* XXXIV (Oct. 1928), 9–29. A pioneer analysis of governmental deliberations concerning legal aspects of the *Trent* seizure that is documented by "Papers Relating to Neutral and Belligerent Rights, 1861–1865," *ibid.,* 77–91.

Bell, Herbert C. F. *Lord Palmerston.* 2 vols. London, 1936. An indispensable biography.

Belmont, August. *A Few Letters and Speeches of the Late Civil War.* New York, 1870. Contains commentary on foreign affairs by a Rothschild agent in New York and his European correspondents.

Beresford-Hope, Alexander J. B. *A Popular View of the American Civil War.* London, 1861. Contains three pro-Southern lectures by a British M.P.

Bernath, Stuart L. *Squall Across the Atlantic.* Berkeley, Calif., 1970. A thorough and judicious treatment of the diplomatic and legal problems emanating from the seizure of blockade-runners along the Confederate coast.

Bevington, Merle M. *The Saturday Review, 1855–1868: Representative Educated Opinion in Victorian England.* Columbia University Studies in English and Comparative Literature, no. 154. New York, 1941. Barely touches on the American Civil War.

Bigelow, John. *Retrospections of An Active Life.* 3 vols. New York, 1909. A spirited and informative memoir by the U.S. consul at Paris.

Black, Jeremiah S., "Mr. Black to Mr. Adams," *The Galaxy* XVII (Jan. 1874), 107–21. A diatribe against Seward that disgraces its author.

Blumenthal, Henry. *France and the United States, Their Diplomatic Re-*

lations, 1789–1914. New York, 1972. An excellent survey based on the diligent research reflected in the author's earlier *Reappraisal of Franco-American Relations, 1830–1871* (Chapel Hill, N.C., 1959).

Bourne, Kenneth. "British Preparations for War with the North, 1861–1862," *English Historical Review* LXXVI (Oct. 1961), 600–32. Offers an illuminating discussion, elaborated in an admirable volume entitled *Britain and the Balance of Power in North America, 1815–1908.* Berkeley, Calif., 1967.

*Brauer, Kinley J. "Seward, American Politics and Anglo-American Relations: The British Perspective," *American Chronicle* I (Feb. 1972), 48–55. Well represents the anti-Seward positions taken by Lyons, Russell, and other British statesmen.

———. "Seward's 'Foreign War Panacea': An Interpretation," *New York History* IV (Apr. 1974), 132–57. May be compared with my own interpretation, presented in a companion volume to this one, entitled *Desperate Diplomacy: William H. Seward's Foreign Policy, 1861.*

Bright, John. "Bright-Sumner Letters, 1861–1872," Massachusetts Historical Society *Proceedings* XLVI (Oct. 1912), 93–164. Collects over forty letters from the English radical leader to Senator Charles Sumner bearing on American affairs.

———. *The Diaries of John Bright.* Ed. by R.A.J. Walling. New York, 1931. Illuminates Bright's pro-Northern stance during the Civil War years.

———. "Letters of John Bright, 1861–1862," Massachusetts Historical Society *Proceedings* XLV (Nov. 1911), 148–59. Includes additional letters to Senator Sumner.

———. *Speeches on Questions of Public Policy by John Bright, M.P.* Ed. by James E. T. Rogers. 2d ed. 2 vols. London, 1869. Reproduces several of Bright's great addresses on the American Civil War.

British Sessional Papers (House of Commons), LXXII. From a useful collection of British government documents, described in Jones, Robert H., "The American Civil War in the British Sessional Papers: Catalogue and Commentary," American Philosophical Society *Proceedings* CVII, no. 5 (15 Oct. 1963), 415–26.

Broom, Walter W. "An Englishman's Thoughts on the Crimes of the South and the Recompense of the North," *Pamphlets Issued by the Loyal Publication Society*, no. 84. New York, 1865. Attacks the Southern Confederacy from a "religious" point of view.

Browne, Francis F. *The Everyday Life of Abraham Lincoln. A Narrative and Descriptive Biography with Pen-Pictures and Personal Recollections by*

Those Who Knew Him. Chicago, 1913. Offers a plethora of unreliable anecdotes.

Browning, Orville H. *The Diary of Orville Hickman Browning.* Ed. by Theodore C. Pease and James G. Randall. 2 vols. Springfield, Ill., 1925. Provides a glimpse of Lincoln during the *Trent* crisis.

Buchanan, James. *The Works of James Buchanan, Comprising His Speeches, State Papers, and Private Correspondence.* Ed. by John B. Moore. 12 vols. Philadelphia, 1908–11. Has letters touching on foreign policy for the years 1861 and 1862.

Bulloch, James D. *The Secret Service of the Confederate States in Europe.* Reprint, 2 vols. New York, 1959. A generally reliable account of Confederate shipbuilding operations in Europe by the man who directed them.

Cain, Marvin R. *Lincoln's Attorney General, Edward Bates of Missouri.* Columbia, 1965. Sheds rather uncertain light on Bates's role in the *Trent* affair.

Carroll, Daniel B. *Henri Mercier and the American Civil War.* Princeton, N.J., 1971. The first scholarly study of the French minister at Washington.

Case, Lynn M., and Warren F. Spencer. *The United States and France: Civil War Diplomacy.* Philadelphia, 1970. Offers an unparalleled analysis of Franco-American relations, 1861–1865.

The Case of Great Britain, As Laid Before the Tribunal of Arbitration Convened at Geneva, Under the Provisions of the Treaty Between the United States of America and Her Majesty the Queen of Great Britain, Concluded at Washington, May 8 1871. 3 vols. in 4. Washington, D.C., 1872. Reproduces many pages of valuable documents relating to Anglo-American diplomatic disputes during the Civil War.

Cavendish, Lady Lucy Lyttleton. *The Diaries of Lady Frederick Cavendish.* 2 vols. New York, 1927. Provides contemporary commentary from Gladstone's niece.

Chase, Salmon P. *Inside Lincoln's Cabinet: The Civil War Diaries of Salmon P. Chase.* Ed. by David Donald. New York, 1954. Tells about discussions of the *Trent* affair in Lincoln's cabinet.

Chesnut, Mary B. *A Diary from Dixie.* Boston, 1949. Offers cogent comments on the personalities of men prominent in Confederate diplomacy, including James M. Mason.

Chevalier, M. Michel. *France, Mexico, and the Confederate States.* New York, 1863. Applauds the French intervention in Mexico as a step toward a Franco-Confederate alliance.

Clapp, Margaret. *Forgotten First Citizen: John Bigelow.* Boston, 1947. A brief biography that lacks French sources in treating the work of the American consul at Paris during the *Trent* crisis.

Cohen, Victor H. "Charles Sumner and the Trent Affair," *Journal of Southern History* XXII (May 1956), 205–19. Useful in estimating how helpful Sumner was in peacekeeping during the *Trent* crisis.

Coleridge, Ernest H. *Life and Correspondence of John Duke Lord Coleridge, Lord Chief Justice of England.* 2 vols. London, 1904. Contains letters exchanged between the Lord Chief Justice and the American correspondent of the Manchester *Guardian.*

Congressional Globe, 37 Cong., 1 sess. and 2 sess. (1861). Contains debates in Congress on Anglo-American relations during the period of the *Trent* affair.

Connell, Brian. *Regina Vs. Palmerston.* Garden City, N.Y., 1961. Prints correspondence between the queen and the prime minister regarding America.

Conway, Moncure D. *Autobiography.* 2 vols. Boston, 1904. Offers a few relevant reminiscences.

Correspondence Concerning Claims Against Great Britain, Transmitted to the Senate of the United States, in Answer to the Resolutions of December 4 and 10, 1867, and of May 27, 1868. 7 vols. Washington, D.C., 1869. A major source of documents for Anglo-American relations during the Civil War.

Corti, Count Egon Caesar. *Maximilian and Charlotte of Mexico.* 2 vols. New York, 1929. A famous work in a crowded field, based on the extensive private archives of Maximilian.

Costi, Angelo M. *Memoir of the Trent Affair.* Washington, D.C., 1865. A pamphlet which tries unsuccessfully to vindicate Wilkes's conduct.

Cowley, Henry R.C. Wellesley, 1st Earl. *Secrets of the Second Empire.* New York, 1929. Also published as *The Paris Embassy During the Second Empire* (London, 1927). This memoir approaches the *Trent* crisis from the vantage point of the British ambassador at Paris.

*Crook, David Paul. *The North, the South, and the Powers: 1861–1865.* New York, 1974. Ably summarizes recent scholarship on the subject of Anglo-American relations during the Civil War.

Crooks, George R. *Life and Letters of the Rev. John M'Clintock, D.D., LL.D., Late President of Drew Theological Seminary.* New York, 1876. Reproduces letters written during the *Trent* crisis by an American working for the Union cause in Paris.

Daly, Maria L. *Diary of a Union Lady, 1861–1865.* Ed. by Harold E. Hammond. New York, 1962. Provides perspective from the wife of an eminent New York judge who was well acquainted with leading American politicians and several foreign envoys.

Dalzell, George W. *The Flight From the Flag: The Continuing Effect of the Civil War Upon the American Carrying Trade.* Chapel Hill, N.C., 1940. An important monograph.

Dana, Richard H. III. *Hospitable England in the Seventies: the Diary of a Young American, 1875–1876.* Boston, 1921. Contains interesting reminiscences of C.F. Adams, Lord Russell, the Duke of Argyll, and others who were leading participants in the *Trent* affair.

————. "The Trent Affair—An Aftermath," with a reply by C.F. Adams, Jr. Massachusetts Historical Society *Proceedings* XLV (Mar. 1912), 508–30. Offers an able criticism of Adams's essay, "The Trent Affair," followed by a petulant rejoinder by Adams.

D'Auvergne, Edmund B. *The English Castles.* New York, 1926. Discusses Pontefract Castle, where C.F. Adams first learned of the *Trent* seizure.

Davis, Jefferson. *The Rise and Fall of the Confederate Government.* 2 vols. New York, 1881. Defends Confederate foreign policy premises.

Donald, David. *Charles Sumner and the Rights of Man.* New York, 1970. The first half of a definitive biography of Sumner.

————. *Lincoln Reconsidered.* New York, 1961. Offers a collection of shrewd essays.

*Drake, Frederick C. "The Cuban Background of the *Trent* Affair," *Civil War History* XIX (Mar. 1973), 29–49. Supplies fresh details regarding the Havana background of the *Trent* affair by drawing upon the author's interesting Ph.D. diss., "The Empire of the Seas: A Biography of Robert Wilson Shufeldt, U.S.N.," Cornell Univ., 1970.

Dudley, Thomas H. "Three Critical Periods in Our Diplomatic Relations with England During the Late War," *Pennsylvania Magazine of History and Biography* XVII (1893), 34–54. A self-congratulatory reminiscence with little to offer on Anglo-American relations before the year 1862.

Dugan, James. *The Great Iron Ship.* New York, 1953. Paints a graphic picture of the transporting of British military reinforcements to Canada.

Dunn, Waldo H. *James Anthony Froude, A Biography, 1857–1894.* Oxford, 1963. Prints a significant letter from J. L. Motley.

DuPont, Samuel F. *Samuel Francis DuPont; A Selection From His Civil War Letters.* Ed. by John D. Hayes. 3 vols. Ithaca, N.Y., 1969. Contains anti-Wilkes comments.

*Ellison, Mary. *Support for Secession: Lancashire and the American Civil*

War. Chicago, 1973. Demolishes the myth that Lancashire cotton workers, owing to anti-slavery feelings and a love for democracy, stubbornly supported the North against a pro-Confederate ruling class in England.

Elton, G.R. *Political History: Principles and Practice*. New York, 1970. Reinforces my own conviction that "mankind prefers its comfortable legends" to historical truth.

Everett, Edward. "The Monroe Doctrine," *Loyal Publication Society* pamphlet no. 34 (Oct. 1863). Refutes allegations that American foreign policy had been full of "studied insults" toward Great Britain.

"Extract from Twisleton to Dwight, 7 Dec 61," Massachusetts Historical Society *Proceedings* XLVII (Nov. 1913), 107–109. Shows that exact information about the crown law officers' advice on the *Trent* affair could have been received in Washington prior to the decision of Lincoln's cabinet whether to release the captured Confederate envoys.

Fairfax, D. MacNeill. "Captain Wilkes's Seizure of Mason and Slidell." In *North to Antietam: Battles and Leaders of the Civil War*. Ed. by R.U. Johnson and C.C. Buel, pp. 135–42. Reprint, New York, 1956. The story of the *Trent* seizure by a leading participant.

Fair-Play [pseud.]. *The True State of the American Question*. London, 1862. A short propaganda pamphlet.

Fay, C.R. *Life and Labour in the Nineteenth Century*. Cambridge, 1947. Used in this book for a single quotation about Cobden.

Ferris, Norman B. "The Prince Consort, 'The Times,' and the 'Trent' Affair," *Civil War History* VI (June 1960), 152–56. Correlates the prince's suggestions for moderating the British ultimatum with editorials from the London *Times*.

Fitzmaurice, Edmond. *The Life of Granville George Leveson-Gower, Second Earl Granville, K.G., 1815–1891*. 2 vols. London, 1905. The standard life.

Forbes, John M. *Letters and Recollections of John Murray Forbes*. Ed. by Sarah Forbes Hughes. 2 vols. Boston, 1899. Especially useful regarding the purchasing and equipping of federal warships in 1861 and regarding Forbes's later mission to England.

Ford, Worthington C. "Goldwin Smith's Visit to the United States in 1864," Massachusetts Historical Society *Proceedings* XLIV (Oct. 1910), 3–12. Appraises Smith's efforts to influence English opinion in favor of the North.

———. "Letters to Governor John A. Andrew in March, 1861," Massachusetts Historical Society *Proceedings* LXII (June 1929), 209–12. Prints letters of interest to Seward scholars.

————. "Sumner-Andrew Letters, 1861," Massachusetts Historical Society *Proceedings* LX (Apr. 1927), 222–35. Discusses Sumner's "strongly wrought up" condition which turned him against his friend C.F. Adams and contributed to his dislike of Seward.

Fox, Gustavas V. *Confidential Correspondence of Gustavas Vasa Fox, Assistant Secretary of the Navy, 1861–1865*. Ed. by R.M. Thompson and Richard Wainwright. 2 vols. and separate index. New York, 1918–19. Disappointing on foreign relations.

Frothingham, Paul R. *Edward Everett, Orator and Statesman*. Boston, 1925. Prints entries from Everett's journal and extracts from his correspondence with C.F. Adams.

Gasparin, Agenor de. *A Word of Peace on the American Question*. London, 1861. An eloquent effort to sway Europeans to support the Union cause.

Gilmore, James R. *Personal Recollections of Abraham Lincoln and the Civil War*. Boston, 1898. A meager source of foreign policy information.

Goddard, Samuel A. *Letters on the American Rebellion*. London, 1870. A collection of pro-Northern essays which appeared in England during the Civil War years.

Graebner, Norman. "Northern Diplomacy and European Neutrality." In *Essays in American Diplomacy*, ed. by Armin Rappaport, pp. 106–20. New York, 1967. An interpretative essay.

Guedalla, Philip. *Gladstone and Palmerston*. London, 1928. Includes one important letter bearing on the *Trent* affair.

————. *Palmerston, 1784–1865*. New York, 1927. A jaunty, sardonic biography which admirably reflects the personality of its subject.

————. *The Queen and Mr. Gladstone, 1845–1879*. London, 1933. Includes a note from Gladstone to Queen Victoria regarding the *Trent* seizure.

Gurowski, Adam. *Diary From March 4, 1861, to November 12, 1862*. Boston, 1862. Contains usually adverse comments on Seward's foreign policy by an eccentric, cynical state department clerk-translator.

Hale, Edward E., Jr. *William H. Seward*. Philadelphia, 1910. A mediocre biography.

Hansard's Parliamentary Debates. 3d ser., CLXII–CLXIII. London, 1861–62. May be consulted for British legislative discussions.

Harper, Robert S. *Lincoln and the Press*. New York, 1951. Has little on foreign relations.

Harris, Thomas L. *The Trent Affair*. Indianapolis, 1896. An unreliable account.

Hay, John. *Lincoln and the Civil War in the Diaries and Letters of John Hay*. Ed. by Tyler Dennett. New York, 1939. A fascinating work but with sparse references to foreign affairs.

Henderson, Daniel. *The Hidden Coasts, A Biography of Admiral Charles Wilkes*. New York, 1953. Unscholarly and lacks objectivity.

Hitsman, J.M. "Winter Troop Movements in Canada in 1862," *Canadian Historical Review* XLIII (1962), 127–35. Adds details to Bourne's studies.

Hobson, J.A. *Richard Cobden, The International Man*. New York, 1919. Prints a selection of Cobden's letters during the *Trent* affair.

Howe, M. A. de Wolfe. *The Life and Letters of George Bancroft*. 2 vols. New York, 1908. Reveals Bancroft as intensely anti-Seward.

Hunter, Robert M. "The Capture of Mason and Slidell," *Annals of the War Written by Leading Participants, North and South*. Philadelphia, 1879. An eyewitness account of the *Trent* seizure.

Huse, Caleb. *Supplies for the Confederate Army, How They Were Obtained in Europe and How Paid For. Personal Reminiscences and Unpublished History*. Boston, 1904. Has little on the *Trent* affair.

Insurgent Privateers in Foreign Ports. 37 Cong., 2 sess., *House Ex. Doc. No. 104*. Provides a few useful documents.

Jeffries, William W. "The Civil War Career of Charles Wilkes," Ph.D. diss., Vanderbilt Univ., 1941, and an article bearing the same title, *Journal of Southern History* XI (Aug. 1945), 324–48. Both examine Wilkes's role in foreign relations with care and perception.

*Jenkins, Brian. *Britain and the War for the Union*. Montreal, 1974. Covers Anglo-American relations for slightly more than the first year of the American Civil War and is especially good on Confederate diplomacy and on Canada.

Jones, John B. *A Rebel War Clerk's Diary*. Ed. by Earl S. Miers. New York, 1958. A condensed version of the original Richmond diary, which repeats comments of Judah Benjamin on the *Trent* affair.

Jordan, Donaldson, and Edwin J. Pratt. *Europe and the American Civil War*. Boston, 1931. Summarizes contemporary English public opinion (but see Mary Ellison's book, cited above).

Kean, Robert G.H. *Inside the Confederate Government, The Diary of Robert Garlick Hill Kean*. Ed. by Edward Younger. New York, 1957. Contains a single important entry on the *Trent* affair.

Klingberg, Frank J. "Harriet Beecher Stowe and Social Reform in England," *American Historical Review* XLIII (Apr. 1938), 542–52. Furnishes a few apt quotations.

Lee, Robert E. *The Wartime Papers of R.E. Lee*. Ed. by Clifford Dowdey. Boston, 1961. Shows that Lee doubted that the *Trent* crisis would lead to an Anglo-American war.

*Lester, Richard J. *Confederate Finance and Purchasing in Great Britain During the American Civil War*. Charlottesville, Va., 1975. Drawn from the author's Ph.D. diss. at the University of Manchester, 1962, and is a good companion volume to Merli's book on Confederate shipbuilding in Great Britain.

Lewis, George C. *Letters of the Right Hon. Sir George Cornewall Lewis, Bart., To Various Friends*. Ed. by the Rev. Sir Gilbert F. Lewis. London, 1870. Reproduces letters of the British secretary for war during the *Trent* crisis.

Lincoln, Abraham. *The Collected Works of Abraham Lincoln*. Ed. by Roy P. Basler. 9 vols. New Brunswick, N.J., 1953. A basic source.

Long, John S. "Glory-Hunting Off Havana: Wilkes and the Trent Affair," *Civil War History* IX (June 1963), 133–44. Drawn from Long's Ph.D. diss., "The Wayward Commander: A Study of the Civil War Career of Charles Wilkes," Univ. of California at Los Angeles, 1953, based on Wilkes papers (LC) and official naval records (NA).

Longfellow, Henry W. *Life of Henry Wadsworth Longfellow, With Extracts from His Journals and Correspondence*. 3 vols. Boston, 1891. Gives impressions of Charles Sumner.

Lossing, Benson J. *Pictorial History of the Civil War in the United States of America*. 3 vols. Philadelphia, 1866–68. A "commemorative" work by a sometimes reliable observer.

Lothrop, Thornton K. *William Henry Seward*. Boston, 1899. An undocumented short biography.

Lutz, Ralph H. "Rudolf Schleiden and the Visit to Richmond, April 25, 1861," *Annual Report of the American Historical Association for the Year 1915*, 209–16. Quotes from the Washington dispatches of the minister from Bremen.

McLaughlin, Andrew C. *Lewis Cass*. Boston, 1899. Relates how the former secretary of state advised Seward to relinquish Mason and Slidell.

McMaster, John B. *Our House Divided, A History of the People of the United States During Lincoln's Administration*. Greenwich, Conn., 1961. A classic survey still worth reading.

Martin, Theodore. *Life of the Prince Consort*. 5 vols. London, 1880. Reproduces the prince's memorandum advising that the *Trent* ultimatum be moderated.

Martineau, John. *The Life of Henry Pelham, Fifth Duke of Newcastle, 1811–1864*. London, 1908. Relates how Seward allegedly threatened England during a conversation with the duke.

Marx, Karl, and Frederick Engels. *The Civil War in the United States*. 3d ed. New York, 1961. Provides a compendium of newspaper articles and letters reflecting a pro-Northern, anti-British bias.

Mason, Virginia. *The Public Life and Diplomatic Correspondence of James M. Mason*. Roanoke, Va., 1903. Prints Mason's private letters during his captivity.

Maxwell, Herbert E. *The Life and Letters of George William Frederick, Fourth Earl of Clarendon*. 2 vols. London, 1913. Contains a few letters exchanged among Whig leaders during the *Trent* crisis.

*Merli, Frank J. *Great Britain and the Confederate Navy*. Bloomington, Ind., 1970. A well-researched analysis of the British government's response to Confederate shipbuilding in England.

Message of the President of the United States to the Two Houses of Congress at the Commencement of the Second Session of the Thirty-Seventh Congress, accompanied by *Papers Relating to Foreign Affairs*. 37 Cong., 2 sess., Sen. Ex. Doc. No. 1. The first volume of the famous "Foreign Relations" series of state department documents.

Mill, John S. *The Contest in America*. Boston, 1862. Offers anti-Confederate arguments by a famous political economist.

Miller, Francis T., ed. *The Photographic History of the Civil War*. VI. Reprint. New York, 1957. Mentions the sinking of the *Peerless*.

Monaghan, Jay. *Diplomat in Carpet Slippers, Abraham Lincoln Deals With Foreign Affairs*. Indianapolis, Ind., 1945. Utilizes suppositions and insinuations in trying to show that Lincoln's hand firmly guided U.S. foreign policy during the Civil War.

Moore, John B. *A Digest of International Law*. 8 vols. Washington, D.C., 1906. Still a valuable source on the legal aspects of Civil War diplomatic disputes.

Moran, Benjamin. *The Journal of Benjamin Moran, 1857–1865*. Ed. by Sarah A. Wallace and Frances E. Gillespie. 2 vols. Chicago, 1949. A gossipy, vitriolic private diary kept by a secretary in the American legation at London, superbly edited.

Morley, John. *The Life of Richard Cobden*. Boston, 1881. Contains some notable extracts from Cobden's correspondence during the *Trent* affair.

———. *The Life of William Ewart Gladstone*. 3 vols. New York, 1903. Disappointing on Gladstone's role in the *Trent* crisis.

Motley, John L. *The Correspondence of John Lothrop Motley.* Ed. by George W. Curtis. 3 vols. New York, 1900. A valuable compilation of the personal correspondence of the American minister in Vienna.

————. *John Lothrop Motley and His Family, Further Letters and Records, Edited by His Daughter and Herbert St. John Mildmay.* London, 1910. Supplements the Curtis edition of Motley's correspondence.

Newton, Thomas L.W. *Lord Lyons, A Record of British Diplomacy.* 2 vols. London, 1913. Presents the British minister in Washington as a consummate diplomat during the American Civil War.

Nicolay, John G., and John Hay. *Abraham Lincoln, A History.* V. New York, 1914. Represents the sixteenth president as a titanic personage.

*Niven, John. *Gideon Welles, Lincoln's Secretary of the Navy.* New York, 1973. An excellent biography that devotes only three pages to the *Trent* affair.

The Official Records of the Union and Confederate Navies in the War of the Rebellion. 30 vols. Washington, D.C., 1894–1914. Has an entire volume (the last one) devoted to Confederate diplomatic documents.

*O'Rourke, Alice. "The Law Officers of the Crown and the *Trent* Affair," *Mid-America* (July 1972), 157–71. Maintains that the queen's legal advisers hardened their position on British neutral rights after learning of the *Trent* "outrage."

Owsley, Frank L. *King Cotton Diplomacy.* 2d ed. Chicago, 1959. A scholarly study of Confederate diplomacy with a Southern bias.

Owsley, Harriet. "Henry Shelton Sanford and Federal Surveillance Abroad, 1861–1865," *Mississippi Valley Historical Review* XLVIII (Sept. 1961), 211–18. Still the best work on Sanford's activities in Europe.

*Paolino, Ernest N. *The Foundations of the American Empire: William Henry Seward and U.S. Foreign Policy.* Ithaca, N.Y., 1973. Depicts Seward as a commercial, rather than a territorial, expansionist who "anticipated the direction of American foreign policy for the next generation and beyond," but who "exhibited no great desire to hasten the annexation of Canada."

Park, Joseph H. "English Workingmen and the American Civil War," *Political Science Quarterly* XXXIX, no. 3 (1924), 432–57. Offers the traditional thesis that English workingmen were uniformly pro-Northern.

Parker, Joel. *International Law: Case of the Trent.* Cambridge, Mass., 1862. Asserts that the crisis should have been treated as a political, rather than as a legal, problem.

Pierce, Edward L. *Memoirs and Letters of Charles Sumner.* 4 vols. Boston,

1877–94. Only hints at Sumner's full role in Civil War foreign relations.

Pope-Hennessy, James. *Monckton Milnes, The Flight of Youth, 1851–1885*. New York, 1955. Touches on Adams's receipt of the news of the *Trent* seizure.

Porter, Horace. *Campaigning with Grant*. 2d ed. Bloomington, Ind., 1961. Has little on diplomatic history.

The Present Condition of Mexico. 37 Cong., 2 sess., *House Ex. Doc. No. 100*. Collects documents treating the preliminary stages of the European intervention and the American attempts to avert it.

Pro Lege [pseud.]. *A Legal View of the Seizure of Messrs. Mason and Slidell*. New York, 1861. Declares that the *Trent* seizure could not be legally justified.

Putnam, George H. "The London 'Times' and the American Civil War," *Putnam's Monthly* V (Nov. 1908), 183–91. Attacks the *Times* as an insidious influence.

———. *Memories of My Youth, 1844–1865*. New York, 1914. Includes colorful but unreliable anecdotes bearing on Anglo-American relations during the Civil War.

Randall, James G. *Lincoln the President*. 4 vols. New York, 1945. A eulogistic biography poor on foreign relations.

Redding, Cyrus. "England and America," *The New Monthly Magazine* CXXIV (Jan. 1862), 63–72. Visualizes mob rule driving the Lincoln administration into war with England.

Reid, T. Wemyss. *The Life, Letters, and Friendships of Richard Monckton Milnes, First Lord Houghton*. 2 vols. London, 1891. Recalls Adams's visit to Fryston Hall at the outset of the *Trent* crisis.

———. *Life of the Right Honourable William Edward Forster*. 2 vols. London, 1888. A weak biography of an able English defender of the Northern cause.

Rhodes, James F. *History of the United States, From the Compromise of 1850 to the Final Restoration of Home Rule at the South in 1877*. 5 vols. New York, 1913–15. Still one of the most reliable Civil War surveys on the subject of foreign relations.

Rice, A.T. "A Famous Diplomatic Despatch," *North American Review* CCCLIII (Apr. 1886), 402–10, plus a 13-page facsimile supplement. Misinterprets the significance of Seward's instruction no. 10 to Adams, dated May 21, 1861.

———. *Reminiscences of Abraham Lincoln by Distinguished Men of His Time*. 8th ed. New York, 1889. Includes an attack on Seward by C.M. Clay.

Ridley, Jasper. *Lord Palmerston*. New York, 1971. Adds little to Bell's biography on the subject of Anglo-American relations during the Civil War years.

Robinson, William M. *The Confederate Privateers*. New Haven, Conn., 1928. The standard monograph on the subject.

Rumbold, Horace. *Recollections of a Diplomatist*. 2 vols. London, 1902. Includes what is probably a spurious story about Palmerston's reaction to the *Trent* seizure.

Russell, John. *The Later Correspondence of Lord John Russell, 1840–1878*. Ed. by G.P. Gooch. 2 vols. London, 1925. Has a few contemporary private letters on the *Trent* affair.

————. *Recollections and Suggestions, 1813–1873*. London, 1875. Adds nothing to the story of the *Trent* affair as related elsewhere.

Russell, Lady John. *Lady John Russell, A Memoir, With Selections From Her Diaries and Correspondence*. Ed. by Desmond McCarthy and Agatha Russell. New York, 1911. Reveals that the Russells were very apprehensive of the outcome of the *Trent* affair.

Russell, William H. *My Diary North and South*. New York, 1863. Best on the early months of 1861.

Sandburg, Carl. *Abraham Lincoln, The War Years*. 4 vols. New York, 1939. Does not allow established historical facts to stand in the way of a good story.

Schmidt, Louis B. "The Influence of Wheat and Cotton on Anglo-American Relations During the Civil War," *Iowa Journal of History and Politics* XVI (July 1918), 400–39. Propounds the "wheat thesis" as an explanation of why England did not intervene in the American Civil War.

Sears, Louis M. *John Slidell*. Durham, N.C., 1925. Presents a scanty summation of Slidell's activities in Paris.

————. "The London *Times*' American Correspondent in 1861: Unpublished Letters of William H. Russell in the First Year of the Civil War," *Historical Outlook* XVI (Oct. 1925), 251–57. Has only two letters from Russell to J.C.B. Davis during the crisis period.

Seitz, Don C. *The James Gordon Bennetts, Father and Son*. Indianapolis, Ind., 1928. Sheds little light on foreign relations.

Seward, Frederick W. *Reminiscences of a War-Time Statesman and Diplomat, 1830–1915*. New York, 1916. Tells how Lincoln and Seward debated what to do about the *Trent* affair.

————. *Seward at Washington, As Senator and Secretary of State. A Memoir of His Life, With Selections From His Letters*. 2 vols. New York, 1891.

Includes Seward family correspondence, the manuscripts of which have disappeared.

Seward, William H. *The Works of William H. Seward.* Ed. by George E. Baker. 5 vols. Boston, 1884. Devotes vol. 5 to Civil War diplomacy without adding much to official sources like the "Foreign Relations" series.

Sideman, Belle B., and Lillian Friedman. *Europe Looks at the Civil War.* New York, 1960. An anthology of European commentary on the Civil War.

Simpson, Evan John. *Atlantic Impact, 1861.* New York, 1952. A short, undocumented "popular" history of the *Trent* affair.

Skelton, Oscar D. *Life and Times of Sir Alexander Tilloch Galt.* Toronto, 1920. Recalls Galt's visit with Lincoln during the *Trent* crisis.

*Smith, Geoffrey S. "Charles Wilkes and the Growth of American Naval Diplomacy." In *Makers of American Diplomacy, From Benjamin Franklin to Alfred Thayer Mahan.* Ed. by Frank J. Merli and Theodore A. Wilson, pp. 135–63. New York, 1974. A short sketch which may grow into a badly needed biography of Wilkes.

Smith, William E. *The Francis Preston Blair Family in Politics.* 2 vols. New York, 1933. Sheds little light on the role of the postmaster general in the *Trent* crisis.

Sowle, Patrick. "A Reappraisal of Seward's Memorandum of April 1, 1861, to Lincoln," *Journal of Southern History* XXXIII (May 1967), 234–39. Argues that Seward planned to publish Lincoln's anticipated acquiescence in his plan of action.

Stacey, C.P. *Canada and the British Army, 1846–1871. A Study in the Practice of Responsible Government.* Toronto, 1963. Indicates that Canada was ill-prepared in 1861 for an Anglo-American war.

The Stanleys of Alderley. Ed. by Nancy Mitford. London, 1939. Has family letters on the *Trent* crisis by a member of the British cabinet.

Temple, Henry W. "William H. Seward," *The American Secretaries of State and Their Diplomacy.* VII. Ed. by Samuel F. Bemis, pp. 3–115. New York, 1927–29. An undocumented biographical essay.

Thornton, Willis. *The Nine Lives of Citizen Train.* New York, 1948. Tells about a colorful American promoter who gave public speeches in England during the *Trent* crisis.

Thouvenel, Edouard A. *Le Secret de l'Empereur.* 2 vols. Paris, 1889. Deals rather sparsely with the American Civil War, mostly in the form of extracts from Thouvenel's letters to the French ambassador in London.

Tilby, A. Wyatt. *Lord John Russell, A Study in Civil and Religious Liberty.* New York, 1931. A short, discursive biography.

Tocqueville, Alexis de. *Democracy in America.* 2 vols. New York, 1955. Was three decades old at the time of the Civil War and still offered insights into the American character.

Toy, Sidney. *The Castles of Great Britain.* London, 1953. Helps to set the scene at Pontefract Castle for Adams's visit there.

Trescot, William H. "The Confederacy and the Declaration of Paris," *American Historical Review* XXIII (July 1918), 826–35. Discusses the negotiation from the vantage point of a participant.

Trevelyan, George M. *The Life of John Bright.* Boston, 1913. A "standard" life with, however, little on the *Trent* affair.

Trimble, William. "Historical Aspects of the Surplus Food Production of the United States, 1862–1902," *Annual Report of the American Historical Association for 1918* I, 223–39. Overstates the "wheat thesis."

Trollope, Anthony. *An Autobiography.* London, 1924. Offers comments by one who "dined with Mr. Seward on the day of the decision."

———. *North America.* London, 1968. A pro-Union book by a popular English novelist who traveled in the United States early in the Civil War.

Twisleton, Mrs. Edward. *Letters of the Hon. Mrs. Edward Twisleton, 1852–62.* London, 1928. Reproduces an interesting letter on the *Trent* question written by a prominent Englishman to his American father-in-law.

Tyrner-Tyrnauer, A.R. *Lincoln and the Emperors.* New York, 1962. Based mostly on information from the Austrian archives and otherwise on secondary sources.

Van Deusen, Glyndon G. *Thurlow Weed, Wizard of the Lobby.* Boston, 1947. A somewhat unsympathetic biography.

———. *William Henry Seward.* New York, 1967. The only authoritative biography.

Victoria, Queen. *The Letters of Queen Victoria, First Series, A Selection From Her Majesty's Correspondence Between the Years 1837 and 1861.* Ed. by A.C. Benson and Viscount Esher. 3 vols. London, 1907. Contains only a handful of communications touching on the American Civil War.

———. *The Letters of Queen Victoria, Second Series, A Selection From Her Majesty's Correspondence and Journal Between the Years 1862 and 1878.* Ed. by George E. Buckle. 2 vols. New York, 1926. Offers little light on the queen's attitude toward the "American question."

Willoughby, C. *The Military Life of H.R.H. George, Duke of Cam-*

bridge. 2 vols. London, 1905. Of marginal value regarding British military preparations.

The War of the Rebellion, A Compilation of the Official Records of the Union and Confederate Armies. 128 vols. Washington, D.C., 1880–1901. Includes a collection of documents related to the *Trent* affair in vol. 115.

Warren, Gordon H. "The Trent Affair, 1861–1862," Ph.D. diss., Indiana Univ., 1969. A workmanlike and generally reliable study.

––––––. "Imperial Dreamer: William Henry Seward and American Destiny." In *Makers of American Diplomacy, From Benjamin Franklin to Alfred Thayer Mahan.* Ed. by F. J. Merli and T. A. Wilson, pp. 195–221. New York, 1974. Characterizes Seward as a reckless, belligerent, and truculent secretary of state.

Weed, Thurlow. *Autobiography of Thurlow Weed.* Ed. by Harriet A. Weed. Boston, 1883. Relates in a self-serving manner how Weed in Paris and London tried to help prevent Anglo-American war.

Welles, Gideon. "The Capture and Release of Mason and Slidell." In *Civil War and Reconstruction. Selected Essays by Gideon Welles.* Comp. by Albert Mordell, pp. 256–79. New York, 1959. A distorted reminiscence.

––––––. *Diary of Gideon Welles, Secretary of the Navy Under Lincoln and Johnson.* Ed. by Howard K. Beale. 3 vols. New York, 1960. Offers a surly and unreliable reminiscence of the period covered by the diary itself (from Aug. 1862 onward), but the 1911 edition is worse because it lacks Beale's careful editing.

––––––. *Lincoln and Seward.* New York, 1874. First published in *The Galaxy* XVI (Oct.–Dec. 1873), 518–30, 687–700, and 793–804, as "Mr. Lincoln and Mr. Seward." A vitriolic attack on Seward by an old political enemy.

West, Richard S., Jr. *Gideon Welles, Lincoln's Navy Department.* Indianapolis, Ind., 1943. A good biography that has recently been eclipsed by Niven's even better book.

Whelan, Joseph G. "William Henry Seward, Expansionist," Ph.D. diss., Univ. of Rochester, 1959. One of the best of many unpublished dissertations and these on Seward.

Williams, John A. "Canada and the Civil War." In *Heard Round the World, The Impact Abroad of the Civil War.* Ed. by Harold Hyman, pp. 259–98. New York, 1969. A brief essay from a Canadian perspective.

Willson, Beckles. *John Slidell and the Confederates in Paris, 1862–1865.* New York, 1932. A lively but unscholarly book.

Winks, Robin W. *Canada and the United States, The Civil War Years.*

Baltimore, 1960. An important contribution to Civil War diplomatic history.

Woldman, Albert A. *Lincoln and the Russians.* Cleveland, 1952. Contains extracts from the correspondence of the wartime Russian minister in Washington.

Woodford, Frank B. *Lewis Cass, The Last Jeffersonian.* New Brunswick, N.J., 1950. A sympathetic biography of one who played a peripheral role in the *Trent* affair.

I would here like to record my gratitude to my daughter, Adrienne, who at the age of thirteen proofread the entire manuscript text of this book. I am also grateful to have received a summer stipend in 1970 from the National Endowment for the Humanities and to have obtained from the Faculty Research Fund at Middle Tennessee State University a grant which helped defray the cost of another summer of research.

Index

The Trent Affair was manually set on the Linotype in eleven-point Granjon with two-point spacing between the lines. Foundry Garamond was selected for display.

The book was designed by Larry Hirst, cast into type and printed letterpress by Heritage Printers, Inc., Charlotte, North Carolina, and bound by The Delmar Company, also of Charlotte. The paper on which the book is printed bears the watermark of the S.D. Warren Company and is designed for an effective life of at least three hundred years.

THE UNIVERSITY OF TENNESSEE PRESS : KNOXVILLE